A BASIC APPROACH TO BASIC

A BASIC APPROACH TO BASIC

Henry Mullish

NEW YORK UNIVERSITY

JOHN WILEY & SONS
New York • Chichester • Brisbane • Toronto

Library of Congress Cataloging in Publication Data:

Mullish, Henry.
  A basic approach to BASIC.

  Includes index.
  1. Basic (Computer program language) I. Title.
QA76.73.B3M84   001.6'425   76-24808
ISBN 0-471-62375-X

Printed in the United States of America

20 19 18 17 16 15 14 13 12 11

To the students of New York University

PREFACE

Few will question the fact that computers have made an indelible mark on twentieth-century education. Not only are they increasingly affecting the content and the process of learning, but advantage is now being taken of their incredible speed by the administrative personnel as well. As the computer becomes an ever-present reality, with closely knit links to the classroom, its presence will change the direction and emphasis of classroom content, possibly to a radical extent. For it invites a reassessment of the range and complexity of problems that can be dealt with in the classroom.

The computer can solve problems only if they are presented in a language the computer can "understand," or "interpret." Of the many programming languages in use today, one of the most flexible and fascinating is BASIC. BASIC is designed to take the mystique out of programming. Written and developed at Dartmouth College, the language is directed at the individual who has the need to solve a problem but is without the professional programmer's skills. The only prerequisite for use of the language is a grasp of high school mathematics. Therefore, anyone, from the high school student right up to the experienced researcher, can take full advantage of BASIC's simplicity and considerable power.

All of the hundred or so programs illustrated in this book were run on the Hewlett-Packard 2000C at New York University. Hundreds of students use this computer daily. In fact, every student in the School of Business is *required* to take and pass a course in BASIC. As a result, many problems related to business and finance, as well as science and mathematics, are represented in this book. The rather large number of questions posed at the ends of the various chapters are directly related to their contents. Many of the questions were actually asked by students themselves or were posed by teachers during lectures or in examinations.

The book is organized in accordance with my personal philosophy of modular learning; that is, teaching a unit and then, using the knowledge gained in the previous unit, progressing to a more advanced topic, whenever such a method is deemed appropriate. At any time, the student should feel perfectly free to jump directly to Chapter Fifteen, where instructions are to be found on how to actually run a program. The BASIC language is so designed that a knowledge of the whole is not necessary for solving a problem in a particular area.

Programming is not a spectator sport. Describing to a person the action of riding a bicycle is all very well but it has its serious limitations. Sooner or later—and the sooner the better—the learner is going to have to actually mount a bicycle and try to ride it. The chances are very good that he'll fall off once or twice, but that's to be expected. There's no other way to make him a proficient cyclist. This analogy is really not far-fetched, for the programming novice also has to get involved some time, and the real, practical learning takes place at the machine. It is quite true that interacting with the computer is not nearly so pleasant as with a human, patient, caring, warm-blooded teacher but then again the computer doesn't lose its patience, no matter how often the user makes a mistake, something that can hardly be said of most teachers.

There are several people I would like to thank for their assistance in putting this book together. Without their cooperation it probably would not have seen the light of day. First is Robert Rosentel, a student and assistant of mine, who patiently checked out each of the programs on the computer terminal. He also typed much of the manuscript, assisted at times by Connie Engle and Jacqueline Murdock. I owe a great debt of gratitude to Steve Tihor, now a student at Princeton University. Steve is gifted with a seemingly unlimited knowledge of computer programming and contributed several programs—the more exotic ones. He also critically edited much of the manuscript and the programs. While paying tribute to these wonderful people I would be remiss if I did not express my thanks to David Blaustein, Roxanne Hoffman, Michael Horowitz, Mike Pompa, Carl Wyman, and Drs. David Korn, Frank Karal, and Tom Stuart, all of the Courant Institute of Mathematical Sciences, N.Y.U. for their most helpful suggestions and contributions.

Last but by no means least, I would like to convey my deep thanks to Mr. Ben R. Bean, John Wiley's alert and affable college representative, who, while looking at an ocean of potential text books, was astute enough to select this as a possible candidate for general use.

An earlier version of this book was used for several years by all the BASIC classes at New York University and it seems to have withstood the test of time. But time does not stand still and there will certainly be a need for future changes and amendments. Any suggestions will be gratefully received and each one will be answered personally.

Henry Mullish

New York University, 1975

CONTENTS

A BASIC APPROACH TO BASIC

CHAPTER ONE

THE DEVELOPMENT OF COMPUTERS

"In the beginning there were no computers . . . "

Few people will question the validity of the above statement even though some of them will suspect it resembles the opening line of the world's best selling book. The fact is that computers, albeit elementary ones, have been used for centuries. If one defines a computer to be a device for aiding computation, computers can be traced to prehistoric times.

In prehistory man used his fingers for counting, which after all, are an aid to computation. This practice was used by the ancient Romans, Greeks, Egyptians, Babylonians, and the Chinese. What is interesting is that the fingers were used not only for counting in much the same way that children do today but also for the basic arithmetic processes of addition, subtraction, multiplication, and division. This fingers (and thumb) reckoning remained in vogue in Europe until the late Middle Ages and in the Orient until modern times.

From the eleventh century B.C., physical, nonmechanical aids to computation were developed. The Chinese used bamboo counting rods and later developed their most widely known and widely used physical aid, the abacus, which came in various forms. Abacuslike devices were used in Egypt, Greece, Rome, China, and South America.

In the seventeenth century John Napier invented a physical aid to multiplication—the famous Naperian rods. Napier is, of course, best known for his invention of logarithms.

The seventeenth century seems to have been particularly prolific, for in 1642 Blaise Pascal invented a calculating device capable of addition and subtraction, which had an important feature—it provided for the automatic "carry" when a 10 had been reached. Baron Gottfried Leibnitz also invented a calculator that automated the process of multiplication and division.

As ingenious as these devices were, they were not entirely reliable simply because the technology of the day was inadequate to the needs. It was not until the early nineteenth century that a reliable calculator was invented and used commercially.

Most of us are familiar with the punched cards that are used on very modern computers. Punched cards are not exactly a new development. The French, back in 1725, developed this principle to a remarkable degree. Punched cards were successfully used by Joseph Marie Jacquard. In 1804 Jacquard invented a loom that was controlled by metal cards with holes punched in them. The complex pattern produced by the loom could be easily changed by substituting other cards. These same principles were incorporated by Charles Babbage of England when he developed mechanical computing equipment under the auspices of the British government. Babbage, in 1822, completed the construction of a so-called difference engine, a special-purpose calculator. Babbage subsequently conceived of a machine he called an "analytical engine" whose design is strikingly similar to that of a modern digital computer. However, Babbage was too far ahead for his time; his ideas could not be implemented by the technology of his day. Babbage came incredibly close to designing the modern computer.

Credit for the invention of electromechanical aids to computation must go to Herman Hollerith, a statistician from Buffalo, New York. He designed an electromechanical device to process data from the official national census of 1890. His device used cards punched with the critical information collected during the census. His efforts expedited the tabulation of the results considerably.

Finally, in the twentieth century, the electronic era began. The first electronic digital computer was known by the acronym* ENIAC (Electronic Numerical Integrator And Computer). It was completed in 1946 at the Moore School of Electrical Engineering of the University of Pennsylvania. Because the ENIAC utilized vacuum tubes for its circuitry, it represented a great advance over the electromechanical methods of computation used earlier. The fact that it had some 18,000 vacuum tubes made the ENIAC the most complex electronic device constructed in its time. It was quite cumbersome judged by modern standards and, of course, relatively slow. It could add nevertheless in 0.2 of a millisecond (about 5000 computations per second), multiply in 2.8 milliseconds and divide in 25 milliseconds. A computer using vacuum tube technology is now referred to as a first-generation computer.

The first commercially available first-generation computer was the UNIVAC I (UNIVersal Automatic Calculator) manufactured by Remington Rand in the 1950s. It was used extensively for scientific purposes and could calculate at the rate of 10,000 additions per second. (The time it takes for one addition is often taken as a representative measure of the speed of a computer.)

The UNIVAC I had a "memory" of 1000 words. This means that it could store either 1000 data items or had 1000 memory locations for computer instructions or a mixture of data and instructions. As useful as it was, in terms of speed and memory size, the scientific world soon found that the UNIVAC was just too slow for the more demanding problems it wanted to solve. Not only that, but its memory was much too small. This is a conclusion which is to be repeated time and again along the road of development to the present-day computers. Suffice it to say that the UNIVAC I now resides in the Smithsonian Institution in Washington, D. C.—obsolete in so short a period of time.

Meanwhile, a company that had hitherto been concerned mainly with typewriters and tabulating equipment, the International Business Machines Corporation (IBM) developed an excellent first-generation computer called the IBM 704 in 1957. It had a memory of 32,000 locations ("words") and could perform 100,000 calculations per second. Later IBM produced another first-generation computer, the IBM 709, which had a speed of 150,000 calculations per second (the memory size remained the same).

In the late 1950s transistors were invented and quickly replaced the thousands of vacuum tubes used in electronic computers. IBM developed a transistorized version of the IBM 709 and called it the IBM 709T, the T signifying "transistorized." Because when spoken 709T sounds like "seven-oh-ninety," this computer became known as the 7090. It used the same 32K (the letter K is often used in place of "thousand") word memory but could perform 200,000 calculations per second. Later IBM modified the 7090 to increase its speed even further, and so was born the IBM 7094 with the speed of about 250,000 calculations per second.

*There seems to be a veritable fascination in the computing community with acronyms. An acronym is simply a word formed from the initial letter(s) that describe a particular unit.

All these developments took place toward the end of the 1950's, and transistor-based computers dominated the field until about 1965. The transistorized computer represents the second generation of computers. It was not until the mid-1960s that the third generation of computers came into being. They are characterized by integrated circuitry coupled with extreme miniaturization.

Two terms with which every programmer or would-be programmer must become familiar are *hardware* and *software*.

1.1 Hardware

Every computer system is comprised of certain equipment, such as the central processing unit (which holds the memory) and auxiliary equipment that may include card readers, teletypewriters, or disk or tape input devices. Together these physical components are called, quite appropriately, hardware.

1.2 Software

Hardware is useless unless computer programs or routines have been written to make it capable of processing data. An analogy could be made with the automobile, a very useful piece of "hardware"; without suitable fuel to make it work the automobile remains immobile and does no good at all (except perhaps for the ecology).

It is generally the responsibility of the computer manufacturer to supply the software, but often it is amended or even improved upon by a diligent software group at a particular installation. The software performs various functions, such as translating man-written computer programs to machine language instructions (the language that the computer actually understands) and controlling the processing of jobs as they go through the system.

CHAPTER TWO

A TOWER OF BABEL?

There are so many computer languages in vogue today why, one is inclined to ask, should one add BASIC* to the ever-expanding list, thereby compounding this virtual Tower of Babel? Is not FORTRAN† and all its versions and subsets sufficient? Why burden the computing community with yet another language? One could answer that FORTRAN is fine for the typical mathematical and scientific problem but fails miserably when one wishes to solve the nonnumerical problem. Textual material or, to use the general description, "character strings" are not particularly amenable to FORTRAN. For such problems then, why not resort to SNOBOL,‡ which was created to process character strings and does so with considerable elegance? It could be argued that SNOBOL lacks the computational facility required for solving a host of character-string problems. In that case why not go to PL/I,§ a widely used language that supposedly combines the mathematical clout of FORTRAN with the ease of manipulation of character strings usually associated with SNOBOL? This is a much more difficult question to answer. Another contender for the dual-purpose language champion would be APL,‖ a language of considerable elegance and power. To use PL/I and APL programmers must have an appreciable degree of sophistication; they must devote considerable time to the study of the language before they can claim "fluency" in it. By fluency we mean a sufficient familiarity with the language to enable one to solve a wide variety of problems without having to pore through manuals at each step when writing and debugging¶ the program.

What was sorely needed was an easy-to-learn language, one with the minimum of commands but yet, at the same time, one that provided the user with sufficient power and flexibility to permit him to solve a great number of different problems. Moreover, from a practical point of view, the language had to possess a repertoire and syntax enabling the average student to learn it quickly say in an hour or two.

As a result of these considerations, BASIC was devised at Dartmouth College where the students tested it and proved it to be extremely successful. In a very short time the user could learn to solve problems of a nontrivial nature quickly. The user can supply appropriate instructions to the computer by simply typing them on a Tele-

---

*Beginner's All-purpose Symbolic Instruction Code.
†FORmula TRANslation
‡StriNg Oriented symBOlic Language.
§Programming Language I.
‖A Programming Language.
¶A term which in computer jargon means finding and eliminating any errors.

type machine connected to the central computer. After the instructions are typed on the Teletype, the solution is calculated, and literally within seconds the results are printed on the Teletype terminal from which the instructions were transmitted. Moreover, a number of users can simultaneously input different problems to the central computer and receive immediate and individual responses because of a special so-called time-sharing arrangement (the computer deals with each terminal, or user, in rapid succession). In so doing, each user is given the impression that he is the sole user, permitting him to proceed at his own pace, oblivious to all the other users who might be sharing the computer with him at that time.

This in itself is not sufficient reason for devising BASIC. It has other inherent advantages too. In most computer languages the user is compelled to state the problem he wishes to solve in a language sometimes somewhat remote from the English language; this is not true in BASIC. Here users quickly learn to express their problems in a certain precise format, each instruction conforming to a rigidly designed syntax closely resembling that of the English language. Should any one of the syntactic rules be violated, the offending instruction is instantly rejected and the user notified of the error by means of an appropriate diagnostic* message. The user is then at liberty to retype the instruction, this time in conformity with the strict syntactic rules. Little or no time elapses between the moment of transmitting an erroneous instruction to the computer and being advised of it.

This rapid response is very important, because by being notified immediately, one wastes a minimal amount of time. Moreover, this instantaneous feedback is one of the critical elements in efficient learning. One soon finds that even if the same mistake is committed time and again, the computer responds in precisely the same cool manner, without irritation. It is as if the computer has infinite patience even though the user producing the error may soon lose patience with himself. While on the subject of errors, it is fairly axiomatic to say that computers do not make mistakes—humans do. The computer itself has no intelligence and, to be honest, does not even know enough to make a mistake! Its IQ is zero and it will obey each one of our instructions no matter how ridiculous it is. It is therefore incumbent upon the programmer to ensure that his program instructions are accurate, appropriate, and assist in the solution of the problem at hand.

Once the mechanics of submitting a BASIC problem to the computer have been mastered—and it really doesn't require very much intellectual dexterity to do so—the user is free to solve a great variety of problems. Each set of instructions becomes known as a program and thus the user becomes elevated to the rank of a programmer.

Experience has proved that programming is a most desirable practice for intellectual development, and some feel that it should be taught to all students even if only as a lesson in self-discipline. In any case, it seems that solving a problem at a teletype leads to efficient learning because of the instantaneous feedback. Both acceptance of an instruction, which represents reward, and its rejection, which represents some mild negative response, are immediate. In addition to that, the level of concentration is usually at its highest when one is actively engaged with the computer, and the interactive mode favors extended contact with the computer. All these factors combine to lead the learner to a high level of comprehension. In other words, the teletype becomes a teaching machine. Experience has shown fairly convincingly that students not only learn well by this process of interacting directly with a computer but also enjoy doing so.

---

*A message to the user advising him of an instruction containing an error and pinpointing the error wherever possible.

However, we should explain here that the student is not, in fact, interacting directly with the computer when he uses the BASIC language. No computer in the world truly understands the language. Although we human beings may write a program in this English-like language we call BASIC, each individual instruction has to be converted or translated into the language of the computer before it can be acted upon. Once translated into the machine's language the computer is able to execute each of the resulting elementary instructions rapidly and efficiently. The conversion to the machine language is usually called *compilation*.

Although the machine language of a particular computer system is identical the world over, the same cannot be said for BASIC systems. They differ among themselves in very much the same way that the English language as we know it differs among the English-speaking nations around the globe. The New Yorker speaks differently from the Texan, the English cockney speaks a different dialect from his Scottish neighbor to the North and the Jamaican's intonation cannot be mistaken for a Canadian's.

And so it is with BASIC. The original language has undergone many changes by both various computer manufacturers and individual installations. Thus we have a wide variety of BASIC dialects all of which are being used simultaneously. For several reasons, including exportability of programs and programmers, it is desirable to arrive at a standard form of the language. Indeed, such an endeavor is currently underway at the American National Standards Institute (ANSI).

Questions

1. What does the acronym BASIC mean?

2. Name another computer language that can handle character strings.
   SNOBOL

3. What is the meaning of the term "time-sharing"?
   The computer deals w/each terminal or user in rapid succession

4. What is a BASIC program?
   Each individual instruction has to be translated into the language of the computer.

5. What is a diagnostic message? *a message to the user advising him of an instruction containing an error and pinpointing the error.*

CHAPTER THREE

THE BASIC PROGRAM

Every instruction in BASIC must be assigned a statement number. In other words each instruction must be preceded by a positive integer such as 1, or 50, or 100, or whatever. Furthermore, each program must be terminated by a numbered END statement. Instructions may be entered in any order because the program is actually executed in the sequence of the ascending order of the statements. For example, the instructions

$$130 \quad \text{Statement 3}$$
$$120 \quad \text{Statement 2}$$
$$110 \quad \text{Statement 1}$$
$$140 \quad \text{END}$$

would be executed in the order 110, 120, 130, and 140. Clearly, the highest numbered statement must always be the END statement and no two statements may have the same number—each statement number must be unique.

Suppose we wanted to have the computer print the message:

THIS IS A BOOK

We could accomplish this by resorting to the PRINT instruction. This instruction is written as follows.

PRINT "THIS IS A BOOK"

where the message to be printed is enclosed in double quotes. The complete program to accomplish this somewhat elementary task is now shown:

```
100   PRINT "THIS IS A BOOK"
150   END
```

In this two-line program the choice of numbering the statements 100 and 150 is quite arbitrary. It is also quite possible to assign consecutive numbers to them although this is not usually done, however natural this would seem to be at this stage. The reason for this is that one could easily forget an instruction that must then be inserted in the middle of a program. If the statements were consecutively numbered, one would be at a loss to do this, since it is not permissible to number statements in the form 100.1, 100.2, etc.

Suppose now we did, in fact, want to insert another line underneath the line we have already indicated. For example, suppose we wanted the printout to be:

THIS IS A BOOK
ON BASIC

What we could do is to assign the additional line the number say, 110, and rewrite the program as shown, taking care to center the second line beneath the first, since this greatly improves the appearance. (A blank is indicated by b.)

100 PRINT "THIS IS A BOOK"
110 PRINT "bbbON BASIC"
150 END

Now if we wanted to separate the two lines of text by a blank line all we need do is to insert another PRINT statement between statements 100 and 110. It can be of the form

PRINT " "

where the pair of double quotes follow consecutively, or what is more usual because it is less work, just the word PRINT by itself. Hence, the amended program might look like this:

100 PRINT "THIS IS A BOOK"
105 PRINT
110 PRINT "bbbON BASIC"
150 END

The program above was actually run on the computer and both the input and output are shown in Program 3-1. Notice that the quotes do not appear on the printout and all zeros are slashed. This is to distinguish them from the letter "O."

Program 3-1

100 PRINT "THIS IS A BOOK"
105 PRINT
110 PRINT "   ON BASIC"
150 END

RUN

THIS IS A BOOK

   ON BASIC

DONE

The word RUN which follows the program is a system command that is typed by the user or programmer to instruct the computer to execute the program. The word DONE is printed automatically by the computer at the termination of execution of every program.

Suppose it were necessary to insert a quotation mark somewhere in the text. We know that the first quote indicates the beginning of the text to be printed and the *next* quote the end, so it is impossible to insert a quotation mark within the text. If quotes are truly necessary, however, one can resort to the apostrophe, which is neither a beginning nor an ending delimiting character.

A simple program to illustrate this point follows. It puts out a short message in which the single apostrophe signifies quotes and performs their usual grammatical function.

Program 3-2

```
1   PRINT "MICHAEL SAID, 'WHERE IS MULLISH'S BASIC BOOK?'."
9999  END

RUN

MICHAEL SAID, 'WHERE IS MULLISH'S BASIC BOOK?'.

DONE
```

Notice that it is perfectly in order to assign the statement 1 to the first program statement and, since the highest statement number allowed is 9999, it is both proper and safe to assign the number 9999 to the END statement.

So much for printing textual material. How can we get the computer to calculate? After all, computers are renowned for their speed of calculation.

For our first example of a problem requiring computation, let us select a simple one. Let us find, for example, the average of two numbers. It is quite true that we could easily solve such a problem without a computer. The most we need is a pencil and a scrap of paper. But right now it is the principle we want to understand. What we learn from solving this simple problem will apply to almost all subsequent problems.

But first some ground rules.

3.1 Assigning Names to Numeric Data

The BASIC language uses data that is invariably referred to by a name. Thus that name assumes a symbolic meaning. It represents a value of some kind or another. In fact an allusion to this is found in the acronym from which the name BASIC is (supposedly) derived. It is a symbolic instruction code.

Numeric data is always assigned a name that is either one of the 26 letters of the English alphabet, or a letter followed by one of the 10 digits of the decimal system, zero through nine. The following would therefore be valid names for numerical data:

$$Y \quad A3 \quad X \quad L1 \quad P6 \quad Z4 \quad C0$$

Suppose we arbitrarily selected the name A to represent the number 11 and the name B to represent the number 2. In BASIC this would be written as:

$$\text{LET A} = 11$$
$$\text{LET B} = 2$$

The numbers 11 and 2 are called *constants*.

These two simple statements, which are clearly understood by the novice, have in fact a deeper significance than is apparent.

The LET statement is known as an *assignment* statement. In the first case above it assigns the value 11 to the symbol A. This implies that the value 11 is stored in the memory of the computer under the symbol A. To the left of the equals sign is written the symbolic name for the location in the computer's memory, into which is stored whatever expression or number appears to the right of the equals sign. It follows that only one name may appear to the left of the equals sign but many may be written to the right.

The significance of the above might not yet be completely meaningful but in a very short while it will be clearly understood. Once the values have been defined we would want to operate upon them using the familiar operations of arithmetic, namely:

Operation	Symbol in BASIC
Addition	+
Subtraction	−
Multiplication	*
Division	/
Exponentiation	↑

Exponentiation is merely the name given to the act of raising a number to a power. For example, x cubed may be written more concisely as x^3, where the superscript 3 is called an exponent. Since it is impossible to type superscripts on the ordinary computer terminal, an arrow pointing upward is used to represent *raising* a number to a power. Thus x^3 is written in BASIC as X↑3.

We can now write our program to find the average of two numbers. We shall call the result C.

Program 3-3

```
100   LET A=11
110   LET B=2
120   LET C=(A+B)/2
130   PRINT "THE AVERAGE = "
140   PRINT C
150   END


RUN



THE AVERAGE =
  6.5


DONE
```

In line 120, where the value of the average is computed, it will be noticed that the expression A + B is enclosed in parentheses. The reason for this is that in BASIC there is an order of precedence (a hierarchy) for arithmetic operations. They are:

Order of Precedence

Lowest priority	+ −
Intermediate priority	* /
Highest priority	↑

In the absence of parentheses, exponentiation is performed before any of the other arithmetic operations. Since multiplication and division have the same priority they are executed in the order in which they occur, from left to right. Similarly for addition and subtraction.

To illustrate this order of precedence, here are some typical algebraic expressions written first without parentheses and then rewritten with parentheses that indicate the manner in which the computer performs each operation, according to the hierarchy denoted above.

(1) $A + B * C$ $A + (B * C)$
(2) $D \uparrow 2 - F * G + H / M$ $((D \uparrow 2) - (F * G)) + (H/M)$
(3) $M * P \uparrow C - F$ $(M * (P \uparrow C)) - F$
(4) $A / B / C * D * E$ $(((A/B)/C) * D) * E$

What does all this have to do with statement 120? Well, if we had written:

$$120 \quad \text{LET } C = A + B / 2$$

we would *not* have calculated the average but rather the quantity $A + B/2$. The value of this expression is 12, clearly not the average of 11 and 2. The reason for this is simply that, in accordance with the order of precedence explained above, division is of a higher priority than addition, and therefore $B/2$ would be computed first. The addition follows immediately. It is imperative, therefore, to surround the expression $A + B$ with parentheses to avoid computing the wrong result. One is always at liberty to use parentheses when one is unsure of the hierarchy or when it serves some other useful purpose; for example to make the problem clearer to the programmer.

Notice that in line 140, C represents a value that is stored in the memory of the computer. Therefore, if C is an item included in a PRINT statement, the letter C itself is not printed, but rather its numeric value. If the letter C were to be enclosed by quotes, the character C would then be printed, but not its numerical value. If the PRINT statement is followed by an arithmetic expression, the expression is evaluated and the result printed.

Of course, Program 3-3 can be criticized for many reasons which we shall soon explain. But the answer of 6.5 obtained is correct and few will complain.

One criticism that may be aimed at the Program 3-3 is that although it works, it works for only one case. That is to say, only when A is equal to eleven, and B is equal to two is the program useful. For any other values of A and B the program is utterly useless. Don't despair—there is a very simple way to change the program so that it will work for many different values of A and B. In other words, we want A and B to be *variable* in value. It is for this reason that A and B are known as *variables.*

We mentioned previously that if a PRINT instruction is followed by an arithmetic expression, it is evaluated first and the result is then printed. This is an unusual feature in programming languages; other more sophisticated computer languages do *not* permit expressions in print instructions.

We now illustrate this feature and also test the rules for the order of precedence of the arithmetic operators. It would be an excellent idea for the reader to avoid looking at the printed results until she has first tried to anticipate them. Remember, if parentheses are present the expression contained within them is computed first. Next the order starts with exponentiation, multiplication, and division (left to right), and addition and subtraction, again from left to right. Here is the program. The final printout will be discussed shortly.

Program 3-4

```
100   PRINT 50-10/2*4+2
110   PRINT
120   PRINT 5/2*5
130   PRINT 5/(2*5)
140   PRINT
```

```
15Ø  PRINT 9/3↑2+1
16Ø  PRINT (9/3)↑2+1
17Ø  PRINT 9/3↑(2+1)
18Ø  PRINT 9/(3↑2+1)
19Ø  PRINT 9/(3↑(2+1))
2ØØ  END


RUN


  32

  12.5
  .5

  2
  1Ø
  .333333
  .9
  .333333

DONE
```

3.2 The READ and DATA Statements

In order to assign different values to variables they may be placed in a DATA statement that may then be read by its related READ statement. This probably seems somewhat circuitous, but a simple illustration will make this concept clear.

Suppose we have a variable named X which is to take on the values 5, 7.2, 6.32, and 4.3 consecutively. These four values may be included in a DATA statement—or four separate DATA statements—and each value may be read by means of the READ statement. In principle it would look like this:

READ X
.
.
.

DATA 5, 7.2, 6.32, 4.3
.
.
.

In the DATA statement the values are separated by a comma. When the READ instruction is acted upon it assigns the first value in the DATA list to X. The dots indicate the operations to be performed on X. But how does X take on subsequent values? That is indeed a good question. We shall now "go to" the answer.

3.3 The GO TO Statement

Ordinarily, each BASIC instruction is acted upon sequentially, in the order of ascending statement numbers. On occasion, however, it is desirable to alter this course of events and "jump" to another point in the sequential flow of instructions. This is known as a *transfer of control* or *branching*. If the transfer takes place without any preconditions being met it is known as an *unconditional* transfer. This is what the GO TO statement does and this is how it is implemented:

        100   READ X
                    .

                    .

                    .

        200   GO TO 100
        300   DATA 5, 7.2, 6.32, 4.3

When the READ instruction is "executed" X takes on the first value 5. When the GO TO is encountered, control is sent unconditionally to statement 100. At statement 100 the READ X is again encountered, but this time X takes on the second value 7.2, erasing the first value 5. This process continues until all the values have been used and the program is terminated automatically (rather inelegantly, but that is not too important right now*) when there are no more data items to be read. Incidentally, the DATA statement may be placed anywhere in the program as long as it precedes the END statement, since "executing" it has no effect on the program—it is merely referred to by the READ statement.

If more than one DATA statement is present in a program the same process takes place; the items are taken in sequential order, first from the first DATA statement (left to right) and so on all the way to the last DATA statement.

Our original program found the average of two numbers; we are now in a position to amend it so that it could read *pairs* of values from one or more DATA statements. It is important to realize that once a program has been set up to solve *one* particular problem it may be amended in the most trivial way to solve tens, hundreds, and even thousands of *similar* problems.

Here is the amended program in which we have used one READ statement to read in three pairs of A and B. When several variables are listed in a READ statement, they must be separated by a comma. By the way, blanks are completely ignored except when placed between quotes in a PRINT statement. To illustrate the point that blanks are ignored, Program 3-5, which follows, has been written deliberately without blanks, even though it is not aesthetically pleasing. The instruction GO TO is typed as GOTO but since the spaces are ignored it is treated as GO TO in the ordinary way. Note also that in line 150 the printed message is followed by a variable name, separated by a comma.

Program 3-5

        100   READA,B
        110   DATA11,2,3.6,4.5,117,432
        120   LETC=(A+B)/2
        130   PRINT"THE AVERAGE OF"
        140   PRINTA,B
        150   PRINT"IS",C
        160   GOTO100
        170   END

---

*What actually happens is that the computer prints out a diagnostic that reads: OUT OF DATA IN LINE 100.

RUN

THE AVERAGE OF
  11   2
IS   6.5
THE AVERAGE OF
  3.6   4.5
IS   4.Ø5
THE AVERAGE OF
  117   432
IS   274.5

OUT OF DATA IN LINE 1ØØ

Program 3-5 is designed to average separately three pairs of numbers, all of which are included in a DATA statement. The first time around the value of A is 11, B is 2. After their average is computed and the values of A, B, and the average are printed, control is sent to statement 100 which causes the next two data items to be read. The previous values of A and B are replaced by the values 3.6 and 4.5. When the average of these two numbers is computed, the last pair of numbers is read, again replacing the previous values for A and B. This program terminates inelegantly because the GO TO is forever sending control to the READ statement and eventually there simply will no longer be any data items left to be read. The "out of data" message is printed and the program is terminated.

What in fact has been set up in this last program is what is known as a *loop*. The loop extends from statement 100 to statement 160. The loop is the fundamental characteristic of computer programming, not just in BASIC but in all computer languages. It is by means of such a loop that the same sequence of operations—no matter how long and involved the sequence might be—may be used repeatedly on a large number of data items. It is safe to say that all programs may be written without loops. However, such a program will not be worth the time and effort required to write it.

Only by examining a program carefully will it become apparent that it is composed of loops. Many programmers like to write a schematic representation of the "flow" of their programs, before they actually begin writing the program in BASIC. Such a schematic outline is called a *flowchart*.

In order to improve the appearance of Program 3-5 let us amend it slightly. Since there are several separate "cases" to the problem, inserting a blank line between indi-

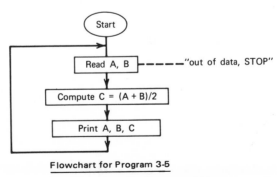

Flowchart for Program 3-5

Flowchart for Program 3-5

vidual cases would be appropriate. This, of course, may be done by including a blank PRINT statement immediately following the instruction to PRINT the average C.

The amended Program 3-5 appears below.

Program 3-6

```
100   READ A,B
110   DATA 11,2,3.6,4.5,117,432
120   LET C=(A+B)/2
130   PRINT "THE AVERAGE OF"
140   PRINT A, "AND",B
150   PRINT "IS",C
160   PRINT
170   GO TO 100
180   END
```

RUN

```
THE AVERAGE OF
  11                AND              2
IS                  6.5

THE AVERAGE OF
  3.6               AND              4.5
IS                  4.05

THE AVERAGE OF
  117               AND              432
IS                  274.5
```

OUT OF DATA IN LINE 100

3.4 Cosmetic Programming

If the output to a program has to look "fancy" it might be a good idea to begin the output with a suitable heading. Perhaps an appropriate title enclosed in a rectangle of asterisks might look attractive and, at the same time, serve a useful purpose. In Program 3-7, a minor amendment to Program 3-6, such a heading has been included. Notice that the GO TO statement does *not* go to statement 100 this time, for if it did, the heading would be printed out each time another pair of data items was read.

Of course, when printing out input data or even the results of computation, one could take pains to ensure that the information conformed to some attractive format. Cosmetic programming is entirely concerned with the way the printed results look. What advantage is there in having attractive looking output? For one thing it is always more pleasant to read and therefore easier to examine for the relevant information, to say nothing of the enjoyment one derives from producing an aesthetically pleasing output.

One can also improve the structure of one's program. One can intersperse appropriate "remark" statements signified by the letters REM (see Chapter 6) throughout the program and thereby aid an outsider in understanding the manner in which it works by reference to its listing. An ample supply of REM statements often serve to remind the original programmer of his own strategy in solving a problem, months and even years after it was written. Thus REM statements provide an excellent means of internally documenting a program.

Program 3-7

```
100   PRINT "*************************"
110   PRINT "* FINDING THE AVERAGE *"
120   PRINT "*                      *"
130   PRINT "* OF PAIRS OF NUMBERS *"
140   PRINT "*************************"
150   PRINT
160   READ A,B
170   DATA 11,2,3.6,4.5,117,432
180   LET C=(A+B)/2
190   PRINT "THE AVERAGE OF"
200   PRINT A,"AND",B
210   PRINT "IS",C
220   PRINT
230   GO TO 160
240   END
```

```
RUN


*************************
* FINDING THE AVERAGE *
*                      *
* OF PAIRS OF NUMBERS *
*************************

THE AVERAGE OF
  11              AND             2
IS              6.5

THE AVERAGE OF
  3.6             AND             4.5
IS              4.05

THE AVERAGE OF
  117             AND             432
IS              274.5


OUT OF DATA IN LINE 160
```

Before leaving this admittedly elementary problem of finding the average pairs of numbers, it would be interesting to consider what results would be obtained if the

READ statement in Program 3-7 were written:

160 READ A, A, B

In the first place, three data items would be read each time the READ statement were executed. What values then would the variables A and B assume? The first A (the first time around) assumes the value 11 (the first item of the data list), but since the second variable name is also A, the second item becomes "stored" in A, erasing the number 11 and replacing it with 2. In effect, the first result would be the average of 2 and 3.6, with the number 11 not even becoming a part of the computation. In the same way, the second (and last) result would be the average of 117 and 432, the number 4.5 being ignored.

3.5 Packing the Printout Closer Together

So far we have used the comma to separate fields to be printed. The effect of using the comma is to have the computer automatically begin printing the next item in the *next variable* field of which there are five across the page. They begin in columns 1, 16, 31, 46, and 61. In order to condense these fields to permit the printing of more information, a semicolon may be substituted for a comma. This has the effect of packing the printouts closer together. If the semicolon is used, up to 12 *numeric* fields can be contained in one output line. However, text appearing in quotes and separated by a semicolon are "concatenated" (joined) together, producing a continuous string of characters that are not separated by spaces. Here is a simple illustration of this feature.

Program 3-8

```
100   PRINT "**********************"
110   PRINT "*                    *"
120   PRINT "* THE COMMA VERSUS  *"
130   PRINT "*                    *"
140   PRINT "* THE      SEMICOLON *"
150   PRINT "*                    *"
160   PRINT "**********************"
170   PRINT
180   LET A=17
190   LET B=21
200   PRINT "A","B"
210   PRINT A,B
220   PRINT
230   PRINT "A";"B"
240   PRINT
250   PRINT "A          B"
260   PRINT A;B
270   END


RUN


**********************
*                    *
* THE COMMA VERSUS  *
*                    *
* THE      SEMICOLON *
*                    *
**********************
```

```
A               B
  17              21


AB


A       B
  17      21


DONE
```

In Program 3-8 A and B are set equal to 17 and 21, respectively. In statement 200 "A" and "B" separated by a comma are printed. As a result the *letters* A and B are printed in the beginning of the first two of the five fields. In line 210, where the *variables* A and B separated again by a comma are printed, the values 17 and 21 are printed again in the first two of the five fields. They are preceded by a blank space.

When, as in line 230, "A"; "B" is printed, the letters AB are printed together without any separation. This might not be the programmer's intended printout. However, printing "AbbbbbB," (where b represents a blank space), followed immediately by a separate print of A; B has the effect of printing AbbbbbB on one line and the values 17 and 21 on the next line, packed closer together.

3.6 Undefined Variables

If a program contains an undefined variable, it would be wishful thinking to expect a correct result. One would hope that the computer would reject such a program. In fact, the program does not detect such an error during the phase known as "compilation,"the phase that is initiated immediately after each line of a program is typed in. If no errors are found during compilation, the program is converted to its binary equivalent, a form which the computer "understands," and the program then goes into its final phase known as "execution." It is during this execution phase that the attempt to use an undefined variable causes the program to "bomb out," as the expression goes. Execution is terminated abruptly and the system prints out the diagnostic: UNDEFINED VALUE ACCESSED IN LINE n.

3.7 Scientific Notation

One sometimes has to work with extremely large numbers and on other occasions with very small numbers. In each case we might have to include a great many zeros to define the number. Since it is both awkward and error-prone to deal with such unwieldy numbers another method was devised for handling them. It is called *scientific notation*, although, strictly speaking, there is nothing unscientific about the conventional method.

The number 1000 may be written as 1.0×10^3. Here are some other numbers written in both their representations.

Conventional Way	Scientific Notation
10,000*	$1. \quad \times 10^4$
−0.0023	$-2.3 \quad \times 10^{-3}$
123400000	1.234×10^8
0.00000012	$1.2 \quad \times 10^{-7}$

*Incidentally, in BASIC commas are never used to separate off the thousands. The number 10,000 would be written simply as 10000.

It will be noticed that in scientific notation the number is represented as a short, positive or negative decimal number times 10 raised to either a positive or a negative power. That power is an indication of how many places to move the decimal left or right.

In BASIC, one is quite free to express numbers in scientific notation. Instead of writing "X10" we substitute the letter E (for exponent), for example

$$10,000 \quad \text{becomes} \quad 1.00000E+04$$
$$-0.0023 \quad \text{becomes} \quad -2.30000E-03$$

Even if you, the programmer, are not interested in defining numbers in scientific notation, the computer will print out certain computed values of numbers (which are ordinarily more than six to seven decimal digits) in scientific notation, so that one has to be familiar with this concept.

3.8   Algebra Is Not BASIC

In algebra a typical expression is

$$y = a + b$$

As we have already learned, such an expression may be written in BASIC as follows:

$$100 \quad \text{LET } Y = A + B$$

In algebra, the above expression could also have been written

$$a + b = y$$

However, one *cannot* write such an expression in BASIC as

$$100 \quad \text{LET } A+B = Y$$

because there can be only one variable name to the left of the equals sign. The reason for this, as you will recall, is that the variable on the left represents a *memory location* in which the expression to the right is *stored*. To the right of the equals sign may be any number of variables. The expression on the right is evaluated, reduced to a single number, and stored in the symbolic location designed on the left.

On the HP-2000C, the word LET may be omitted from the assignment statement. In other words instead of typing

$$100 \quad \text{LET } A = B$$

you could type:

$$100 \quad A = B$$

However, this is not done anywhere in the programs illustrated in this book because some BASIC systems will not accept an assignment statement without the word LET.

The Moment of Truth

By this time you should be ready to actually run a simple program on the computer. When this is done for the first time it is truly an exciting moment. During such a moment, however, one is more apt to make mistakes. It is for this reason that we suggest that you should first look at Chapter fifteen, where you will learn how to "get onto the computer" and to correct any program errors should they occur.

QUICK REFERENCE GUIDE TO CHAPTER THREE

Item	General Form	Examples
1. Variable name	Letters A–Z	X Q A
	Letters followed by digits 0–9	I3 W2 B0
2. Constants	Integer (signed or unsigned)	19 −3 +12
	Decimal number	1.2 −3.4 .33
	Scientific notation	1.23E+12 −4.5E−04 1.056E3
3. Operators	$+ \quad - \quad * \quad / \quad \uparrow$	
4. Expression	*Constant*	8 −14 .3
	Variable name	X5 T U2
	Arithmetic expression	3.14−R↑2 X/3 (A+B)*C
5. Assignment statement	*Line number* LET *variable name = expression*	100 LET A = 3
		200 LET B9 = X↑2
		300 LET X5 = A + B/C − D
6. PRINT statement	*Line number* PRINT	100 PRINT
	Line number PRINT *"literal"*	200 PRINT "ABC"
	Line number PRINT *expression*	300 PRINT A9 + 7
		400 PRINT Q1,X,Z
		500 PRINT B; Y2, A6/B9
7. READ statement	*Line number* READ *variable name(s)*	100 READ X
		200 READ A1,A2,A3,W
8. DATA statement	*Line number* DATA *constant(s)*	100 DATA 43
		200 DATA 5,17,4,−68
		300 DATA 9,1.23,−2.015E4
9. GO TO statement	*Line number* GO TO *line number*	100 GO TO 416
10. END statement	*Line number* END	9999 END

Questions

1. What is the output of the following program?

```
10  DATA 5,3,4
30  PRINT "D =", D
20  READ A,B,C
53  LET D = (F + G + H)/3
99  PRINT "D =", D
110 END
32  READ F,G,H
49  DATA 11,12,13
25  LET D = (A + B + C)/3
```

2. Write a BASIC program to print a star-shaped figure with stars (asterisks).

3. Which of the following variable names are illegal?

   (a) X   (f) X6   *letter has to be first*
   (b) P   (g) V8
   (c) R   (h) .7
   (d) ALPHA   (i) -W
   (e) 6X   (j) TT

4. Identify the errors in the following BASIC program:

   20 LET XW = -25
   25 LET 6C = 4.567
   30 K = XW + 6C + A - B
   40 PRINT K

5. What is the minimum number of DATA statements required in a program with four READ statements?

6. Write the algebraic equivalents of the following expressions:

   (a) 5 * A
   (b) B - C / D
   (c) E + F * G
   (d) E↑2 - F↑3 + X↑4
   (e) (H + I↑J)/K + 1

7. Convert the following algebraic equations to BASIC:

   (a) $a = b + c$ ** multiplication*
   (b) $d = e - f$
   (c) $g = ijk$
   (d) $m = \dfrac{n + p}{q} - 4$
   (e) $r = s^t - u^4$
   (f) $v = w^{2.3} x^{4.7} y$
   (g) $z = \dfrac{s - t}{c - d}$ *( ) first*
   (h) $p + q = r$

8. Rewrite the following statements more succinctly:

   (a) 100 LET A = B * B * B * B * B
   (b) 342 LET C = D * D * D
   (c) 981 LET E = F + F + F + F
   (d)   6 LET G = H - H - H - H
   (e)   71 LET I = 123 * 0

9. What statement is always associated with the READ statement? Where may it be placed in a program?

10. What statement transfers control to another part of a program unconditionally?

11. In what order are items on a DATA statement read?

12. What is accomplished, if anything, by the following program?

    20 GO TO 40
    40 GO TO 20
    60 END

13. Predict the results you would obtain from the following program:

    10 READ R
    20 LET C = 2 * 3.14159 * R
    30 PRINT C, R
    40 GO TO 10
    50 DATA 3,4,5,6,7
    60 END

14. Predict the output of the following program:

    100 LET A = 3
    110 LET B = 2
    120 LET C = 1
    130 LET D = B ↑ C * A + B / C − A * B
    140 PRINT "D="; D
    150 END

15. Convert each of the following numbers to scientific notation:

    (a) 1.35
    (b) 12345.678
    (c) 876.1234
    (d) −999.9
    (e) −0.000002345
    (f) 555.5555

16. There is an error in one of the following conversions to scientific notation. Find it, circle it and rewrite it correctly.

    (a) 36.28   3.628E1
    (b) −496.159   −4.96159E2
    (c) 444.444   4.44444E2
    (d) −0.00123   −0.123E3
    (e) −88.88912   −8.888912E1

17. Pretend you are a computer. Upon executing the following program what results would you print out?

    10 READ A,B
    20 LET C = A * B
    30 PRINT A,B,C
    40 GO TO 10
    50 DATA 2,4,−1,4,3,6
    60 END

18. Indicate whether the following statements are true (T) or false (F):

    (a) BASIC is an acronym for Beginner's All-purpose System for Intelligent Computers.

    (b) A diagnostic message is an attempt by the computer to indicate what is wrong with a program.

    (c) The last statement in every program is the word DONE.

    (d) An integer number like 131,482 must appear in a DATA statement exactly as shown, with a comma separating off the thousands.

    (e) The GO TO statement unconditionally transfers control to another part of the program.

19. Evaluate the following BASIC expressions:

    (a) $(2+3)/10 * 2$

    (b) $4\uparrow2*3/(5+3)$

    (c) $(2\uparrow((4*5+4)/8))\uparrow2$

    (d) $10/2 + 3\uparrow2 - 5$

    (e) $(15 + 9/3)/6$

    (f) $2\uparrow(3+ 2 / 2) + 8 / 2$

    (g) $5 + 4 + 3 - 6 + 10 / 5$

    (h) $4 * 2 * 5 / 10$

    (i) $(15 / 3) \uparrow 2 * 4 + 25 / 5$

    (j) $4 * 2 \uparrow 3 + 4 / 4$

20. Indicate whether the following BASIC instructions are invalid (I) or valid (V).

    (a)   100   READ X,Y,Z

    (b)   482   PRINT A,B,C

    (c)   352   GO TO 14.6

    (d)   4   LET X = ((3*A) + 4) - (C$\uparrow$2- B)

    (e)   10   DATA 4,6,7,4.5,C

    (f)   47   LET C = (A + B) / (X * Y)

    (g)   123   LET D = (X + Y) (Z * B)

    (h) 4001   READ, A, B

    (i)   14   READ A,A,B,C,B

    (j)   76   READY

CHAPTER FOUR

THE CONDITIONAL CLAUSE

In everyday commercial dealings one encounters situations where the cost of an item is conditional upon the quantity purchased. Naturally, the more items purchased the lower the cost per item. A typical but hypothetical example would be:

1–5 items	35¢ each
6–20 items	33¢ each
21–50 items	30¢ each
over 50 items	25¢ each

The above cost scale could be written as follows:

1. if 1 to 5 items are purchased, then the cost is 35¢ each
2. if 6 to 20 items are purchased, then the cost is 33¢ each
3. if 21 to 50 items are purchased, then the cost is 30¢ each
4. if over 50 items are purchased, then the cost is 25¢ each

Perhaps an item may come with or without certain extras. If the extras are included then the cost would be more. Or if the bill is paid within a certain period, say within 10 days after delivery then a discount might be offered.

4.1 The IF/THEN Statement

In each of the above situations the key words are "if" and "then." And, in BASIC, when we want to take a certain path depending on some condition, we also use the words "if" and "then." This has the form:

IF (expression) THEN (go to statement number).

This might look strange at first, but a few simple examples will help to clarify it. Study the following program statement:

100 IF X = 5 THEN 200

The above statement numbered 100 asks: "Is the value of X equal to 5?" If it is, then the statement has the effect of "GO TO 200." If, however, the value of X is *not* equal to 5, the THEN clause is ignored and control is transferred to the *statement immediately following statement 100*, whatever it happens to be.

Let us now look at another example.

24

```
350  IF W = 10 THEN 1000
360  LET A = 5
        .
        .
        .

1000  LET T = 4
        .
        .
        .
```

Statement 350 says that if W is equal to 10 then control is sent directly to statement 1000, where T is set equal to 4. The program then continues from this line. If, on the other hand, W is *not* equal to 10 then control flows on to the next statement, which is numbered 360, where A is set equal to 5 and the statements in this path are executed.

A word of warning. There is an almost irresistible temptation for the novice to write IF ... THEN GO TO .... Although this meaning is true in principle, such a statement will be rejected by the HP-2000 computer. Think GO TO, but don't write it!

Armed with this IF/THEN statement, we can now write a program where, by means of a GO TO statement, we can successively read a series of data items and yet terminate the program elegantly. But how?

We can make the *last* item of data some special quantity and, in the program, test whether each of the items is equal to that special quantity. Suppose, for example, we are dealing with positive numbers only, such as ID numbers, heights, weights, or IQs. We could insert an artificial negative score, such as -9, at the end of the data, and when the IF/THEN statement detects the presence of this negative number, it would act as a signal that all the *real* data has been read.

As a simple illustration of the use of this so-called trailer technique, we shall write a program containing a DATA statement consisting of various positive numbers. At the end of the positive numbers we shall place the number -9, as an indicator of the end of data. The problem will be to determine how many positive items are present. In other words, simply count the positive numbers.

Since we are going to count items, we must select a variable name to represent the count. Let us call this variable C and set its value to zero at the beginning of the program. This is analogous to the automobile manufacturers in Detroit who set the odometer of a new car to zero before dispatching it to a customer. The practice of setting a variable to a fixed value like zero is called *initialization*.

Now in order to update the value of C we shall have to include the statement

LET C = C + 1

where the variable C appears on both sides of the equals sign. At first glance this looks like a perfectly preposterous statement. How can C be equal to C + 1? In fact, however, this statement makes a lot of sense in BASIC. To understand it completely, let us look at the expression to the *right* of the equals sign. It says:

C + 1

But C was initially set to zero. When 1 is added to it, it becomes 0 + 1 = 1. Now this value 1 is "stored" in whatever is written to the *left* of the equals sign. But that also is the variable name C.

In other words, what was previously zero now becomes 1. When the expression C + 1 is encountered the second time, the *current* value of C is 1. Once 1 is added to it and is stored in C, the new value of C becomes 2. This process continues and, in effect, acts as a counter. Here is how such a technique is implemented in a BASIC program.

What follows is a program that *attempts* to solve the problem. It contains a DATA statement with seven elements, followed by the trailing −9. However, according to the output, eight elements were found rather than seven.

✓ **Program 4-1**

```
100   PRINT "*********************"
110   PRINT "* AN ATTEMPT AT THE *"
120   PRINT "*                   *"
130   PRINT "* TRAILER TECHNIQUE *"
140   PRINT "*                   *"
150   PRINT "*********************"
160   PRINT
170   LET C=0
180   READ X
190   DATA 3,5,7,142,12,19,8,-9
200   LET C=C+1
210   IF X=-9 THEN 230
220   GO TO 180
230   PRINT C, "DATA ITEMS HAVE BEEN READ."
250   END


RUN


*********************
* AN ATTEMPT AT THE *
*                   *
* TRAILER TECHNIQUE *
*                   *
*********************


8               DATA ITEMS HAVE BEEN READ.

DONE
```

The "attempt" at the trailer technique as shown in Program 4-1 failed because 1 was added to the counter C before it was established whether or not the current data item was the trailing item. Since the count was incremented by 1 first, the −9, which is not really a data item but rather a signal or flag indicating no more data items follow, was included in the count—in error. Therefore the printout states that there are 8 data items rather than 7. Here is good reason for not believing everything that comes out of a computer!

Errors of logic are the responsibility of the programmer. One cannot expect the computer to detect such errors. Some teachers like to remind students of the most famous cry GIGO, another acronym, which stands for "garbage in, garbage out!"

In the next attempt—a successful one this time—the test for −9 is made before the count is incremented. On this occasion the correct number is printed out.

Program 4-2

```
100   PRINT "***************"
110   PRINT "* THE TRAILER *"
120   PRINT "*  TECHNIQUE  *"
130   PRINT "***************"
135   LET C=0
150   READ X
160   DATA 3,5,7,142,12,19,8,-9
170   IF X=-9 THEN 200
180   LET C=C+1
190   GO TO 150
200   PRINT C, "DATA ITEMS HAVE BEEN READ."
210   END
```

RUN


```
***************
* THE TRAILER *
*  TECHNIQUE  *
***************
   7                    DATA ITEMS HAVE BEEN READ.
```

DONE

In an IF statement the equal sign is called a *relational operator*. Other relational operators are $\#$ or $<>$ (not equal), $>$ (greater than), $<$ (less than, $>=$ (greater than or equal), and $<=$ (less than or equal).

4.2 The RESTORE Statement

We have seen how, using the trailer technique, we can determine by means of the IF statement whether all of the data items have been read. But what if we wanted to reread those same data items for subsequent processing? In other words we would like to, in a sense, "restore" the data. As you might have guessed, the way in which this is done in BASIC is by means of the RESTORE statement.

The following program illustrates the use of the RESTORE statement. It is composed of two loops and is complex enough to warrant the drawing of a flowchart. (You should know that diamond-shaped boxes are conventionally used to denote conditional branches.)

The variable T totals the value of the X's, and the variable K represents the number of X's present. The variable K therefore acts as a counter. The average of the X's is stored in the variable A. Once this is calculated (in line number 260) it is possible to reread each value of X by resorting to the RESTORE statement. After the RESTORE statement has been executed it is possible to compute the number of X values less than the average (L), equal to the average (E), and greater than the average (G).

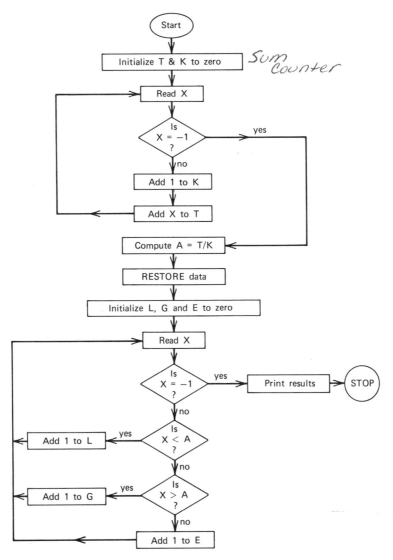

Flowchart for Program 4-3

Program 4-3

```
100  PRINT "********************"
110  PRINT "*                  *"
120  PRINT "* ILLUSTRATION OF *"
130  PRINT "*                  *"
140  PRINT "* THE    RESTORE *"
150  PRINT "*                  *"
160  PRINT "********************"
170  PRINT
180  LET T=0
190  LET K=0
200  READ X
210  DATA 28,13,5,71,35,41,24,32,17,-1
220  IF X=-1 THEN 260
```

```
230   LET K=K+1
240   LET T=T+X
250   GO TO 200
260   LET A=T/K
270   RESTORE
280   LET L=0
290   LET G=0
300   LET E=0
310   READ X
320   IF X=-1 THEN 410
330   IF X<A THEN 370
340   IF X>A THEN 390
350   LET E=E+1
360   GO TO 310
370   LET L=L+1
380   GO TO 310
390   LET G=G+1
400   GO TO 310
410   PRINT "THE AVERAGE OF THE X'S =",A
420   PRINT L, "ITEMS ARE LESS THAN THE AVERAGE"
430   PRINT E, "ITEMS ARE EQUAL TO THE AVERAGE"
440   PRINT G, "ITEMS ARE GREATER THAN THE AVERAGE"
450   END
```

RUN

```
*******************
*                 *
* ILLUSTRATION OF *
*                 *
* THE     RESTORE *
*                 *
*******************
```

```
THE AVERAGE OF THE X'S =          29.5556
    5                ITEMS ARE LESS THAN THE AVERAGE
    0                ITEMS ARE EQUAL TO THE AVERAGE
    4                ITEMS ARE GREATER THAN THE AVERAGE
```

DONE

4.3 The INPUT Statement

When data one wishes to use are known in advance, one can merely include them in a DATA statement. On occasion, however, this is quite inconvenient. One often wishes to feed in data at the terminal during execution of the program. For this purpose BASIC provides the INPUT statement which has the effect of printing out a question mark and pauses until the user has typed in a value.

Program 4-4 is designed to give someone sitting at the Teletype the opportunity to type in a temperature on the centigrade scale. The computer will convert it to its equivalent temperature on the Fahrenheit scale. Also, the program will permit him to go from Fahrenheit to centigrade, if desired.

Since the effect of executing an INPUT instruction is the printing of nothing more than a question mark, it is a very good idea to print some message indicating to the user what he has to do upon seeing the question mark. If he does nothing, the Teletype will simply sit there idle.

The first question that comes to mind is what kind of conversion has to be done; C to F or F to C? Once that has been established, one would use another INPUT statement to provide for the typing in of the temperature to be converted.

Obviously, one would write a program that will solve for more than one case. With the use of a GO TO statement we can easily make the program work for an infinite number of cases. How can we arrange for termination of the program once we have input all the data? This can be done by typing in a third number in response to a question that is normally answered by one of two replies. This third number, when detected, can send control to the END statement, which has the effect of terminating the program. Notice carefully the method used in the program.

The general formula for converting temperature to and from centigrade and Fahrenheit is:

$$\frac{C}{5} = \frac{F - 32}{9}$$

from which can be derived the two separate formulas:

(1)
$$C = \frac{5F - 160}{9}$$

(2)
$$F = \frac{9C + 160}{5}$$

Notice the logic beginning in statement 200 of program 4-4. If K is set equal to 1 the desired conversion is from °C to °F. It is for this reason that control is sent to statement 250, which instructs the user to type in his centigrade temperature. If K is not equal to 1, the next statement in line, statement 210, is executed. This checks to see whether K is equal to 2. If it is, control goes to statement 300 which asks the user to type in the Fahrenheit temperature to be converted. If K is not equal to 1 or 2 control "falls down" or "falls through" to statement 220 which tests if K is equal to 3. If it is, control is sent to the END statement, which terminates the program. If, on the other hand, K is not equal to 1, 2, or 3, something is wrong. The user was initially instructed to type in 1, 2, or 3 and if the test at statement 220 fails, something other than 1, 2, or 3 must have been typed in. The strategy adopted in this case is to print some reminder to the user (statement 230) and send control immediately to statement 150, which prints out the required descriptive information, again permitting the user to input another value for K.

It probably would not be a good idea to go to the beginning of the program since the heading would be printed out again and this would be just a waste of time—and paper.

One of the traps associated with INPUT loops, a trap into which beginning programmers sometimes fall, is to omit a provision for exiting from the program. If such provision is not made, control is continually sent to the INPUT statement. Thus an *infinite* loop is set up. No matter what is typed in, getting out of the loop proves to be impossible, short of severing the connection to the computer!

However, two complementary methods of escape from a loop have been provided by the HP-2000C system. They are:

1. When the teletype prints the question mark in response to the execution of the INPUT statement, rather than typing in a value, the "control" button (which is described in detail in Chapter Fifteen) should be held down while the key labeled C is pressed. This will not print the letter C, but instead control is sent to the END statement after the carriage return is pressed. The word DONE is printed and the program aborted.

2. At any time that the computer is *not* waiting for input from the terminal, pressing the "break" button (also described in Chapter Fifteen) and holding it down for at least $\frac{1}{10}$ of a second, but no more than one second, will also abort the program. If this procedure is followed the word STOP is printed.

An additional element could be inserted into Program 4-4 to add to its sophistication. A record could be kept of the number of invalid values entered and, after a certain maximum, some appropriate message could be printed and the program terminated.

Program 4-4

```
100  PRINT "****************"
110  PRINT "*TEMPERATURE*"
120  PRINT "* CONVERSION *"
130  PRINT "*   PROBLEM   *"
140  PRINT "****************"
150  PRINT
160  PRINT "FOR CONVERSION FROM C TO F, TYPE 1"
170  PRINT "FOR CONVERSION FROM F TO C, TYPE 2"
180  PRINT "TO TERMINATE PROGRAM, TYPE 3"
190  INPUT K
200  IF K=1 THEN 250
210  IF K=2 THEN 300
220  IF K=3 THEN 350
230  PRINT "PLEASE TYPE IN 1, 2, OR 3"
240  GO TO 150
250  PRINT "PLEASE TYPE IN YOUR CENTIGRADE TEMPERATURE"
260  INPUT C
270  LET F=(9*C+160)/5
280  PRINT "EQUIVALENT FAHRENHEIT TEMPERATURE IS ",F
290  GO TO 150
300  PRINT "PLEASE TYPE IN YOUR FAHRENHEIT TEMPERATURE"
310  INPUT F
320  LET C=(5*F-160)/9
330  PRINT "EQUIVALENT CENTIGRADE TEMPERATURE IS ",C
340  GO TO 150
350  END


RUN


****************
*TEMPERATURE*
* CONVERSION *
*   PROBLEM   *
****************
```

FOR CONVERSION FROM C TO F, TYPE 1
FOR CONVERSION FROM F TO C, TYPE 2
TO TERMINATE PROGRAM, TYPE 3
?1
PLEASE TYPE IN YOUR CENTIGRADE TEMPERATURE
?Ø
EQUIVALENT FAHRENHEIT TEMPERATURE IS   32

FOR CONVERSION FROM C TO F, TYPE 1
FOR CONVERSION FROM F TO C, TYPE 2
TO TERMINATE PROGRAM, TYPE 3
?1
PLEASE TYPE IN YOUR CENTIGRADE TEMPERATURE
?1ØØ
EQUIVALENT FAHRENHEIT TEMPERATURE IS   212

FOR CONVERSION FROM C TO F, TYPE 1
FOR CONVERSION FROM F TO C, TYPE 2
TO TERMINATE PROGRAM, TYPE 3
?1
PLEASE TYPE IN YOUR CENTIGRADE TEMPERATURE
?-4Ø
EQUIVALENT FAHRENHEIT TEMPERATURE IS   -4Ø

FOR CONVERSION FROM C TO F, TYPE 1
FOR CONVERSION FROM F TO C, TYPE 2
TO TERMINATE PROGRAM, TYPE 3
?2
PLEASE TYPE IN YOUR FAHRENHEIT TEMPERATURE
?-4Ø
EQUIVALENT CENTIGRADE TEMPERATURE IS   -4Ø

FOR CONVERSION FROM C TO F, TYPE 1
FOR CONVERSION FROM F TO C, TYPE 2
TO TERMINATE PROGRAM, TYPE 3
?7
PLEASE TYPE IN 1, 2, OR 3

FOR CONVERSION FROM C TO F, TYPE 1
FOR CONVERSION FROM F TO C, TYPE 2
TO TERMINATE PROGRAM, TYPE 3
?2
PLEASE TYPE IN YOUR FAHRENHEIT TEMPERATURE
?212
EQUIVALENT CENTIGRADE TEMPERATURE IS   1ØØ

FOR CONVERSION FROM C TO F, TYPE 1
FOR CONVERSION FROM F TO C, TYPE 2
TO TERMINATE PROGRAM, TYPE 3
?32
PLEASE TYPE IN 1, 2, OR 3

```
FOR CONVERSION FROM C TO F, TYPE 1
FOR CONVERSION FROM F TO C, TYPE 2
TO TERMINATE PROGRAM, TYPE 3
?2
PLEASE TYPE IN YOUR FAHRENHEIT TEMPERATURE
?32
EQUIVALENT CENTIGRADE TEMPERATURE IS              Ø

FOR CONVERSION FROM C TO F, TYPE 1
FOR CONVERSION FROM F TO C, TYPE 2
TO TERMINATE PROGRAM, TYPE 3
?3

DONE
```

QUICK REFERENCE GUIDE TO CHAPTER FOUR

Item	General Form	Examples
1. Relational operators	=, # or $<>$, $>$, $<$, $>=$, $<=$	
2. Relational expression	*Expression relational operator expression*	$A > B$ $C + D < E$ $F >= 9$
3. IF/THEN	*Line number* IF *relational expression* THEN *line number*	100 IF A=5 THEN 422 200 IF B$>$C THEN 216 300 IF D+E↑F $<=$ 60.5 THEN 321
4. INPUT	*Line number* INPUT *variable name(s)*	100 INPUT N 200 INPUT X,Y,Z
5. RESTORE	*Line number* RESTORE	100 RESTORE

Questions

1. Which of the following program statements is invalid? State your reasons.

   (a) 123   IF A $>=$ B THEN 234   *OK*

   (b) 420   IF C = D + E THEN 430.1 — *No decimal statement*

   (c) 341   IF F $<>$ G THEN 143   *OK*

   (d) 298   IF H # I THEN GO TO 100 — *No GOTO*

   (e) 361   IF J =$<$ K THEN 362 — *Signs backwards*

   (f) 499   IF L $>$ M THEN 499 — *OK, but a Loop*

   (g) 348   IF N $<$ P THEN MAYBE 200 — *NO MAYBE*

   (h) 119   IF Q #= R THEN 120 — *one or the other*

   (i) 262   IF S + T = U – V THEN 263 — *OK (but 262 → 263 to close syntacticly correct)*

   (j) 999   IF W = Z THEN END — *Line# for END*

   (k) 311   IF A + B – C $<$ J + K ↑ 2 = 4 THEN 6 — *Can't stick too much in 1 statement*

2. What is the meaning of the statement:

   100   LET A = A + 1

3. What is the effect of the INPUT statement?

4. What is wrong with the following program segment?

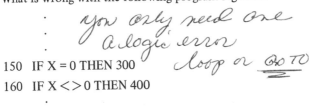

   ·
   ·
   ·

150 IF X = 0 THEN 300
160 IF X <> 0 THEN 400

   ·
   ·
   ·

5. What criticism could be made of the following program segment?

   ·
   ·
   ·

230 IF X # 10 THEN 240
240 PRINT X

   ·
   ·
   ·

6. Write a program that READs five positive numbers and finds the arithmetic mean (average).

7. Write an elegant program to print out the message 'BASIC IS FUN' 20 times, on successive lines. (The print statement containing the message should appear only once.)

8. The sum of the first n squares is given by the formula

$$s = \frac{n(n + 1)(2n + 1)}{6}$$

Write a program that READs a series of values of n and computes the sum of the squares for each value of n.

9. Write a program to compute $x = y^3 z^4$ if $a^3 + b^4$ is equal to zero; otherwise compute $x = a^5 y^4 b^3 z^2$, using the values:

$a = 1, \quad b = -1, \quad y = 10, \quad z = 0.1$

$a = 7, \quad b = -5, \quad y = 17, \quad z = -3.14.$

10. Write a program to READ 10 numbers and separately add the positive and negative numbers. Print the sum of the positive numbers, the sum of the negative numbers, and the product of both. Use these numbers: 5, -6, -2, -12, 15, 50, 63, -7, 4, 21.

11. The DATA statements to a program contain the number of checks drawn and the minimum balance during the month for four checking accounts:

A/C No.	Number of Checks	Minimum Balance(s)
1	3	42.00
2	12	111.30
3	15	33.19
4	7	218.50

Write a program to compute the service charge by the following rule: If the minimum balance is equal to or greater than $100 there is no service charge. However, if it is less than $100 the charge is 10¢ per check, with a 75¢ minimum.

12. What output would you expect from the following program and can you identify the name of the sequence generated?

```
100  LET A = 1
110  LET B = 1
120  PRINT A;
130  PRINT B;
140  LET A = A + B
150  LET B = A + B
160  IF B < 100 THEN 120
170  END
```

13. Write the output that would be printed from the following program.

```
100  LET A = 3
110  LET A = A + 1
120  PRINT "A= "; A
130  END
```

A =
4

14. Write a program that will permit a user to type in at the terminal a weight in kilograms (using the INPUT statement). The program should convert the value into pounds and ounces (2.2 pounds = 1 kilogram, 16 ounces = 1 pound). A negative value should terminate the program.

15. Assume the following formulas:

(a) Circumference of a circle: $C = 2\pi r$

(b) Area of a circle: $A = \pi r^2$

(c) Volume of a sphere: $V = (4/3) \pi r^3$

Write a program that uses a list of different values of the radius in a DATA statement to print out a table. The table should have a suitable heading, begin with a sequence number, followed by the value of the radius, circumference, area, and volume.

16. What output is printed when the following program is run?

```
10   LET N = 0
20   LET T = 4
30   LET T = T - 1
40   LET N = N + 1
50   IF T = 0 THEN 140
60   IF N = 2 THEN 100
70   IF N > 2 THEN 120
80   PRINT N*N, T*N
90   GO TO 30
100  PRINT N+T, N-T
110  GO TO 30
120  PRINT T*T, T*N
```

130 GO TO 30

140 END

17. Write a BASIC program that reads three numbers representing the lengths of the sides of a rectangular box and compute the volume of the box. Print out the lengths of the sides, the volume, and the sequential case number. Assume the data is input by means of an INPUT statement. Terminate the program upon reading three zeros after the last case.

18. Write a BASIC program that computes and prints out the average of an arbitrary number of positive integers. Assume the positive integers appear in a DATA statement at the end of which is a number less than zero.

19. Explain exactly what output is produced by the following program.

10 LET A = 4

20 READ X

30 IF X = 6 THEN 90

40 LET A = A + 2

50 LET S = A + X

60 PRINT A, X, "S= ", S

70 GO TO 20

80 DATA 2,3,6,4,6

90 PRINT "STOP"

100 END

20. The C & S Manufacturing Company sells chairs and sofas to its distributors according to the schedule shown to the right. Each week the company processes the orders received from its distributors and computes the amounts to be charged.

Quantity	Chairs	Sofas
0–49	$ 50	$ 200
50–99	45	175
100–199	40	150
>199	35	125

Write a BASIC program that prints out the following information for each distributor: (1) ID number; (2) number of chairs ordered; (3) price of chairs; (4) number of sofas ordered; (5) price of sofas, and (6) price of chairs and sofas. Also print out the sums of the items in (3), (5), and (6). Assume the input data is given in the order ID number, number of chairs ordered, and number of sofas ordered. Terminate the program upon reading a negative ID number. Prepare a heading and label your output. Assume the following DATA statement:

184, 25, 50, 212, 75, 25, 412, 150, 25, 515, 200, 150, 614, 100, 250, 788, 200, 200, 813, 75, 50, 919, 175, 50, -100, 0, 0,

21. Indicate whether the following BASIC statements are valid (V) or invalid (I):

(a)   10 LET C = C + 1

(b)   47 IF J < K THEN 12

(c)   63 IF A + S = 12 THEN 17

(d)   67 LET C1 = C + 1

(e)   146 IF A*J-K > 4*A-B+C = L THEN 20

(f)   86 LET C = C - 1

(g)   112   IF J =< 0 THEN 999

(h)   87   IF H >< I THEN 412

(i)   100   IF D = 0 THEN END

(j)   520   LET A = A/2

(k)   780   LET B = B*2+1

(l)   890   IF 3*0 > 1 * 0 THEN 35

(m) 980   IF W <= K THEN GO TO 100

(n)   444   IF Y↑2 – 2 + (J–K ↑ 3) < Y↑2 – 2 – (J–K↑4) THEN 29

(o)   33   INPUT N

(p)   77   INPUTS 1

(q)   777   INPUT A7

(r)   2440 INPUTT

(s)   846   INPUT 7

(t)   807   IF (D↑2–3) ↑ K = 42.7 THEN 101

22. Indicate whether the following statements are true (T) or false (F):

(a) Errors in the logic of a program often go undetected by the compiler.

(b) The INPUT statement will cause a program to stop indefinitely while waiting for input.

(c) If the computer is waiting for a response to an INPUT statement, pressing the BREAK button will terminate the program.

(d) The IF/THEN statement is an example of conditional transfer of control.

(e) The statement:

LET C1 = C + 1

will automatically keep a count.

REM STATEMENTS — EXPLAIN SOME OF LOGIC.

IF C <> INT(C) THEN

CHAPTER FIVE

FOR THE NEXT LOOP . . .

In Chapter Three we were introduced to the concept of a loop. In each of the subsequent programs (or in most of them anyway) we used a loop to repeat a series of instructions. This is the essence of computer programming.

BASIC provides a remarkably simple yet efficient way to handle loops. Before describing it, however, examine the following program and try to determine *exactly* what output would be produced, without being told *anything* about the program. Here is the first version of the program:

Program 5-1

```
100  LET I = 1
110  PRINT" HAVE A NICE DAY"
120  LET I = I + 1
130  IF I < 100 THEN 110
140  END
```

Did you conclude that the program would print out the phrase: "Have a nice day" many times? If you did, you are perfectly correct. But exactly how many times?— 99? 100? 101?

Is the next version any different?

Program 5-2

```
100  LET I = 1
110  PRINT "HAVE A NICE DAY"
120  IF I = 100 THEN 150
130  LET I = I + 1
140  GO TO 110
150  END
```

And is Program 5-3 different?

Program 5-3

```
100  LET I = 0
110  PRINT "HAVE A NICE DAY"
120  IF I > 100 THEN 150
130  LET I = I + 1
140  GO TO 110
150  END
```

Admittedly, this is very confusing. Each of these programs looks very much like the other. There simply isn't any rule of thumb to aid one in arriving at the correct conclusion. One has to follow the logic very carefully and perform the instructions exactly as the computer would. Rather than comparing I with 100 each time why not substitute the number 3 and decide on the basis of that finding.

The need to know the exact answer may seem of little consequence to the reader at this point. After all, is it really important to know in advance how many times any action, computation or text is printed? The answer is a decided "yes!" It is invariably of paramount importance to know precisely how many times a loop is executed. But does one have to indulge in such brain stretching each time? Fortunately for us BASIC provides us with a very easy solution. It is called the FOR/NEXT loop, which explains the title of this chapter.

5.1 The FOR/NEXT Loop

The following version of the program, which uses a FOR/NEXT loop, prints out the salutation "Have a nice day" exactly 100 times.

Program 5-4

```
100  FOR I = 1 TO 100
110  PRINT "HAVE A NICE DAY"
120  NEXT I
130  END
```

It is short, concise, exact, and a paragon of simplicity. Study it carefully.

In line 100 an index arbitrarily called I is set to 1. The PRINT instruction is then executed and when NEXT I is reached I is incremented to 2. The question is now *automatically* asked: is I greater than 100? If not, control returns to line 110, printing out the phrase for the second time. This process continues until I is, in fact, greater than 100. At that point, the loop is said to be satisfied, and control is passed to the statement following the NEXT I instruction. At this point the phrase will have been printed out 100 times.

The format of the FOR/NEXT loop is as follows:

FOR *index variable* = *initial value* TO *final value*
.
.
.

NEXT *same index variable*

So that the following are all valid FOR/NEXT loops:

(1)   FOR I = 1 TO 156
.
.
.

NEXT I

(2)   FOR J1 = X TO 73
.
.
.

NEXT J1

(3)   FOR X = Y ↑ Z TO A ↑ 3
           .
           .
           .
           NEXT X

(4)   FOR T = -3 TO 19
           .
           .
           .
           NEXT T

Since blanks are ignored, the following, despite its appearance, is perfectly valid:

(5)   FORM = 1 TO 15
           .
           .

           NEXT M

And now here are some *invalid* examples of FOR/NEXT loops:

(1)   FOR I = 1 TO 10
           .
           .
           NEXT J

(2)   FOR K = 10 TO 1
           .
           .
           NEXT K

[This will ignore the loop entirely.]

(3)   FOUR L = 1 TO N
           .
           .
           NEXT L

(4)   FOR M = 1 TWO 10
           .
           .
           NEXT M

(5)   FOR P = FROM 1 TO 10
           .
           .
           .
           NEXT P

5.2 Stepping a Loop in Increments Other than One

The statement:

FOR I = 1 TO 10

is exactly equivalent to the alternate form:

FOR I = 1 TO 10 STEP 1

Since more often than not it is required to increment the index variable in steps of 1 the STEP 1 clause may be and usually is omitted entirely.

In order to increment a FOR/NEXT loop in steps of 2, one would simply write:

FOR I = 1 TO 10 STEP 2

The values of I would include 1, 3, 5, 7, and 9. Similarly, the statement:

FOR I = 2 TO 10 STEP 2

would include 2, 4, 6, 8, and 10 for the values of I. Program 5-5 adds the odd numbers from 1 to 99 and then sums the even numbers from 2 to 100. The sum of these two totals is the sum of all the integers from 1 to 100. This result is confirmed by the well-known Gaussian formula:

$$S = \frac{n(n+1)}{2}.$$

Program 5-5

```
100   PRINT "**************************"
110   PRINT "*                        *"
120   PRINT "*  INCREMENTING A LOOP   *"
130   PRINT "*                        *"
140   PRINT "*  IN STEPS OTHER THAN 1 *"
150   PRINT "*                        *"
160   PRINT "**************************"
170   PRINT
180   LET S1=0
190   FOR I=1 TO 99 STEP 2
200   LET S1=S1+I
210   NEXT I
220   PRINT "THE SUM OF THE ODD INTEGERS FROM 1 TO 99 = "; S1
230   LET S2=0
240   FOR I=2 TO 100 STEP 2
250   LET S2=S2+I
260   NEXT I
270   PRINT "THE SUM OF THE EVEN INTEGERS FROM 2 TO 100 = "; S2
280   LET S=S1+S2
290   LET S3=(100*101)/2
300   PRINT
310   PRINT "THE SUM OF THE INTEGERS FROM 1 TO 100 USING LOOPS = "; S
320   PRINT
330   PRINT "THE SUM OF THE INTEGERS FROM 1 TO 100 USING FORMULA="; S3
340   END
```

RUN

```
*************************
*                       *
*  INCREMENTING  A  LOOP  *
*                       *
*  IN STEPS OTHER THAN 1  *
*                       *
*************************
```

THE SUM OF THE ODD INTEGERS FROM 1 to 99 = 2500
THE SUM OF THE EVEN INTEGERS FROM 2 TO 100 = 2550

THE SUM OF THE INTEGERS FROM 1 TO 100 USING LOOPS = 5050

THE SUM OF THE INTEGERS FROM 1 TO 100 USING FORMULA = 5050

DONE

   Just a word of explanation about Program 5-5. It will be noticed that not only is the index I used for counting purposes but it is also used within a computation.
   IF it is desired to increment the value of the index by a step of 5, it is done typically as shown:

FOR I = 1 TO 50 STEP 5

   In Program 5-6 we use a well-known drinking song to illustrate the fact that the index of a FOR/NEXT loop can be made to "go backward." In the program the index I begins at 4 and goes to 1 in steps of -1. The functions of TAB and LIN features that are included are fairly self-evident. If they are not, they are explained in detail a little later on in this book.

Program 5-6

```
100  PRINT "******************"
110  PRINT "*                *"
120  PRINT "* A LOOPED SONG *"
130  PRINT "*                *"
140  PRINT "******************"
150  PRINT
160  FOR I=4 TO 1 STEP -1
170  PRINT I; "BOTTLES OF BEER ON THE WALL,"
180  PRINT I; "BOTTLES OF BEER,"
190  PRINT TAB (6); "IF ONE OF THE BOTTLES SHOULD HAPPEN TO FALL,"
200  PRINT I-1; "BOTTLES OF BEER ON THE WALL."
210  PRINT LIN(2)
220  NEXT I
230  END
```

RUN

```
*****************
*               *
* A LOOPED SONG *
*               *
*****************
```

4   BOTTLES OF BEER ON THE WALL,
4   BOTTLES OF BEER,
      IF ONE OF THE BOTTLES SHOULD HAPPEN TO FALL,
3   BOTTLES OF BEER ON THE WALL,

3   BOTTLES OF BEER ON THE WALL,
3   BOTTLES OF BEER,
      IF ONE OF THE BOTTLES SHOULD HAPPEN TO FALL,
2   BOTTLES OF BEER ON THE WALL.

2   BOTTLES OF BEER ON THE WALL,
2   BOTTLES OF BEER,
      IF ONE OF THE BOTTLES SHOULD HAPPEN TO FALL,
1   BOTTLES OF BEER ON THE WALL.

1   BOTTLES OF BEER ON THE WALL,
1   BOTTLES OF BEER,
      IF ONE OF THE BOTTLES SHOULD HAPPEN TO FALL,
Ø   BOTTLES OF BEER ON THE WALL.

DONE

QUICK REFERENCE GUIDE TO CHAPTER FIVE

Item	General Form	Examples
1. FOR statement	*Line number* FOR *variable name* = *expression* TO *expression*	100 FOR I = 1 TO 10 200 FOR W = J TO K
	Line number FOR *variable name* = *expression* TO *expression* STEP *expression*	100 FOR I = 1 TO 10 STEP 2 200 FOR S=T TO U STEP V
2. NEXT statement	*Line number* NEXT *variable name*	100 NEXT I 200 NEXT W2

Questions

1. Must the increment of a FOR/NEXT loop always be in steps of 1? If not, how may it be changed?

2. What is accomplished by the following program and how will the program terminate?

   10   FOR I = 1 TO 12

   20   READ R

30   LET C = 2 * 3.14159 * R

40   PRINT C, R

50   NEXT I

60   DATA 5, 3, 2, 11, 4, 6, 7.3

70   END

3. Circle the following BASIC statements that would create trouble:

   (a)   50   FOR K = 0 TO 25

   (b)   60   FOR P3 = 1 TO 1

   (c)   70   FOR L = -1 TO 100

   (d)   80   FOR I = 3.5 TO 10 STEP .35

   (e)   90   FOR J = 0 TO 50.1 STEP 1.6

   (f)   100   FOR R = 10 TO 50 STEP -10

   (g)   110   FOR Q = -50 TO -100 STEP -2

   (h)   120   FOR T = -40 TO -100 STEP 10

   (i)   130   FOR K = 1 THRU 10

   (j)   140   FOR PD = 10 TO 99

   (k)   150   FOR 3X = 10 TO 44 STEP -5

   (l)   160   FOR S = 25, 35 STEP .5

   (m)   170   FOR S FROM 5 TO 25

4. Write a BASIC program that evaluates the expression

$$y = \frac{x^2}{x^2 + 4}$$

for values of X from 1 to 100 in steps of 1. Print out the values of X and Y in columns.

5. What is the output of the following program?

   10   FOR J=2 TO 6 STEP 2

   20   LET A=(J+1)*J/2

   30   PRINT " J=", J, "A=", A

   40   NEXT J

   50   PRINT A, A*A, A↑3

   60   END

6. Which of the following BASIC statements are invalid (I) or valid (V):

   (a)   44   FOR J = 3, 10

   (b)   35   FOR I = 1 TO 10 NEXT I

   (c)   258   FORK = -4 TO 6 STEP 3

   (d)   354   FOR X = 100 TO 7 STEP -1

   (e)   198   FORM3 = ATOM

7. Determine the printed results from the following program segments:

   (a)   100   FOR I = 1 TO 3

          110   LET X = I

```
           120  NEXT I
           130  PRINT X

(b)   100  LET X = 0
      110  FOR I = 1 TO 3
      120  LET X = X + I
      130  NEXT I
      140  PRINT X

(c)   100  LET X = 0
      110  FOR I = 1 TO 3 STEP 1
      120  LET X = X + I
      130  NEXT I
      140  PRINT X

(d)   100  LET X = 0
      110  FOR I = 1 TO 3 STEP 2
      120  LET X = X + I
      130  NEXT I
      140  PRINT X

(e)   100  LET X = 6
      110  FOR J = 1 TO 4
      120  LET X = X - J
      130  NEXT J
      140  PRINT X

(f)   100  LET X = 0
      110  FOR K = 4 TO 1 STEP -1
      120  LET X = X + 1
      130  NEXT K
      140  PRINT X

(g)   100  LET X = 4
      110  FOR J = 1 TO 8 STEP 3
      120  LET X = -X + J
      130  NEXT J
      140  PRINT X

(h)   100  FOR K = 1 TO 7 STEP 2
      110  LET X = K - 1
      120  NEXT K
      130  PRINT X
```

CHAPTER SIX

STANDARD LIBRARY FUNCTIONS

Certain arithmetic operations are performed very frequently. For example, one might want to take the square root of a number, or the absolute value of an expression, or the logarithm to base e. One could resort to writing clever programs that generate these commonly used functions, but it would be most wasteful of human talent and time to do so. Instead, these and many other functions have been *preprogrammed* and are readily available to the programmer.

Here is a list of some of the mathematical functions and their meanings, followed by some examples of how they are used. Notice that all the function names are composed of three letters.

Function Name	Purpose
ABS	The absolute value of an expression
EXP	The constant e raised to the power of the expression value
INT	The largest integer $\leq$ to the expression
LOG	The logarithm of the expression to the base e
RND	A random number between 0 and 1
SQR	The positive square root
SGN	Returns a 1 if the expression is greater than 0; a 0 if the expression equals 0 and a −1 if the expression is less than 0.
SIN	The sine of the expression (in radians)
COS	The cosine " "
TAN	The tangent " "
ATN	The arctangent " "

All these functions may be used as expressions or as parts of expressions. Here are some examples of some mathematical expressions using these functions and how they would be represented in BASIC.

(1) $y = |a|$
           LET Y = ABS(A)

(2) $x = e^v$
           LET X = EXP(V)

(3) b = largest integer resulting from 106/31
                                  LET B = INT(106/31)
(4) $c = \log_e d^2 f$
                                  LET C = LOG(D ↑ 2 * F)

[The LOG expression must have a positive value or a terminal (fatal) error will occur.]

(5) g = random number between 0 and 1
                                  LET G = RND(0)

(A sequence of random numbers is repeatable if it follows a call to RND with a given negative argument.)

(6) $h = \sqrt{ij}$
                                  LET H = SQR(I * J)

(The SQR expression must have a positive value or it will cause a terminal error.)

(7) $k = \sin(m)$
                                  LET K = SIN(M)
(8) $n = \cos(p)$
                                  LET N = COS(P)
(9) $q = \tan(r)$
                                  LET Q = TAN(R)
(10) $s = \arctan(t)$
                                  LET S = ATN(T)

It is pointed out that it is illegal to write a function on the left side of an assignment statement.

6.1   Using the SQR Function

The most frequently used supplied function is probably the square root, designated SQR in BASIC. When the SQR function is "invoked" the square root of its argument (i.e., whatever is contained within the parentheses immediately following it) is calculated automatically. Later we describe a method to arrive at the square root without using the SQR function, but this is done not for expediency but for the benefit derived from the exercise. It happens to be quite an interesting procedure.

6.2   Solving a Quadratic Equation

Imagine the following situation in a classroom:

Teacher: Think of a number.
          (Teacher writes x)
Student: (Thinks of the number 3 and writes it down).
Teacher: Multiply your number by itself.
          (Teacher writes down x^2.)
Student: (Writes 9.)
Teacher: Add to your result four times the original number.
          (Teacher writes $x^2 + 4x$.)
Student: (Writes 9 + 12 = 21.)
Teacher: Subtract two from your result.
          (Teacher writes $x^2 + 4x - 2$.)
Student: (Writes down 21 - 2 = 19.)
Teacher: What is your final result?
Student: (triumphantly) 19.

The teacher now has enough information to determine the student's original number. The information is written in this form:

$$x^2 + 4x - 2 = 19$$

It is recognized immediately as a quadratic equation since the highest power of x present is 2. However, to solve the equation, the expression on the left must equal zero. To do this the teacher merely subtracts 19 from both sides of the equation, which yields the new form of the equation:

$$x^2 + 4x - 21 = 0$$

Once the equation is in this form, the famous quadratic equation formula can be applied:

$$x_1, x_2 = \frac{-b \pm \sqrt{b^2 - 4ac}}{2a}$$

where, referring to the equation,

$$a = \text{coefficient of } x^2 = 1$$
$$b = \text{coefficient of } x \ = 4$$
$$c = \text{constant} \qquad = -21$$

The "roots" of the equation are found by "plugging" these values into the formula:

$$x_1, x_2 = \frac{-4 \pm \sqrt{4^2 - 4 \times 1 \times (-21)}}{2 \qquad 1}$$

$$= \frac{-4 \pm \sqrt{16 + 84}}{2}$$

$$\frac{-4 \pm \sqrt{100}}{2}$$

$$= \frac{-4 \pm 10}{2} = -7 \text{ or } 3$$

Of course, it is the latter answer, 3, which is sought. (To every quadratic equation there are two roots.)

While on the subject of quadratic equations it might be a good idea to mention that the expression "under the radical," that is, $b^2 - 4ac$, is known as the *discriminant*. It is so named for a very good reason; by means of it one can discriminate in advance between the different kinds of solutions possible using quadratic equations. If the discriminant is positive, there are two real roots. If the discriminant is exactly equal to zero, there are still two roots but they are identical. If the discriminant is negative, the roots are "complex" and to find them one must resort to "complex" arithmetic. Actually, this is an unfortunate term since it is not a complex problem to solve. The term "complex" merely indicates that the number referred to is made up of two separate parts, a real and an imaginary part, rather than the single part to which most of us are accustomed.

As long as a quadratic is set equal to zero, all that one needs to solve it are the values of the coefficients a, b, and c, as used in the formula. Armed with these three values, we can solve the quadratic equation either by reading them by means of a READ and its related DATA statement, or by resorting to an INPUT statement. We shall solve quadratic equations by both methods.

Rather than taking only one case (representing a single quadratic equation), we shall solve several equations with the following values for a, b, and c:

(1)	1	2	−1
(2)	1	−2	4
(3)	3	2	9
(4)	1	−2	1

To exit from the computer elegantly, we shall include a trailing set of data items, say, A = 0, B = 0, and C = 0. When these values are encountered, it will mean that all the data has been read. In effect, the DATA statement, or statements, will contain what will appear to be five sets of data. For the time being the only advantage to this is that we will avoid the computer printout telling us that we are out of data.

In writing the program it would be most natural to call the coefficients a, b, and c by their capitalized names A, B, and C. In fact, only the uppercase letters are available on the Teletype machine. The names A, B, and C must be separated by commas when they appear as part of the READ statement. If blanks were used as separators they would be ignored and the variable names A, B, and C would become reduced to the *single* unacceptable variable name ABC. In the same way, each of the data items in the DATA statement must be separated by commas.

Here is our first program for solving the quadratic equations.

Program 6-1

```
100  PRINT "*********************"
110  PRINT "*SOLVING QUADRATIC*"
120  PRINT "*     EQUATIONS     *"
130  PRINT "*                   *"
140  PRINT "*********************"
150  PRINT
160  READ A,B,C
170  DATA 1,2,-1,1,-2,4
180  DATA 3,2,9,1,-2,1
190  DATA 0,0,0
200  IF A<>0 THEN 240
210  IF B<>0 THEN 240
220  IF C<>0 THEN 240
230  GO TO 360
240  LET D=B↑2-4*A*C
250  IF D<0 THEN 320
260  LET X1=(-B+SQR(D))/(2*A)
270  LET X2=(-B-SQR(D))/(2*A)
280  PRINT
290  PRINT "A=";A;"B=";B;"C=";C
300  PRINT "ROOT 1 =";X1,"ROOT 2 =";X2
310  GO TO 150
320  PRINT "A=";A;"B=";B;"C=";C
330  PRINT "THE RESULTS OF THIS QUADRATIC ARE COMPLEX"
340  PRINT "THIS CASE IS THEREFORE IGNORED"
350  GO TO 150
360  END

RUN
```

```
**********************
*SOLVING QUADRATIC*
*     EQUATIONS     *
*                   *
**********************


A= 1      B= 2      C=-1
ROOT 1 = .414214                    ROOT 2 =-2.41421


A= 1      B=-1      C= 4
THE RESULTS OF THIS QUADRATIC ARE COMPLEX
THIS CASE IS THEREFORE IGNORED


A= 3      B= 2      C= 9
THE RESULTS OF THIS QUADRATIC ARE COMPLEX
THIS CASE IS THEREFORE IGNORED


A= 1      B=-2      C= 1
ROOT 1 = 1      ROOT 2 = 1
```

DONE

6.3 The Logical Operators

There are three separate and consecutive IF statements in Program 6-1. Their purpose is to detect the presence of the special case where A, B, and C are all equal to zero—the trailer data items. It is instructive to examine closely these three IF's and to be quite sure why, in each case, the coefficient is tested to see whether it is *not* equal to zero rather than *equal* to zero.

6.3.1 The AND Operator

One can replace these three IF statements in BASIC with a single IF written in the following way:

IF A = 0 AND B = 0 AND C = 0 THEN 230

Only if all three parts of the expression are true, *at the same time*, is the expression as a whole true. The insertion of the operator AND combines the preceding and the following partial expression. If any one of the members is false, the whole expression is false. This AND operator is one of the three *logical* operators in BASIC. A logical value, as opposed to a numeric value, is either "true" or "false." Any nonzero expression value is "true" and any expression whose value is zero is "false."

The reader is cautioned against writing the above compound IF statement as:

IF A AND B AND C = 0 THEN 230

This is not invalid from the syntactical point of view but unfortunately it does not test what is intended. This is interpreted as meaning: if A is a nonzero value (true) and B also has a nonzero value and C is equal to zero, then the expression as a whole is true and control therefore passes to statement 230.

There are two other logical operators, the OR and the NOT. Here are some examples of these.

(1)	360	IF G3 OR T1 THEN 160
(2)	119	PRINT M OR N
(3)	483	IF NOT X4 THEN 100
(4)	29	PRINT NOT L

6.3.2 The OR Operator

For an expression containing an OR to be true, at least one of its members must be true. In (1) above control passes to statement 160 if either G3 or T1 is true, that is, has a nonzero value. In (2) if M or N (or both) is true the expression is true and a 1 would be printed. Otherwise a 0 is printed.

6.3.3 The NOT Operator

The NOT operator reverses the truth value of that variable to its right. In (3) above, statement 100 takes control only if the logical value of X4 is zero, in which case NOT X4 becomes true, and the expression also becomes true. Similarly, in (4) if the logical value of L is false (zero), NOT L becomes 1 and the 1 would be printed.

These logical operators are extremely useful and will be used throughout this text.

Here are some examples of valid compound IF statements:

(1)	100	IF A = B AND C = D THEN 200
(2)	150	IF E > F OR G < H THEN 300
(3)	200	IF I <= J AND K = L AND M >= N THEN 400
(4)	250	IF P # Q OR R > S AND T < > U THEN 500
(5)	300	IF NOT (V = W AND Y > Z) THEN 600
(6)	350	IF X < 3 AND X = 4 THEN 700

In (1) above, control is sent to line 200 only if A and B are equal at the same time that C is equal to D.

Control is sent to line 300 in (2) if either E is greater than F or G is less than H. Only one of these conditions must be satisfied but if both are true, control still is passed to line 300.

In example (3), if I is less than or equal to J and K is equal to L, and M is greater or equal to N—only if these conditions are true *at the same time*, is control sent to line 400. The AND carries the connotation of simultaneity. If any one of these conditions is false, the whole expression becomes false, and control is not passed to line 400 but rather to the next statement in sequence.

Example (4) is a little more complicated to follow because it contains both an AND and an OR logical operator. When both operators appear in the same expression, as in this example, the AND takes precedence over the OR. That means that the subexpression

(a)   R > S AND T < > U

is examined first. It then takes on the value "true" or "false" depending upon the values of R, S, T, and U. Only then is the subexpression

(b)   P # Q OR $\begin{bmatrix} \text{"true"} \\ \text{or} \\ \text{"false"} \end{bmatrix}$

evaluated. Let us assume that subexpression (a) is "true." Then subexpression (b) will be "true" regardless of the values of P and Q, since they are connected with an OR operator. If, however, the value of (a) is "false" then the entire expression is "false" if P is equal to Q and is true if, in fact, P is not equal to Q.

The only other point worth making with respect to this example is that it illustrates both forms of the "not equal" sign. Both are equally acceptable to the HP-2000C.

Example (5) uses the logical operator NOT. It has the effect of negating the truth value of whatever follows it. It takes precedence over both the AND and the OR. It is for this reason that the parentheses are necessary in the case shown. If V is equal to W and Y is greater than Z (making the parenthesized expression "true") the NOT has the effect of converting it to "false."

In the last example (6) we had an overt contradiction. It can never be true that X is both less than 3 and *simultaneously* equal to 4. Therefore, although the example is syntactically valid it will always return a "false" value.

All the above relationships may be summarized in the following "truth tables."

6.4   The Truth Tables

The AND Table

A B	A AND B
T T	T
T F	F
F T	F
F F	F

The OR Table

A B	A OR B
T T	T
T F	T
F T	T
F F	F

The NOT Table

A	NOT A
T	F
F	T

6.5   The MIN and MAX Functions

BASIC provides two special operators called MIN and MAX. The operator MIN selects the smaller, or minimum value of two given expressions, and the MAX operator selects the maximum.

Program 6-2 is a simple illustration of these two operators. The alert observer will notice that since the READ instruction reads *two* data items each time it is executed, two trailer items are needed, either of which may be tested. If only one trailer item were included in this case, the program would have terminated with an out-of-data diagnostic.

Program 6-2

```
100  PRINT "******************"
110  PRINT "*                *"
120  PRINT "*ILLUSTRATION OF *"
130  PRINT "*                *"
140  PRINT "* MIN  AND  MAX *"
150  PRINT "*                *"
160  PRINT "******************"
170  PRINT
180  READ X,Y
190  DATA 5,3,4,2,7,5,16,4,3,-9,-9
200  IF X=-9 THEN 270
210  LET A=X MIN Y
220  PRINT "THE MINIMUM OF";X;"AND";Y;"IS";A
230  LET B=X MAX Y
240  PRINT "THE MAXIMUM OF";X;"AND";Y;"IS":B
250  PRINT
260  GO TO 180
270  END
```

RUN

```
******************
*                *
*ILLUSTRATION OF *
*                *
* MIN  AND  MAX *
*                *
******************
```

THE MINIMUM OF 5	AND 3	IS 3
THE MAXIMUM OF 5	AND 3	IS 5
THE MINIMUM OF 4	AND 2	IS 2
THE MAXIMUM OF 4	AND 2	IS 4
THE MINIMUM OF 7	AND 5	IS 5
THE MAXIMUM OF 7	AND 5	IS 7
THE MINIMUM OF 16	AND 4.3	IS 4.3
THE MAXIMUM OF 16	AND 4.3	IS 16

DONE

6.6   Introduction to Character Strings

So far we have dealt only with numeric data. This was quite appropriate since we have been concerned until now with numerical operations. But nonnumeric data also exist although one cannot perform numeric operations upon them. The nonnumeric data which BASIC is equipped to handle are known as "character strings." A character string is any character(s) (typed on the Teletype machine) enclosed between double quotes.

In order to distinguish between numeric data and string data the variables associated with string data are *always* denoted by a single letter of the alphabet followed by the dollar sign. Such a variable can hold exactly one character which, as pointed out above, must be enclosed by double quotes.

Program 6-3 serves as simple introduction to the notion of character strings. Its purpose is to read in and count a series of one-letter character strings representing the five vowels of the English alphabet. The character "S" (stop) is arbitrarily assigned to play the role of the trailer. Since there is a considerable amount of counting to be done each of the counters (K, A1, E1, I1, O1, U1) must be initialized to zero. In BASIC this may be done in a single statement, as shown in line 200.

The name C$ is assigned to the data items, each of which is examined in turn to determine which of the vowels it is. Once this has been established a 1 is added to the appropriate counter.

Program 6-3

```
100   PRINT "**************************"
110   PRINT "*                        *"
120   PRINT "* ILLUSTRATION OF SOME   *"
130   PRINT "*                        *"
140   PRINT "* SIMPLE      CHARACTER  *"
150   PRINT "*                        *"
160   PRINT "*            STRINGS      *"
170   PRINT "*                        *"
180   PRINT "**************************"
190   PRINT
200   LET K=A1=E1=I1=O1=U1=0
210   READ C$
220   DATA "A","U","I","I","E","E","O","U","A","A","U","S"
230   IF C$="S" THEN 410
240   LET K=K+1
250   IF C$="A" THEN 310
260   IF C$="E" THEN 330
270   IF C$="I" THEN 350
280   IF C$="O" THEN 370
290   IF C$="U" THEN 390
300   GO TO 210
310   LET A1=A1+1
320   GO TO 210
330   LET E1=E1+1
340   GO TO 210
350   LET I1=I1+1
360   GO TO 210
370   LET O1=O1+1
```

```
380  GO TO 210
390  LET U1=U1+1
400  GO TO 210
410  PRINT "THERE ARE" ;K;" CHARACTER DATA ITEMS"
420  PRINT
430  PRINT A1,"A'S"
440  PRINT E1,"E'S"
450  PRINT I1,"I'S"
460  PRINT O1,"O'S"
470  PRINT U1,"U'S"
480  PRINT "_____"
490  LET K1=A1+E1+I1+O1+U1
500  PRINT K1
510  PRINT "_____"
520  END
```

RUN


```
*************************
*                       *
* ILLUSTRATION OF SOME  *
*                       *
* SIMPLE     CHARACTER  *
*                       *
*          STRINGS      *
*                       *
*************************
```


THERE ARE 11   CHARACTER DATA ITEMS

```
3                   A'S
2                   E'S
2                   I'S
1                   O'S
3                   U'S
----------
11
----------
```


DONE

We return to this question of character strings in greater detail in Chapter Twelve, where we deal with strings greater than one character in length.

6.7 A Reevaluation of the Quadratic Equation Solver

Returning to our original quadratic equation on page 00; if an expression, like the discriminant, is to be used in several different places, it is usually a good idea to evaluate it once and thereafter to refer merely to that evaluation. It is not only easier to program this way, but also saves time and effort (and requires less valuable computer time). For this reason the discriminant was defined to be D.

There are many ways of *incorrectly* writing the statement for finding the "roots" of the quadratic equation. Here are only some of them. Be sure that the reasons they are incorrect are quite clear.

(1)   X1 = − B + SQR(D) / 2 * A
(2)   X1 = (− B + SQR(D) / 2 * A
(3)   X1 = (− B + SQR(D))/ 2 * A

As far as the computer is concerned (1) and (3) above would be accepted as valid by the compiler but would produce incorrect and therefore worthless results. In (1) the result X1 would be algebraically equivalent to:

$$-b + \left(\frac{\sqrt{b^2 - 4ac}}{2} \right) a$$

while the equivalent algebraic expression for (3) would be:

$$\left(\frac{-b + \sqrt{b^2 - 4ac}}{2} \right) a$$

No result would be computed for (2) because the compiler would detect the fact that the expression contains unbalanced parentheses. As a result, the statement would simply be rejected.

A rendering into BASIC of an "approximation" or a "close likeness" to an algebraic formula is just not good enough. It has to be correct in all its parts for the results to be meaningful. Therefore, great attention has to be given to the smallest detail; such is the nature of programming.

6.8   An Improved Quadratic Equation Solver

When a negative discriminant was encountered in the quadratic equation program above, (Program 6-1) the associated values of A, B, and C were printed out together with a statement that because the roots were complex the case was ignored. However, in the next program we actually compute the roots, even if the discriminant is negative. This means that we resort to complex arithmetic in which numbers are represented by a real part and an imaginary part.

For the benefit of the interested reader, the complex roots are calculated according to the following logic. The general formula for solving quadratic equations is, as stated earlier,

$$x_1, x_2 = \frac{-b \pm \sqrt{b^2 - 4ac}}{2a}$$

This is equivalent to:

$$\frac{-b}{2a} \pm \frac{\sqrt{b^2 - 4ac}}{2a}$$

If the discriminant is negative, its absolute value is taken using the ABS (absolute) function. When this function is used, both parts of the formula may be reduced to a single number. The first part, which presents no problem, is $-b/2a$, and the second part, $\sqrt{b^2 - 4ac}/2a$, can now also be reduced to a single number because the discriminant is no longer negative. One root of the equation is given by the real part $(-b/2a)$ and the imaginary part by $\sqrt{b^2 - 4ac}/2a$. The second root has the *same* real part as the first but the sign of the imaginary portion is opposite from that of the first root. The imaginary parts are referred to as *conjugates*. This is the manner in which the complex roots have been calculated in the following program.

Notice that in line 430 the user is asked whether he would like to continue. A "yes" is indicated by "Y" and a "no" by "N." Anything else typed in will be detected in line 490 where an appropriate message is printed. The next line of coding sends control to line 440 which again prints the method of responding to the question. Entry of "N" will send control to statement 510, which will terminate the program.

Program 6-4

```
100  PRINT "***************************"
110  PRINT "*                         *"
120  PRINT "* AN IMPROVED QUADRATIC *"
130  PRINT "*     EQUATION SOLVER      *"
140  PRINT "*                         *"
150  PRINT "***************************"
160  PRINT
170  INPUT A,B,C
180  PRINT
190  PRINT
200  IF A=Ø AND B=Ø AND C=Ø THEN 430
210  IF A=Ø THEN 380
220  LET D=B↑2-4*A*C
230  IF D<Ø THEN 300
240  LET X1=(-B+SQR(D))/(2*A)
250  LET X2=(-B-SQR(D))/(2*A)
260  PRINT "A=" ;A, "B=" ;B, "C=" ;C
270  PRINT
280  PRINT "ROOT 1=" ;X1, "ROOT 2=" ;X2
290  GO TO 420
300  LET M=ABS(D)
310  LET N=SQR(M)/(2*A)
320  LET P=-B/(2*A)
330  PRINT "A=" ;A, "B=" ;B, "C=" ;C
340  PRINT
350  PRINT "ROOT 1=" ;P;"+" ;N; "I"
360  PRINT "ROOT 2=" ;P;"-" ;N; "I"
370  GO TO 420
380  LET X=-C/B
390  PRINT "A=" ;A, "B=" ;B, "C="C
400  PRINT
410  PRINT "X=" ;X
420  PRINT LIN(2)
430  PRINT "WOULD YOU LIKE TO CONTINUE"
440  PRINT "(TYPE Y FOR YES, N FOR NO)";
450  INPUT A$
460  IF A$="Y" THEN 160
470  IF A$="N" THEN 510
480  PRINT
```

```
490  PRINT "YOU OBVIOUSLY MISUNDERSTOOD THE INSTRUCTIONS"
500  GO TO 440
510  END


RUN



***************************
*                         *
* AN IMPROVED QUADRATIC *
*     EQUATION SOLVER     *
*                         *
***************************



?1,-1,-12

A= 1              B=-1              C=-12

ROOT 1= 4      ROOT 2=-3




WOULD YOU LIKE TO CONTINUE
(TYPE Y FOR YES, N FOR NO)?Y

?12,2,46


A= 12             B= 2              C= 46

ROOT 1=-8.33333E-02      + 1.95612      I
ROOT 2=-8.33333E-02      - 1.95612      I




WOULD YOU LIKE TO CONTINUE
(TYPE Y FOR YES, N FOR NO)?Y

?32,2,87


A= 32             B= 2              C= 87

ROOT 1=-.03125           + 1.64857      I
ROOT 2=-.03125           - 1.64857      I
```

WOULD YOU LIKE TO CONTINUE
(TYPE Y FOR YES, N FOR NO)?∅
YOU OBVIOUSLY MISUNDERSTOOD THE INSTRUCTIONS
(TYPE Y FOR YES, N FOR NO)?Y

?∅,46,-92

A= ∅   B= 46   C=-92

X= 2

WOULD YOU LIKE TO CONTINUE
(TYPE Y FOR YES, N FOR NO)?N

DONE

Finally, it should be stated that if the value of A is equal to zero, the equation is not a quadratic but rather a linear equation. In such a case the value of the single root is calculated by:

$$X = - C/B$$

The new, improved program for solving quadratic equations just presented permits the user to type in his data at the terminal. This obviously points to the use of the INPUT statement. A loop is set up such that each time around control goes to that INPUT statement. The question that had to be answered was: How will we get out of this loop to terminate the program? This is taken care of near the end of the program.

The value of A has to be tested individually to determine whether it is a.quadratic or a linear equation that is to be solved.

Note very carefully that the input statement reads

INPUT A, B, C

This means that when the Teletype machine prints out the single question mark and comes to a halt, the user must type in *three* values separated by commas. We will later build into the program instructions to the user advising him of this so that he will experience the minimum difficulty when running the program. Perhaps the reader would like to amend the program himself.

6.9   Ulam's Conjecture

A mathematician of note named Stanislav Ulam from the University of Colorado hypothesized that any positive, whole number (integer) would always converge to 1 if treated in the following manner: If it is odd, multiply it by three and add one; if it is even, divide it by two. This procedure is then applied to the result of each calculation.

Let us select, for example, the number seven. Here is the sequence of results that are yielded as it converges to the number 1.

7   22   11   34   17   52   26   13   40   20   10   5   16   8   4   2   1

The question arises: Does *every* number converge to 1 when treated this way? No one really knows, although computers have been used to test numbers running into the millions. So far, all those tested have converged to one.

The following program is not designed to prove whether all numbers converge to 1 according to Ulam's conjecture but rather to provide a user seated at the terminal with the opportunity to type in a number of her choice to be tested to see whether it converges to 1 or not.

The major problem that confronts a programmer is how to get the computer to know whether a number is odd or even. We human beings can tell immediately but the computer doesn't have our unique intelligence.

A simple way to overcome this problem is to take the number and divide it by two. If the integer portion of this result is now multiplied by two it will equal the original number only if the original number was even. For if the number was odd, say 7, dividing it by two gives 3.5. Multiplying the integer portion by two yields 6 with is *not* equal to the original number, 7. The INT function may therefore be used to great advantage. In Program 6-5 all of the intermediate steps except the final figure 1 are printed. It is left to the reader to modify the program so that the last step also is printed.

Program 6-5

```
100   PRINT "***************"
110   PRINT "*    ULAM'S    *"
120   PRINT "*CONJECTURE*"
130   PRINT "***************"
140   PRINT
150   PRINT "PLEASE TYPE IN YOUR VALUE OF N AFTER THE QUESTION
          MARK"
160   PRINT "(TO TERMINATE PROGRAM, PLEASE TYPE IN ANY NEGATIVE
          NUMBER)"
170   INPUT N
180   IF N<0 THEN 330
190   PRINT "THANK YOU."
200   PRINT
210   PRINT N
220   IF INT(N/2)*2-N<0 THEN 270
230   REM: N IS EVEN
240   LET N=N/2
250   IF N=1 THEN 300
260   GO TO 210
270   REM: N IS ODD
280   LET N=N*3+1
290   GO TO 210
300   PRINT
310   PRINT "ULAM'S CONJECTURE CONFIRMED"
320   GO TO 140
330   END
```

RUN

```
*************
*   ULAM'S   *
*CONJECTURE*
*************
```

PLEASE TYPE IN YOUR VALUE OF N AFTER THE QUESTION MARK
(TO TERMINATE PROGRAM, PLEASE TYPE IN ANY NEGATIVE NUMBER)
?7
THANK YOU.

7
22
11
34
17
52
26
13
4Ø
2Ø
1Ø
5
16
8
4
2

ULAM'S CONJECTURE CONFIRMED

PLEASE TYPE IN YOUR VALUE OF N AFTER THE QUESTION MARK
(TO TERMINATE PROGRAM, PLEASE TYPE IN ANY NEGATIVE NUMBER)
?15
THANK YOU.

15
46
23
7Ø
35
1Ø6
53
16Ø
8Ø
4Ø
2Ø
1Ø
5
16
8
4
2

ULAM'S CONJECTURE CONFIRMED

PLEASE TYPE IN YOUR VALUE OF N AFTER THE QUESTION MARK
(TO TERMINATE PROGRAM, PLEASE TYPE IN ANY NEGATIVE NUMBER)
?8
THANK YOU.

8
4
2

ULAM'S CONJECTURE CONFIRMED

PLEASE TYPE IN YOUR VALUE OF N AFTER THE QUESTION MARK
(TO TERMINATE PROGRAM, PLEASE TYPE IN ANY NEGATIVE NUMBER)
?-1

DONE

6.10 The REMark Statement

To help the reader follow the logic of Program 6-5, certain remarks have been included at critical junctures. This is done by means of the REM statement which, although it takes a statement number, is completely ignored during processing. Therefore, after the letters REM anything at all may follow. It is by this means that the program may be internally documented.

6.11 The Swing of the Pendulum

Many of us have studied the phenomenon of the swinging pendulum in one of our physics courses. We learned that the longer the pendulum, the longer it took to make one complete swing. We could calculate the *period* of the pendulum, that is, the time it took for one complete swing, by clocking the time for say, 20 swings, and dividing this by 20 to arrive at the average time for one complete swing. Given this time and the length of the pendulum one could calculate the pull of gravity by referring to a version of the formula:

$$T = 2\pi \sqrt{\frac{l}{g}}, \quad \text{namely} \quad g = \frac{4\pi^2 l}{T^2}$$

where

T is the time in seconds for one complete swing
π is the constant 3.14159
l is the length in centimeters of the pendulum
g is the gravitational constant (acceleration due to gravity) in centimeters per second, per second.

For any given point on the surface of the earth, the value of g is constant and is usually given as 981 cm/sec^2. Armed with this information and the length of the pendulum, it is not difficult to calculate the value of T. A modern pocket calculator would furnish the answer in a matter of seconds.

If the values of l were known in advance, they could be included in a DATA statement and read by a READ statement. Suppose, however, it was necessary to have a program set up so that a user could have the option to type in his value of *l*? Such a program is fairly easy to write; Program 6-6 is a first attempt.

Program 6-6

```
100  PRINT "*****************"
110  PRINT "* THE PENDULUM *"
120  PRINT "*               *"
130  PRINT "*    PROBLEM    *"
140  PRINT "*****************"
150  PRINT
160  PRINT "PLEASE TYPE IN YOUR VALUE OF L"
170  PRINT "(TO TERMINATE PROGRAM, TYPE IN ANY NEGATIVE VALUE)"
180  INPUT L
190  IF L<0 THEN 240
200  LET T=2*3.14159*SQR(L/981)
210  PRINT "FOR THE LENGTH" ;L;"CENTIMETERS"
220  PRINT "THE PERIOD OF THE PENDULUM IS" ;T;"SECONDS."
230  GO TO 150
240  END


RUN

*****************
* THE PENDULUM *
*               *
*    PROBLEM    *
*****************


PLEASE TYPE IN YOUR VALUE OF L
(TO TERMINATE PROGRAM, TYPE IN ANY NEGATIVE VALUE)
?981
FOR THE LENGTH 981 CENTIMETERS
THE PERIOD OF THE PENDULUM IS 6.28318      SECONDS.


PLEASE TYPE IN YOUR VALUE OF L
(TO TERMINATE PROGRAM, TYPE IN ANY NEGATIVE VALUE)
?63
FOR THE LENGTH 63 CENTIMETERS
THE PERIOD OF THE PENDULUM IS 1.59226      SECONDS.


PLEASE TYPE IN YOUR VALUE OF L
(TO TERMINATE PROGRAM, TYPE IN ANY NEGATIVE VALUE)
?2.5
FOR THE LENGTH 2.5 CENTIMETERS
THE PERIOD OF THE PENDULUM IS .317187      SECONDS.


PLEASE TYPE IN YOUR VALUE OF L
(TO TERMINATE PROGRAM, TYPE IN ANY NEGATIVE VALUE)
?162.456
FOR THE LENGTH 162.456 CENTIMETERS
THE PERIOD OF THE PENDULUM IS 2.5569      SECONDS.
```

PLEASE TYPE IN YOUR VALUE OF L
(TO TERMINATE PROGRAM, TYPE IN ANY NEGATIVE VALUE)
?-99

DONE

The strategy used to terminate the program is the typing in of a negative value for *l*, a very convenient device since it is difficult to imagine a pendulum with negative length. The first case tested was a length of 981 centimeters. This was quite deliberate since unless this gives a result for *T* of 2π, there is a "bug" in the program (i.e., the program contains an error). Since the computed value is, in fact, equal to twice π it confirms that, from a computational point of view, we have a good working program, one that does not require "debugging."

6.12 Printing Out a Table of Results

Suppose now it were necessary to calculate not just a dozen or so values of *T*, but hundreds or even thousands of values. It might not be convenient to set up endlessly long DATA statements or even to insist that the user type in her values of *l* at the Teletype as in the previous program, since she would be condemned to endless hours at the terminal. There is, however, a neat way to solve the problem. We could decide upon a minimum and a maximum value of *l*. Starting with the minimum value, we could compute its value of *T* and then add some *increment*, that is, a small value like 0.0001, to the minimum and compute the new *T*, continuing this procedure until we reached the maximum. If the minimum is 1, the maximum 1000, and the increment 0.0001, no fewer than an incredible 9,990,001 separate results would be calculated!

Here is such a program where the user decides upon the minimum, maximum, and increment at the Teletype. What prints out is a table of results with suitable headings. Naturally, we selected a small range of values for the sake of space.

Program 6-7

```
100  PRINT "**********************"
110  PRINT "* A TABLE OF RESULTS*"
120  PRINT "*                   *"
130  PRINT "*        FOR THE     *"
140  PRINT "*                   *"
150  PRINT "* PENDULUM PROBLEM*"
160  PRINT "**********************"
170  PRINT
180  PRINT "PLEASE TYPE IN YOUR MINIMUM, MAXIMUM, AND INCREMENT"
190  PRINT "              SEPARATED BY COMMAS."
200  INPUT S,B,I
210  PRINT "LENGTH", "PERIOD"
220  PRINT "_____", "_____"
230  PRINT
240  LET L=S
250  LET T=2*3.14159*SQR(L/981)
260  PRINT L,T
270  LET L=L+I
280  IF L>B THEN 300
290  GO TO 250
300  PRINT
```

```
310  PRINT "THIS IS THE END OF THE TABLE"
320  END
```

RUN

```
**********************
* A TABLE OF RESULTS*
*                    *
*        FOR THE     *
*                    *
* PENDULUM PROBLEM*
**********************
```

PLEASE TYPE IN YOUR MINIMUM, MAXIMUM, AND INCREMENT
              SEPARATED BY COMMAS.

?100,105,.25

LENGTH	PERIOD
100	2.00606
100.25	2.00857
100.5	2.01107
100.75	2.01357
101	2.01607
101.25	2.01856
101.5	2.02105
101.75	2.02354
102	2.02603
102.25	2.02851
102.5	2.03099
102.75	2.03346
103	2.03593
103.25	2.0384
103.5	2.04087
103.75	2.04333
104	2.04579
104.25	2.04825
104.5	2.0507
104.75	2.05316
105	2.05561

THIS IS THE END OF THE TABLE

DONE

In the above program, we selected the letter S (for small) to represent the minimum, B (for big) for the maximum—selecting L (for large) would have conflicted with the variable name selected for the length of the pendulum—and I for the increment. First, the value of L is set to the minimum and its value of T calculated. The current value of L is incremented by I. Immediately afterward, a test is made to determine whether the new value of L exceeds the maximum. (If this test were not made, the program would go on forever and the table printed would be endless!) Once the table is completed, a closing message is typed out and the program is terminated.

6.13 Anticipating Users' Errors

Referring to Program 6-7, the question is posed: What would have happened if the user had, either deliberately or inadvertently, entered the minimum and maximum in the wrong order? The answer is that the value of T only for the real maximum would be calculated and printed, and the program would terminate with a table consisting of a single line of results only. Examine the program carefully to ascertain that this is, in fact, what would happen!

It is possible to build into the program a test to determine whether such a mistake has, in fact, occurred. And if such a mistake is detected it is also possible to correct it. One can simply insert as IF test of the form:

IF S > B THEN

This test would immediately determine if the minimum and maximum had been switched. However, having determined that they had been switched, we would want to correct for it within the program. In order to accomplish this task, great care must be taken. A first attempt might be the following:

```
100   IF S > B THEN 110
110   LET S = B
120   LET B = S
            .
            .
            .
```

This attempt is useless for several reasons. In the first place, after the IF test, control goes to statement 110 whether or not S is greater than B. Moreover, as soon as the value of B is assigned to S the value of S is assigned to B, *making them both the same value*. Substituting

```
110   LET B = S
120   LET S = B
```

would result in a similar catastrophe. In such a situation—and the situation is always cropping up in computer programming—whenever one wishes to exchange two values, one uses another memory location in which to temporarily store either one of the two values. It is something like holding a book in one hand and a pencil in the other. In order to switch them (without resorting to juggling and with the condition that only one object can be in one hand at any time) one can merely place either the book or pencil on the table and transfer the other object to the opposite hand. With the free hand the object that was placed on the table can now be picked up and it will be seen that the objects are now held in the opposite hands. This is very similar to the standard method used in programming. It is incorporated in Program 6-8, which allows for the minimum and maximum to be reversed in order. The program prints out a short message to this effect and continues on its merry way to print the desired table of results.

Are we approaching some kind of artificial intelligence with this program? After all, we are making an inanimate object, the computer, test for human errors, correct any errors it finds, advise the human of the error, and provide the intended results.

What follows is a listing of the program that was run twice. The first time the data was correctly entered, and on the second run the minimum and maximum were deliberately interchanged.

Program 6-8

```
100  PRINT "'***********************************'"
110  PRINT "* A MORE SOPHISTICATED PROGRAM *"
120  PRINT "* FOR  PRINTING  OUT  A  TABLE  OF *"
130  PRINT "*    RESULTS FOR THE PENDULUM    *"
140  PRINT "*            PROBLEM             *"
150  PRINT "'***********************************'"
160  PRINT
170  PRINT "PLEASE TYPE IN YOUR MINIMUM, MAXIMUM, AND INCREMENT"
180  PRINT "                 SEPARATED BY COMMAS."
190  INPUT S,B,I
200  IF S<B THEN 280
210  LET X=S
220  LET S=B
230  LET B=X
240  PRINT "OOPS, IT SEEMS YOU HAVE SWITCHED THE MINIMUM FOR THE MAXIMUM"
250  PRINT "THAT'S O.K., WE HAVE TAKEN CARE OF IT FOR YOU."
260  PRINT "HERE IS YOUR TABLE OF RESULTS."
270  PRINT
280  PRINT "LENGTH", "PERIOD"
290  PRINT "_ _ _ _ _ _", "_ _ _ _ _ _"
300  PRINT
310  LET L=S
320  LET T=2*3.14159*SQR(L/981)
330  PRINT L,T
340  LET L=L+I
350  IF L>B THEN 370
360  GO TO 320
370  PRINT
380  PRINT "THIS IS THE END OF THE TABLE"
390  END
```

RUN

```
***********************************
* A MORE SOPHISTICATED PROGRAM *
*FOR  PRINTING  OUT  A  TABLE  OF*
*    RESULTS FOR THE PENDULUM    *
*            PROBLEM             *
***********************************

PLEASE TYPE IN YOUR MINIMUM, MAXIMUM, AND INCREMENT
                 SEPARATED BY COMMAS.
?100,105,.25
LENGTH          PERIOD
_ _ _ _ _ _     _ _ _ _ _ _


100             2.00606
100.25          2.00857
100.5           2.01107
100.75          2.01357
```

101	2.01607
101.25	2.01856
101.5	2.02105
101.75	2.02354
102	2.02603
102.25	2.02851
102.5	2.03099
102.75	2.03346
103	2.03593
103.25	2.0384
103.5	2.04087
103.75	2.04333
104	2.04579
104.25	2.04825
104.5	2.0507
104.75	2.05316
105	2.05561

THIS IS THE END OF THE TABLE

DONE

RUN


```
**********************************
* A MORE SOPHISTICATED PROGRAM *
* FOR  PRINTING  OUT  A  TABLE  OF *
*     RESULTS FOR THE PENDULUM     *
*                PROBLEM                *
**********************************
```

PLEASE TYPE IN YOUR MINIMUM, MAXIMUM, AND INCREMENT
                    SEPARATED BY COMMAS.
?105,100,.25
OOPS, IT SEEMS YOU HAVE SWITCHED THE MINIMUM FOR THE MAXIMUM
THAT'S O.K., WE HAVE TAKEN CARE OF IT FOR YOU.
HERE IS YOUR TABLE OF RESULTS.

LENGTH	PERIOD
- - - - - -	- - - - - -
100	2.00606
100.25	2.00857
100.5	2.01107
100.75	2.01357
101	2.01607
101.25	2.01856
101.5	2.02105
101.75	2.02354
102	2.02603
102.25	2.02851

102.5	2.03099
102.75	2.03346
103	2.03593
103.25	2.0384
103.5	2.04087
103.75	2.04333
104	2.04579
104.25	2.04825
104.5	2.0507
104.75	2.05316
105	2.05561

THIS IS THE END OF THE TABLE

DONE

6.14 The Compound Interest Problem

There seems to be a tendency on the part of programmers to make use of idle time by indulging in mental fantasies such as: how much would a $100 gift I was given at birth have amounted to if it had been invested at the time at, say, 5% interest and compounded annually for 20 years. With BASIC available to us this kind of problem can be solved quite easily, for BASIC is a particularly suitable language for solving problems involving formulas. To solve the above problem we use the compound interest formula. It is:

$$\text{Amount} = P(1 + r)^n$$

where P is the original amount invested (principal), r is the rate of interest, and n is the number of years the principal is compounded annually.

After the first year the interest amounts to $5, which is then added to the original $100. The interest for the second year is then based on the total of $100 plus the $5 interest.

Program 6-9 reads in the value of the original investment P, and the rate of interest R, with N as the number of years the principal is invested. Just a point regarding the typing in of the rate. If the rate is 7% the value to be typed in is 0.07 since 7% means 7/100, which is equal to 0.07. Notice that an asterisk *must* be included after P in statement 250, even though it does not appear in the formula. Implied multiplication simply is not permitted in BASIC even though it is in algebra.

From the output it will be seen that an investment of $100 with interest compounded annually at 5% for 20 years becomes $265.33. Once the first result has been computed the user is asked if he wishes to solve another problem. (Again, Y represents "yes" and N stands for "no"; any other response to this question causes a polite but definite printout, and the user is given another chance.) Finally, when the user wishes to leave the Teletype he is "told" by the computer: "Looking forward to seeing you again." (A little courtesy and friendliness in this mechanical age is not at all out of place.)

Program 6-9

```
100  PRINT "**************************"
110  PRINT "*                        *"
120  PRINT "*  COMPUTING COMPOUND    *"
130  PRINT "*                        *"
```

```
140  PRINT "*            INTEREST          *"
150  PRINT "*                              *"
160  PRINT "******************************"
170  PRINT
180  PRINT "PLEASE TYPE IN THE PRINCIPAL, RATE OF INTEREST,"
190  PRINT "AND THE NUMBER OF YEARS."
200  PRINT "(IN THAT ORDER AND SEPARATED BY COMMAS.)"
210  PRINT
220  INPUT P,R,N
230  PRINT "THANK YOU KINDLY."
240  PRINT
250  LET A=P*(1+R)↑N
260  PRINT "THE PRINCIPAL HAS NOW BECOME $"; A
270  PRINT
280  PRINT "WOULD YOU LIKE TO SOLVE ANOTHER PROBLEM?"
290  PRINT "TYPE 'Y' FOR YES, AND 'N' FOR NO."
300  PRINT
310  INPUT Q$
320  IF Q$="Y" THEN 180
330  IF Q$="N" THEN 360
340  PRINT "PARDON ME, BUT I THINK YOU HAVE MISREAD THE INSTRUCTIONS."
350  GO TO 290
360  PRINT "LOOKING FORWARD TO SEEING YOU AGAIN."
370  END


RUN


**************************
*                        *
*  COMPUTING COMPOUND  *
*                        *
*         INTEREST       *
*                        *
**************************


PLEASE TYPE IN THE PRINCIPAL, RATE OF INTEREST,
AND THE NUMBER OF YEARS.
(IN THAT ORDER AND SEPARATED BY COMMAS.)

?100, .05,20
THANK YOU KINDLY.

THE PRINCIPAL HAS NOW BECOME $  265.33

WOULD YOU LIKE TO SOLVE ANOTHER PROBLEM?
TYPE 'Y' FOR YES, AND 'N' FOR NO.
?Y
PLEASE TYPE IN THE PRINCIPAL, RATE OF INTEREST,
AND THE NUMBER OF YEARS.
(IN THAT ORDER AND SEPARATED BY COMMAS.)
```

?5ØØ, .10,12
THANK YOU KINDLY.

THE PRINCIPAL HAS NOW BECOME $ 1569.21

WOULD YOU LIKE TO SOLVE ANOTHER PROBLEM?
TYPE 'Y' FOR YES, AND 'N' FOR NO.

?M
PARDON ME, BUT I THINK YOU HAVE MISREAD THE INSTRUCTIONS.
TYPE 'Y' FOR YES, and 'N' FOR NO.

?Y
PLEASE TYPE IN THE PRINCIPAL, RATE OF INTEREST,
AND THE NUMBER OF YEARS.
(IN THAT ORDER AND SEPARATED BY COMMAS.)

?1ØØØ, .12,25
THANK YOU KINDLY.

THE PRINCIPAL HAS NOW BECOME $ 17ØØ0.1

WOULD YOU LIKE TO SOLVE ANOTHER PROBLEM?
TYPE 'Y' FOR YES, AND 'N' FOR NO.

?N
LOOKING FORWARD TO SEEING YOU AGAIN.

DONE

6.15   A Modified Version of the Compound Interest Problem

It could be argued that Program 6-9 is rather simplistic. After all, it seems to allow only for an investment that is compounded *annually*. Suppose the $100 were compounded quarterly instead of annually? In that case the interest rate would have to be divided by 4. Therefore the rate that would have to be typed in would be $0.05 \div 4 = 0.0125$. Also the value of N would have to be changed because N reflects the number of interest periods. For each year an investment compounded quarterly has *four* interest periods. Therefore an investment over a period of 20 years would require an entry of $20 \times 4 = 80$ for the value N. If this entry were made Program 6-9 would be quite satisfactory, but it might be too difficult for some people, particularly those to whom anything mathematical is anathema. So for the benefit of these hapless souls Program 6-9 was rewritten, this time requiring the user to devote very little thought to the problem. Notice the tender, solicitous responses the computer prints each time data is entered. Do you approve of this kind of programming?

```
1ØØ  PRINT "************************"
11Ø  PRINT "*                      *"
12Ø  PRINT "*  MODIFIED COMPOUND   *"
13Ø  PRINT "*                      *"
14Ø  PRINT "*   INTEREST PROBLEM   *"
15Ø  PRINT "*                      *"
16Ø  PRINT "************************"
```

```
170  PRINT
180  PRINT "HI, WE'RE READY TO SERVE YOU."
190  PRINT
200  PRINT "HOW MUCH DO YOU WANT TO INVEST";
210  INPUT P
220  IF P < Ø THEN 61Ø
230  PRINT
240  PRINT "SO YOU WANT TO INVEST $"; P; "?"
250  PRINT
260  PRINT "AT WHAT RATE OF INTEREST";
270  INPUT R
280  PRINT
290  IF R <= Ø THEN 64Ø
300  PRINT "AH YES, YOU WANT TO INVEST IT AT"; R; "%"
310  LET R=R*.Ø1
320  PRINT
330  PRINT "AND HOW MANY INTEREST PERIODS"
340  PRINT "(IF IT'S SEMI-ANUALLY TYPE 2; QUARTERLY TYPE 4, ETC.)";
350  INPUT N
360  IF N <= Ø THEN 67Ø
370  PRINT
380  PRINT "I SEE, EACH YEAR YOU WANT IT COMPOUNDED"; N;" TIME(S)."
390  PRINT
400  PRINT "FOR HOW MANY YEARS:";
410  INPUT Y
420  IF Y <= Ø THEN 7ØØ
430  PRINT
440  PRINT "FINE, FOR"; Y;" YEAR(S)."
450  PRINT
460  PRINT "NOW THAT YOU HAVE SUPPLIED ALL THE REQUIRED INFORMATION,"
470  PRINT "IT IS NOW POSSIBLE TO COMPUTE THE RESULTS."
480  PRINT
490  LET A=P*(1+R/N) ↑ (N*Y)
500  LET I=A-P
510  PRINT "THE ORIGINAL INVESTMENT OF $"; P
520  PRINT "NOW AMOUNTS TO $"; A
530  PRINT
540  PRINT "THE INTEREST IS THEREFORE $"; I
550  PRINT
560  PRINT "WOULD YOU LIKE TO SOLVE ANOTHER PROBLEM"
570  PRINT "(TYPE 1 FOR YES; 2 FOR NO)";
580  INPUT Q
590  IF Q=1 THEN 19Ø
600  GO TO 72Ø
610  PRINT "ARE YOU SURE YOU TYPED THE RIGHT PRINCIPAL?  PLEASE";
620  PRINT " TRY AGAIN."
630  GO TO 19Ø
640  PRINT "ARE YOU SURE YOU TYPED THE CORRECT RATE?  PLEASE";
650  PRINT "TRY AGAIN."
660  GO TO 25Ø
670  PRINT "WOULD YOU MIND CHECKING THE NUMBER OF INTEREST PERIODS?"
```

```
680   PRINT "PLEASE TRY AGAIN."
690   GO TO 320
700   PRINT "HOW MANY YEARS? PLEASE TRY AGAIN,"
710   GO TO 390
720   PRINT "WELL, IT HAS BEEN RATHER JOLLY.  SEE YOU AGAIN."
730   END
```

```
***********************
*                     *
* MODIFIED COMPOUND   *
*                     *
*   INTEREST PROBLEM  *
*                     *
***********************
```

HI, WE'RE READY TO SERVE YOU.

HOW MUCH DO YOU WANT TO INVEST?100

SO YOU WANT TO INVEST $ 100   ?

AT WHAT RATE OF INTEREST?5

AH YES, YOU WANT TO INVEST IT AT 5   %

AND HOW MANY INTEREST PERIODS
(IF IT'S SEMI-ANNUALLY TYPE 2; QUARTERLY TYPE 4, ETC.)? 1

I SEE, EACH YEAR YOU WANT IT COMPOUNDED 1   TIME(S).

FOR HOW MANY YEARS?20
FINE, FOR 20   YEAR(S).

NOW THAT YOU HAVE SUPPLIED ALL THE REQUIRED INFORMATION,
IT IS NOW POSSIBLE TO COMPUTE THE RESULTS.

THE ORIGINAL INVESTMENT OF $ 100
NOW AMOUNTS TO $ 265.33

THE INTEREST IS THEREFORE $ 165.33

WOULD YOU LIKE TO SOLVE ANOTHER PROBLEM
(TYPE 1 FOR YES; 2 FOR NO)?1

HOW MUCH DO YOU WANT TO INVEST? 500

SO YOU WANT TO INVEST $ 500   ?

AT WHAT RATE OF INTEREST?10

AH YES, YOU WANT TO INVEST IT AT 10   %

AND HOW MANY INTEREST PERIODS
(IF IT'S SEMI-ANNUALLY TYPE 2; QUARTERLY TYPE 4, ETC.)?1

I SEE, EACH YEAR YOU WANT IT COMPOUNDED 1   TIME(S).

FOR NOW MANY YEARS?12

FINE, FOR 12   YEAR(S).

NOW THAT YOU HAVE SUPPLIED ALL THE REQUIRED INFORMATION.
IT IS NOW POSSIBLE TO COMPUTE THE RESULTS.

THE ORIGINAL INVESTMENT OF $ 500
NOW AMOUNTS TO $ 1569.21

THE INTEREST IS THEREFORE $ 1069.21

WOULD YOU LIKE TO SOLVE ANOTHER PROBLEM
(TYPE 1 FOR YES; 2 FOR NO)?1

HOW MUCH DO YOU WANT TO INVEST?-12
ARE YOU SURE YOU TYPED THE RIGHT PRINCIPAL? PLEASE TRY AGAIN.

HOW MUCH DO YOU WANT TO INVEST? 1000

SO YOU WANT TO INVEST $ 1000   ?

AT WHAT RATE OF INTEREST?-13

ARE YOU SURE YOU TYPED THE CORRECT RATE? PLEASE TRY AGAIN.

AT WHAT RATE OF INTEREST? 25

AH YES, YOU WANT TO INVEST IT AT 25   %

AND HOW MANY INTEREST PERIODS
(IF IT'S SEMI-ANNUALLY TYPE 2; QUARTERLY TYPE 4, ETC.)?-2
WOULD YOU MIND CHECKING THE NUMBER OF INTEREST PERIODS?
PLEASE TRY AGAIN.

AND HOW MANY INTEREST PERIODS
(IF IT'S SEMI-ANNUALLY TYPE 2; QUARTERLY TYPE 4, ETC.)? 4

I SEE, EACH YEAR YOU WANT IT COMPOUNDED 4   TIME(S).

FOR HOW MANY YEARS? 3

FINE, FOR 3   YEAR(S).

NOW THAT YOU HAVE SUPPLIED ALL THE REQUIRED INFORMATION,
IT IS NOW POSSIBLE TO COMPUTE THE RESULTS.

THE ORIGINAL INVESTMENT OF $ 1000
NOW AMOUNTS TO $ 2069.89

THE INTEREST IS THEREFORE $ 1069.89

WOULD YOU LIKE TO SOLVE ANOTHER PROBLEM
(TYPE 1 FOR YES; 2 FOR NO)?2
WELL, IT HAS BEEN RATHER JOLLY. SEE YOU AGAIN.

DONE

6.16 The Newton-Raphson Scheme

To find the square root of a number in BASIC, one usually uses the SQR function that has been illustrated several times in the book so far. Of course, one could also raise the number to the power 0.5, in which case the square root will be calculated by means of logarithms; but this is not nearly as efficient as the SQR function.

The curious programmer might have wondered how the SQR function actually works. When the SQR function is "invoked," a special set of preprogrammed instructions is executed, and the result is the desired square root. The computer manufacturer is responsible for the design of those preprogrammed instructions. It might be instructive to the reader to become acquainted with a method of computing the square root. The method we are about to describe is known as the Newton-Raphson scheme.

Suppose we wanted to know the square root of 100. Let us "guess" that its square root is 1, even though this is a fairly dumb guess. Now according to the Newton-Raphson scheme, the new, more accurate guess is found by substituting into the formula:

$$\text{New guess} = \tfrac{1}{2}\left(\text{old guess} + \frac{100}{\text{old guess}}\right) = \tfrac{1}{2} \cdot 101 = 50.5.$$

This value of 50.5 is then substituted into the *same* formula to produce a new guess. The process is repeated until the new guess converges to the square root. In Program 6-11 we shall print out each intermediate result so that the reader will develop an understanding of the process. When printing out the answer, the program will also print out the value of the square root yielded by the SQR function, and the value by raising the number to the power 0.5. Any negative value of N will terminate the program.

To test for convergence, the absolute value of $X^2/N - 1$ is compared with an arbitrarily defined small number (epsilon) of 0.00001. If the latest value of X was such that $X^2/N - 1$ was less than or equal to 0.00001 this value of X was taken as the square root.

A careful examination of the three results obtained for $N = 9$ indicates that although the Newton-Raphson method and the SQR function both give a result of exactly 3 for the square root of 9, the value of N raised to the power 0.5 is printed as 3. on the output sheet. This indicates that the computed value was slightly more than 3 but less than 3.0000001. This number, however, is too long to be printed by the system.

Program 6-11

```
100  PRINT "************************"
110  PRINT "*                      *"
120  PRINT "* THE NEWTON-RAPHSON   *"
```

```
130  PRINT "*           METHOD          *"
140  PRINT "*                           *"
150  PRINT "*************************"
160  PRINT
170  PRINT "PLEASE TYPE IN YOUR VALUE OF N"
180  PRINT "(TO TERMINATE PROGRAM, TYPE IN ANY NEGATIVE VALUE)"
190  PRINT
200  INPUT N
210  IF N<Ø THEN 34Ø
220  PRINT
230  PRINT "THANK YOU."
240  LET X=1
250  LET X=.5*(X+N/X)
260  PRINT X
270  IF ABS(X*X/N-1)<=.ØØØØ1 THEN 29Ø
280  GO TO 25Ø
290  PRINT
300  PRINT "NEWTON-RAPHSON RESULT = "; X
310  PRINT "RESULT USING SQR FUNCTION ="; SQR(N)
320  PRINT "RESULT RAISING N TO THE POWER Ø.5 = "; N↑.5
330  GO TO 19Ø
340  END
```

RUN

```
*************************
*                       *
*  THE NEWTON-RAPHSON    *
*         METHOD         *
*                       *
*************************
```

PLEASE TYPE IN YOUR VALUE OF N
(TO TERMINATE PROGRAM, TYPE IN ANY NEGATIVE VALUE)

?2

THANK YOU.
 1.5
 1.41667
 1.41422

NEWTON-RAPHSON RESULT = 1.41422
RESULT USING SQR FUNCTION = 1.41421
RESULT RAISING N TO THE POWER Ø.5 = 1.41421

?9

THANK YOU.
 5
 3.4

```
3.02353
3.00009
3
```

```
NEWTON-RAPHSON RESULT = 3
RESULT USING SQR FUNCTION = 3
RESULT RAISING N TO THE POWER 0.5 = 3.
```

?-999

DONE

6.17 Finding the Sine of an Angle by the Taylor Power Series Expansion

If an angle is expressed in radians, one can easily find the sine of that angle in BASIC by using the standard library function SIN. For example, one need only type:

$$LET\ X = SIN(Y)$$

Once again a preprogrammed set of instructions is called into operation each time the SIN function is invoked. These instructions are based on a formula borrowed from numerical analysis. The sine of an angle of x radians is given by the Taylor power series expansion as:

$$\text{sine } x = x - \frac{x^3}{3!} + \frac{x^5}{5!} - \frac{x^7}{7!} + \ldots$$

This series continues indefinitely and, as with the method used to find the square root using the Newton-Raphson technique, we accept an approximation to the correct solution when a certain convergence criterion is satisfied.

Let us take a good look at the formula. There are several points worth noticing.

1. The sign of each term alternates from positive to negative.
2. The exponent of x in each term is raised successively in steps of 2. Moreover, the power of x in each numerator is equal to the number whose factorial appears in the denominator.
3. The absolute value of each term decreases going from left to right.

This series may be easily programmed. The computation of further terms can be terminated when the absolute value of a given term is equal to or smaller than some arbitrary epsilon. The value of each term of the series is computed using the result of the previous term. This is of particular importance in the computation of the factorial.

When the value of S in the program converges to the sine of X, the value of S is printed out together with the value given by the SIN function for comparison purposes. To terminate the program a value of 99999 radians for x should be entered.

Program 6-12

```
100  PRINT "*************************"
110  PRINT "*                       *"
120  PRINT "* THE SINE OF AN ANGLE  *"
130  PRINT "*        BY THE         *"
140  PRINT "*     TAYLOR SERIES     *"
150  PRINT "*                       *"
160  PRINT "*************************"
```

```
170  PRINT
180  PRINT "PLEASE TYPE IN YOUR VALUE OF X (IN RADIANS)"
190  "(TO TERMINATE PROGRAM, TYPE IN 99999)"
200  PRINT
210  INPUT X
220  IF X=99999. THEN 380
230  PRINT "THANK YOU."
240  PRINT
250  LET T=X
260  LET S=X
270  LET N=1
280  LET N=N+2
290  LET T=(-T*X↑2)/(N*(N-1))
300  LET S=S+T
310  IF ABS(T) <= .00001 THEN 330
320  GO TO 280
330  PRINT
340  PRINT "THE VALUE OF X IN RADIANS = "; X
350  PRINT "THE SINE OF X = "; S
360  PRINT "THE SIN(X) VALUE ="; SIN(X)
370  GO TO 170
380  END


RUN


*************************
*                       *
* THE SINE OF AN ANGLE  *
*        BY THE         *
*      TAYLOR SERIES    *
*                       *
*************************


PLEASE TYPE IN YOUR VALUE OF X (IN RADIANS)
(TO TERMINATE PROGRAM, TYPE IN 99999)

?.1
THANK YOU.


THE VALUE OF X IN RADIANS =  .1
THE SINE OF X = 9.98334E-02
THE SIN(X) VALUE = 9.98334E-02

PLEASE TYPE IN YOUR VALUE OF X (IN RADIANS)
(TO TERMINATE PROGRAM, TYPE IN 99999)

?.2
THANK YOU.
```

```
        THE VALUE OF X IN RADIANS =  .2
        THE SINE OF X =  .198669
        THE SIN(X) VALUE =   .198669

        PLEASE TYPE IN YOUR VALUE OF X (IN RADIANS)
        (TO TERMINATE PROGRAM, TYPE IN 99999)

        ?.3
        THANK YOU.


        THE VALUE OF X IN RADIANS =  .3
        THE SINE OF X =  .29552
        THE SIN(X) VALUE =  .29552

        PLEASE TYPE IN YOUR VALUE OF X (IN RADIANS)
        (TO TERMINATE PROGRAM, TYPE IN 99999)

        ?.8
        THANK YOU.


        THE VALUE OF X IN RADIANS =  .8
        THE SINE OF X =  .717356
        THE SIN(X) VALUE =  .717356

        PLEASE TYPE IN YOUR VALUE OF X (IN RADIANS)
        (TO TERMINATE PROGRAM, TYPE IN 99999)

        ?99999

        DONE
```

6.18   The Russian Peasant Method of Multiplication

A novel method of multiplying two integers is the so-called Russian peasant method. There is evidence that the method was used both in ancient Egypt and China. The method is interesting for it involves only division by two and multiplication by two, followed by straight addition.

Suppose we wanted to find the product of the numbers 19 and 23. We would write down these two numbers in two columns. On the left we would write the number 19 and on the right the number 23. Each number on the left is divided by two, ignoring any remainder (truncating). Each time a divison takes place the corresponding number on the right is multiplied by two. This process continues until the number on the left is reduced to 1. The table would look like this.

```
            19 X   23
             9     46
             4     92
             2    184
             1    368
```

Now, each time an even number appears on the left its corresponding number on the right is crossed out. The right-hand column would now appear as:

$$23$$
$$46$$
$$\cancel{92}$$
$$\cancel{184}$$
$$368$$

The remaining numbers are now added and the sum, believe it or not, is the product of 19 × 23.

Russian Peasant Method	*Straight Multiplication*
23	23
46	19
368	230
437	207
	437

Program 6-13 reads in a series of pairs of numbers, A and B. A value of A = 0 indicates it is a trailer. Notice that the trailer must be composed of two items not one, even though only one of them is tested. The reason for this is that the READ statement in line 200 reads a *pair* at a time. Incidentally, it is also worth noting that the trailer has been put in a separate DATA statement. The reason for this is that if additional data were to be included, the first DATA statement could be amended without disturbing the trailer.

Returning to the program itself, A and B are both set equal to another variable, because their values will be changing during the course of the computation and the original values are needed for the final printout.

The test this time to determine whether A is odd or even is to subtract A/2 from the integer portion of A/2. If the difference is zero, A is even. If it is even, A is tested to see whether it is equal to 1, for if it is, that's the end of the calculation. If it isn't, A is divided by 2 and truncated if necessary. Then the value of B is doubled. If A turns out to be odd, a running total of B is kept.

The output confirms that the method works correctly on each pair selected. The method does in fact work for all negative and positive numbers. It is particularly interesting that the method is very close to the standard way by which multiplication is accomplished on modern computers.

Program 6-13

```
100  PRINT "**************************"
110  PRINT "*                        *"
120  PRINT "*  THE RUSSIAN PEASANT  *"
130  PRINT "*                        *"
140  PRINT "*  METHOD TO MULTIPLY  *"
150  PRINT "*                        *"
160  PRINT "*     TWO NUMBERS        *"
170  PRINT "*                        *"
180  PRINT "**************************"
190  PRINT
200  READ A,B
210  DATA 4,7,5,6,15,-27,19,23
```

```
220  DATA, Ø,Ø
230  IF A=Ø THEN 380
240  LET X=A
250  LET Y=B
260  LET P=A*B
270  LET S=Ø
280  IF INT(A/2)-A/2=Ø THEN 300
290  LET S=S+B
300  IF A=1 THEN 340
310  LET A=INT(A/2)
320  LET B=B*2
330  GO TO 280
340  PRINT "THE PRODUCT OF THE TWO NUMBERS"; X; "AND"; Y; "IS"; P
350  PRINT "BY THE RUSSIAN PEASANT METHOD, THE PRODUCT  IS. "; S
360  PRINT
370  GO TO 19Ø
380  END
```

```
*************************
*                       *
*  THE RUSSIAN PEASANT  *
*                       *
*  METHOD  TO MULTIPLY  *
*                       *
*      TWO NUMBERS      *
*                       *
*************************
```

```
THE PRODUCT OF THE TWO NUMBERS 4     AND  7    IS  28
BY THE RUSSIAN PEASANT METHOD, THE PRODUCT  IS   28


THE PRODUCT OF THE TWO NUMBERS 5     AND  6    IS  3Ø
BY THE RUSSIAN PEASANT METHOD, THE PRODUCT  IS   3Ø


THE PRODUCT OF THE TWO NUMBERS 15    AND- 27   IS- 4Ø5
BY THE RUSSIAN PEASANT METHOD, THE PRODUCT  IS  - 4Ø5


THE PRODUCT OF THE TWO NUMBERS 19    AND  23   IS  437
BY THE RUSSIAN PEASANT METHOD, THE PRODUCT  IS   437
```

6.19 Computer Precision—Or the Lack Thereof

Most people have come to associate computers with absolute accuracy. As desirable as this would be, the fact is that, depending on the data and how it is handled, we often have to settle for an approximation to the correct answer. One reason for this is the computer stores data and does arithmetic in the binary system where the only two digits used are 0 and 1 rather than in the decimal system where the digits 0 through 9 are used. Conversion from one system to the other is done every time input is read in and output is printed out. Whereas in the decimal system the value 0.1 is an exact quantity, when this number is converted into binary it becomes an infinitely repeated binary fraction. But the memory location into which this number is stored is *not* of infinite length. As a result only a portion of the fraction is retained in memory. This really means that the stored number is actually *smaller* than the number we intended to store.

To illustrate this point we present a simple program in which the value 0.1 is summed 10,000 times within a FOR/NEXT loop. (Notice that we write 10,000 without the comma in a program!) One might expect the result to be 10000 × .1 = 1000. A glance at the output however will indicate otherwise.

Program 6-14

```
100  PRINT "**************************"
110  PRINT "*                        *"
120  PRINT "* ILLUSTRATION    OF    A *"
130  PRINT "*                        *"
140  PRINT "* COMPUTER INACCURACY *"
150  PRINT "*                        *"
160  PRINT "**************************"
170  PRINT
180  LET S=0
190  FOR I=1 TO 10000
200  LET S=S+.1
210  NEXT I
220  PRINT S
230  END


RUN


**************************
*                        *
* ILLUSTRATION    OF    A *
*                        *
* COMPUTER INACCURACY *
*                        *
**************************

   999.829

DONE
```

6.20 Repeated Square Roots

If you have access to a pocket calculator with a square root button it would be most instructive if not downright fun to key in a number—any positive number—and find its square root by touching the square root function button. If the button is touched again the display will contain the square root of the square root—the fourth root. If the square root button is punched repeatedly, one will observe that the number in the display approaches 1 and, if continued long enough, actually reaches 1. In mathematics it is said that the number *converges* to 1. If the original number selected is between zero and 1 it is quite possible that it will not actually reach 1 but will get "locked in" at a number slightly less than 1, but that depends on the calculator. Calculators suffer from some of the same kind of deficiencies that computers do. After all, the display and memory of both instruments are of finite size.

We are quite familiar by this time with the square root function SQR which is available to us on the BASIC system. Advantage of it is taken in Program 6-15, where we play a game with the computer. The idea is to type in a number and to guess how many times one has to go through the square root sequence before it converges to 1.

But will it converge to 1 exactly? In view of what has been said about having on occasion to settle for close approximations, it seems clear that this is such a situation. What we have to settle for is not convergence to 1 exactly but to some *programmer defined* approximation. If we decide that any result equal to 1, plus or minus say 0.00001 (1 ± 0.00001), will satisfy our criterion for "the final square root" then such a determination would have to be incorporated into the program.

In other words, what we are saying is that if the *absolute value* of 1 minus our result is greater than or equal to the arbitrarily defined tiny value of 0.00001 (called *epsilon*) the result has not, according to our definition, converged to 1.

In Program 6-15 the user is asked to type in an original positive number X. Then the user is asked to type in her guess G for the number of "iterations" she thinks it will take through the square root routine to converge to 1. In line 290 the value X is duplicated under the name N. This is done because in the very next statement the value of X is changed to the square root of X. Notice that X appears on both sides of the equals sign. The counter K is then incremented by 1.

The test is now made to see whether X has converged to 1 according to our criterion. If it has not, control is sent back to line 300 where the operation is repeated. When the condition is eventually satisfied and X does converge to 1 the guess for the required number of iterations is compared with the actual number K. If they agree the counter for "right guess" R is incremented by 1. If not, 1 is added to the "wrong" counter W. Finally, when a negative number is inputted for X, a tally of the results and the percentage of correct guesses is printed.

The program was run twice to illustrate the second possible response obtainable.

Program 6-15

```
100   PRINT "***************************"
110   PRINT "*                         *"
120   PRINT "*  REPEATED SQUARE ROOT  *"
130   PRINT "*                         *"
140   PRINT "***************************"
150   LET W=R=Ø
160   PRINT
170   PRINT
180   LET K=Ø
190   PRINT "PICK A NUMBER THAT YOU WANT SQUARE ROOTED TO DEATH (TO ";
200   PRINT "TERMINATE PROGRAM, TYPE ANY NEGATIVE NUMBER)";
210   INPUT X
220   IF X<Ø THEN 420
230   PRINT
240   PRINT "NOW TYPE IN YOUR GUESS FOR THE NUMBER OF ITERATIONS IT";
250   PRINT "TAKES FOR YOUR NUMBER TO REACH ONE";
260   INPUT G
270   PRINT
280   PRINT
```

```
290  LET N=X
300  LET X=SQR(X)
310  LET K=K+1
320  IF ABS (1- X) >= .00001 THEN 300
330  IF K=G THEN 380
340  PRINT "YOUR GUESS WAS INCORRECT! IT TOOK "; K; "ITERATIONS";
350  PRINT "FOR "; N " TO REACH 1."
360  LET W=W+1
370  GO TO 160
380  PRINT "CONGRATULATIONS! YOU HAVE CORRECTLY GUESSED THAT IT";
390  PRINT "TAKES "; K; " ITERATIONS FOR "; N; "TO REACH 1."
400  LET R=R+1
410  GO TO 160
420  PRINT LIN(3)
430  LET P1=(R/(W+R)) * 100
440  IF P1=100 THEN 480
450  PRINT "OUT OF ";W+R; "GUESSES, YOU GOT "W;"CORRECT, A SCORE OF"
460  PRINT P1; "% CORRECT"
470  GO TO 490
480  PRINT "YOU GOT 100% CORRECT, BUT NO MORE!!"
490  END
```

```
RUN

***************************
*                         *
*  REPEATED SQUARE ROOT  *
*                         *
***************************


PICK A NUMBER THAT YOU WANT SQUARE ROOTED TO DEATH (TO
TERMINATE PROGRAM, TYPE ANY NEGATIVE NUMBER)?45

NOW TYPE IN YOUR GUESS FOR THE NUMBER OF ITERATIONS IT
TAKES FOR YOUR NUMBER TO REACH ONE?19


CONGRATULATIONS!  YOU HAVE CORRECTLY GUESSED THAT IT TAKES  19
   ITERATIONS FOR  45    TO REACH 1.


PICK A NUMBER THAT YOU WANT SQUARE ROOTED TO DEATH (TO
TERMINATE PROGRAM, TYPE ANY NEGATIVE NUMBER)?43

NOW TYPE IN YOUR GUESS FOR THE NUMBER OF ITERATIONS IT
TAKES FOR YOUR NUMBER TO REACH ONE?32


YOUR GUESS WAS INCORRECT!  IT TOOK  19     ITERATIONS FOR  43
   TO REACH 1.
```

PICK A NUMBER THAT YOU WANT SQUARE ROOTED TO DEATH (TO
TERMINATE PROGRAM, TYPE ANY NEGATIVE NUMBER)?-1

OUT OF 2   GUESSES, YOU GOT 1   CORRECT, A SCORE OF
  50   % CORRECT

DONE

6.21   The Random Function

For many kinds of problems it is most convenient to have the computer supply random data. This is particularly so in the study of probability where one might be interested in say, investigating the frequency with which heads or tails shows up in the tossing of a coin. Execution of the instruction:

$$\text{LET X = RND(1)}$$

will produce a decimal number between 0 and 1, but not including 1. The number in parentheses, the argument, must not be negative but has no direct bearing on the random number generated; it must, nevertheless, be included. So we could have written RND(0), RND(1.2), RND(1.2E5), etc., or even RND(I), RND(Z↑2), etc. provided these arguments are predefined.

6.22   The Tossing of a Coin

A typical number returned by the random number generator RND is 0.012345. How can such a number be regarded as a head or a tail? A simple and direct solution would be to consider any number between 0 and .5 a head and any other number a tail. Here is a simple illustrative program to show how the tossing of a coin may be simulated. Program 6-16 was run twice to show the different results.

Program 6-16

```
100  PRINT "****************"
110  PRINT "*              *"
120  PRINT "*  THE TOSSING *"
130  PRINT "*              *"
140  PRINT "*  OF   A  COIN *"
150  PRINT "*              *"
160  PRINT "****************"
170  PRINT
180  FOR I=1 TO 10
190  LET X=RND(1)
200  IF X<.5 THEN 230
210  PRINT "THE RANDOM NUMBER"; X; "REPRESENTS TAILS."
220  GO TO 240
230  PRINT "THE RANDOM NUMBER"; X; "REPRESENTS HEADS."
240  NEXT I
250  END
```


RUN

```
***************
*             *
*  THE TOSSING *
*             *
*  OF   A   COIN *
*             *
***************
```

THE RANDOM NUMBER 9.Ø8822E-Ø2   REPRESENTS HEADS.
THE RANDOM NUMBER .823271   REPRESENTS TAILS.
THE RANDOM NUMBER .38Ø885   REPRESENTS HEADS.
THE RANDOM NUMBER .26Ø817   REPRESENTS HEADS.
THE RANDOM NUMBER .88987   REPRESENTS TAILS.
THE RANDOM NUMBER .643376   REPRESENTS TAILS.
THE RANDOM NUMBER .434ØØ6   REPRESENTS HEADS.
THE RANDOM NUMBER .76Ø714   REPRESENTS TAILS.
THE RANDOM NUMBER .51Ø599   REPRESENTS TAILS.
THE RANDOM NUMBER .827595   REPRESENTS TAILS.

DONE

RUN


```
***************
*             *
*  THE TOSSING *
*             *
*  OF   A   COIN *
*             *
***************
```

THE RANDOM NUMBER .658411   REPRESENTS TAILS.
THE RANDOM NUMBER .976321   REPRESENTS TAILS.
THE RANDOM NUMBER 9.54954E-Ø2   REPRESENTS HEADS.
THE RANDOM NUMBER .738969   REPRESENTS TAILS.
THE RANDOM NUMBER .1Ø8688   REPRESENTS HEADS.
THE RANDOM NUMBER .55ØØ61   REPRESENTS TAILS.
THE RANDOM NUMBER .243Ø83   REPRESENTS HEADS.
THE RANDOM NUMBER .2Ø29Ø2   REPRESENTS HEADS.
THE RANDOM NUMBER .757804   REPRESENTS TAILS.
THE RANDOM NUMBER .563Ø58   REPRESENTS TAILS.

6.23 Simulating the Throwing of a Die

As is well known to gamblers young and old, professional and amateur, a die is a cube of six sides and each side is marked with one to six dots. Not only can the RND function simulate the tossing of a coin but it may also be used to simulate the throwing of a die.

One approach could be to obtain a random number and assign one of the numbers 1 to 6 to it according to the following table:

Generated Number N	Die Value
$0 <= N < 1/6$	1
$1/6 <= N < 2/6$	2
$2/6 <= N < 3/6$	3
$3/6 <= N < 4/6$	4
$4/6 <= N < 5/6$	5
$5/6 <= N < 6/6$	6

Using this approach each generated number would be tested to determine which die value to assign to it. This would require at least five IF statements together with its associated logic.

The astute reader will observe a pattern in the above table. The numerator of the second fraction on each line is *identical* to the associated die value. To eliminate the denominator 6, therefore, all we have to do is to multiply the fraction by 6. Thus the table above may be transformed into

Generated Number $(N * 6)$	Die Value
$0 <= N * 6 < 1$	1
$1 <= N * 6 < 2$	2
$2 <= N * 6 < 3$	3
$3 <= N * 6 < 4$	4
$4 <= N * 6 < 5$	5
$5 <= N * 6 < 6$	6

The number $N * 6$ which we now have still contains a fractional portion that does not interest us. To eliminate it we may merely resort to the integer fucntion INT. However, this would yield the integers 0, 1, 2, 3, 4, and 5 and these are not exactly the numbers in which we are interested. We *are* interested in these numbers *plus* 1.

This is the essence of Program 6-17, which simulates the throwing of a die 24 times.

Program 6-17

```
100  PRINT "*****************************"
110  PRINT "*                           *"
120  PRINT "*   THE SIMULATION OF THE   *"
130  PRINT "*                           *"
140  PRINT "* THROWING   OF   A   DIE *"
150  PRINT "*                           *"
160  PRINT "*****************************"
170  PRINT
180  FOR I=1 TO 24
190  LET X=INT (RND(1)*6)+1
200  PRINT X;
210  NEXT I
220  END
```

RUN

```
* * * * * * * * * * * * * * * * * * * * * * * * * * * *
*                                           *
*    THE SIMULATION OF THE     *
*                                           *
*  THROWING     OF    A    DIE *
*                                           *
* * * * * * * * * * * * * * * * * * * * * * * * * * * *
```

5	3	2	1	3	5	5	6	2	3	6	3
4	3	5	1	6	5	4	3	5	2	1	1

DONE

6.24 Simulating a Pair of Dice

The famous game, craps, is played with a pair of dice. If it is possible to simulate the throwing of a single die, surely it is possible to simulate the throwing of a pair of dice.

At first blush one might think that generating the numbers 2 through 12 might suffice. However we shall soon see that this approach falls somewhat short of the mark. The random numbers generated by RND are uniformly distributed between 0 and 1. This means that if the numbers 2 through 12 are generated by means of a single random number generator, the likelihood of each of the numbers occurring is about the same. However, the number 7, for example, could show up in the actual throwing of a pair of dice in six different ways, represented as shown:

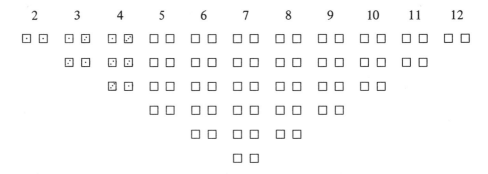

Partial blowup:

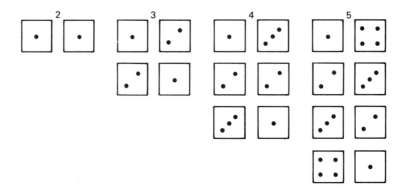

```
* * * * * * * * * * * * * * * * * * * * * * * * * * * *
*                                                   *
*  RESTARTING THE RANDOM  *
*                                                   *
*  NUMBER           SEQUENCE  *
*                                                   *
* * * * * * * * * * * * * * * * * * * * * * * * * * * *
```

THE RANDOM NUMBER .529432 REPRESENTS TAILS.
THE RANDOM NUMBER .225555 REPRESENTS HEADS.
THE RANDOM NUMBER .329078 REPRESENTS HEADS.
THE RANDOM NUMBER .306689 REPRESENTS HEADS.
THE RANDOM NUMBER .537845 REPRESENTS TAILS.
THE RANDOM NUMBER .696617 REPRESENTS TAILS.
THE RANDOM NUMBER .940248 REPRESENTS TAILS.
THE RANDOM NUMBER 8.94691E-02 REPRESENTS HEADS.
THE RANDOM NUMBER 9.68938E-02 REPRESENTS HEADS.
THE RANDOM NUMBER .64532 REPRESENTS TAILS.

QUICK REFERENCE GUIDE TO CHAPTER SIX

Item	General Form	Examples
1. Built-in function	See page 46	SQR(5) INT(7.8)
2. Logical connectors	AND OR NOT	
3. Compound IF statement	*Line number* IF *relational expression logic connector relational expression* THEN *line number*	100 IF A=B AND C=0 THEN 150 200 IF E>F OR G<=H THEN 250 300 IF NOT (E>F OR G<=H) THEN 350
4. The REMark statement	*Line number* REM *anything*	100 REM THIS IS JUST A REMARK
5. String variable	*Letter* $	A$ R$ Z$
6. String DATA statement	*Line number* DATA *string constants*	100 DATA "A", "B", "Z", "%" "$", "."

Questions

1. Make three general statements about the standard functions.

2. What answers would you expect from the following instructions:

 (a) LET Q = SQR(100)

 (b) LET X = SQR(9)

 (c) LET Y = 144

    LET Z = SQR(Y)

 (d) LET A = 2

    LET B = 3

    LET C = SQR((A * B)↑2)

 (e) LET D = SQR(-5)

3. What base is associated with the LOG function? Does BASIC have a logarithm function with another base?

4. Write a program that READs in five sets of A, B, and C, representing the coefficients of quadratic equations. Solve the quadratic equations for both real and complex roots. In addition, if A = 0 for any case, solve that linear equation.

5. Write a program that READs in three integers at a time. Test whether they are Pythagorean triplets. ($A^2 = B^2 + C^2$; in any order).

6. Assume DATA statements contain a list of two integers J and K. Write a program that counts

   (a)   the total number of such pairs

   (b)   the number of pairs in which the value of J equals K, and the ratio, in *percent* of such identical pairs to the total.

7. Referring to Ulam's conjecture, write a program that permits a user sitting at the Teletype console to enter an integer value. The program should check that the number typed in goes to one, but instead of printing out intermediate stages it should count how many such stages are necessary. This number and some appropriate message should be printed out at the termination of each case. REMark statements should be interspersed liberally throughout the program.

8. Write a program to compute the period of a pendulum for lengths of 5 to 7 feet in increments of 0.1 foot. You may use the formula in Section 6.11, with the constant $g = 32$ ft per second, per second.

9. The formula for finding the cube root of a number, according to the Newton-Raphson technique is

$$\text{New guess} = \frac{1}{3}\left(2 \times \text{old guess} + \frac{N}{(\text{old guess})^2}\right)$$

Write a program similar to Program 6-11 to compute the cube root of N using the Newton-Raphson method. Since there is no standard cube root function, you need only print as output the Newton-Raphson cube root and $N \uparrow (1/3)$ for each N.

10. The Taylor polynomial for the cosine of x (in radians) is

$$\cos x = 1 - \frac{x^2}{2!} + \frac{x^4}{4!} - \frac{x^6}{6!} + \ldots$$

Write a program similar to Program 6-12 that calculates and prints cosine x and compares the result with that of the standard library function COS(X).

11. The Taylor polynomial for e^x is

$$e^x = 1 + x + \frac{x^2}{2!} + \frac{x^3}{3!} \ldots$$

Write a program similar to Program 6-12 that calculates and prints e^x and compares the result with EXP(X).

12. Write a program to INPUT an angle x. Compute its sine, by the Taylor polynomial, counting the number of iterations necessary and compare the result with SIN(X). Calculate the cosine using the trigonometric identity $\sin^2 x + \cos^2 x = 1$ and com-

pare it with COS (X). Finally, compute the tangent using the trigonometric definition tan x = sin x/cos x and compare this value with TAN (X).

13. The cashiers manning the checkout counters in the Krazee Supermarket chain are paid in the following fashion. Whenever a total is computed the "cents" portion goes to the cashier and the integral portion goes to the management. Select a list of about 10 items and compute:

    (a) the supermarket's take

    (b) the cashier's take

    (c) the percentage of the cashier's take to that of the supermarket.

14. At the moment in New York City the taxis charge fares according to the following schedule (excluding waiting time):

    $$65 \; ¢ \quad \text{for the first 1/6 mile}$$
    $$10 \; ¢ \quad \text{for each additional 1/6 mile}$$

    Write a program that reads in as input the distance traveled by a fare and the percentage tip. The program should allow for any number of fares and, in each case, should compute the charge according to the meter, the amount of the tip, and the total paid to the driver for each ride. At the termination of the program, the printout should include the total metered distance covered, the total charge according to the meter, the total of the tips, and the percentage of total tips to total metered charges.

15. With an eye to the inevitable changeover to the metric system write a program that reads in as input a distance expressed in kilometers. Convert this number to miles, yards, feet, and inches, using the conversion factor:

    $$1 \text{ km} \equiv 0.62137 \text{ miles}$$

    For example, 32,567 kilometers is equivalent to 20,237 miles, 233 yards, 2 feet, and 3.0 inches.   The program should terminate when a negative number is inputted.

16. Imagine you are a computer instructed with the program that follows. What results would you print?

    ```
    10   READ N
    20   IF N<0 THEN 120
    30   READ X
    40   IF N<4 AND X>25 THEN 80
    50   IF X >= 25 THEN 100
    60   PRINT N,X
    70   GO TO 10
    80   PRINT N,SQR (X)
    90   GO TO 10
    100  PRINT N,X*X
    110  GO TO 10
    120  PRINT "COMPLETE"
    130  DATA 6,9,2,16,5,25,-1
    140  END
    ```

17. Try to deduce the output of the following program.   Then confirm your conclusion by running it on the computer.

    1∅ LET A=4
    2∅ LET B=2
    3∅ LET C=∅
    4∅ LET D=-2
    5∅ PRINT (A>B) AND (C>D)
    6∅ PRINT (A>B) AND (C<D)
    7∅ PRINT A OR B,B=D, NOT C
    8∅ END

18. Write a BASIC program that calculates and prints out the value (at the end of N years) of a $1000.00 investment, compounded annually, at the following rates of interest: 2%, 4%, 6%, 8%. Assume N takes on values from 1 to 16 years.

    Your output should have a suitable heading and be properly labeled. Arrange your output as follows:

                                    HEADING

Year	2%	4%	6%	8%
1	1020.	1040.	1060.	1080.
.	.	.	.	.
.	.	.	.	.
.	.	.	.	.
16				

19. The workers in a certain factory are paid straight time for the first 40 hours worked in a week, at time and a half for the next 20 hours, and at double time for all remaining hours. Write a BASIC program that will perform the following functions:

    (a) Calculate the salary of each worker.
    (b) Print out the worker's ID number, the number of hours worked, the hourly wage rate, and the worker's salary.
    (c) Calculate the sum of the salaries paid at the straight-time rate, the sum paid at time and a half, and the sum paid at double time. Also calculate the sum of all the salaries paid to the workers by the factory.
    (d) Print out the items calculated in (c).
    (e) Label all output.

    Assume the data input is given in the following form:

    ID #, Hours worked, Hourly rate   Ditto   ...   0, 0, 0
    ‾‾‾‾‾‾‾‾‾‾‾‾‾‾‾‾‾‾‾‾‾‾‾‾‾‾‾‾‾   ‾‾‾‾‾‾   ‾‾‾‾‾‾‾
            Worker #1   Worker   Terminal Data
                                        #2   (Trailer)

    Use the following data:

            12, 40, 3.53, 14, 40, 4.57, 17, 35, 3.53, 19, 50, 4.57,
            23, 65, 3.53, 27, 40, 6.73, 32, 30, 4.57, 38, 62, 4.57,
            44, 55, 6.73, 49, 45, 3.53, 62, 70, 3.53, 73, 52, 6.73,
            0, 0,   0

20. Write a program to simulate the casting of two dice. Your program should do the following: (1) Explain to the user what your program does and how to use it; (2) for a given value of N (N = number of times the dice are to be cast), print the outcomes of each die and their sum for each cast; and (3) terminate your program by printing GOODBYE when a negative number is typed in for N.

21. The purpose of the program below is to convert a series of Fahrenheit temperatures to the corresponding centigrade values and to print the two columns of figures. The equation for conversion is $C = 5(F - 32)/9$.

```
 1   REM CONVERT F TO TEMPERATURE
10   PRINT "F", "C"
15   REM GET FIRST AND LAST F AND INCREMENT
20   INPUT X, Y, Z
25   DATA 32, 77, 9
30   FOR F = X TO Y STEP Z
35   REM CONVERT F TO C
40   LET C = F - 32 * (5 / 9)
45   REM ROUND TO NEAREST TENTH OF A DEGREE
50   LET C = INT (C + .5) * 10) / 10
55   PRINT F, C;
60   NEXT F
65   GO TO 5
```

There are five errors in the above program. Try to find them and state clearly the reason(s) why each is, in fact, an error.

22. Write a program that reads in as input a positive integer. The program should scan the number for the presence of the digit 8 placed anywhere within the number. [Hint: Extract the right-most digit by repeated use of the INT function.]

23. A positive integer is said to be "prime" if its only factors are itself and 1. If a number is not prime it is called "composite." What follows is a program to test whether a number is prime or composite. However, portions of statements 60 and 80 have been omitted. Try to deduce what they should read.

```
 10   INPUT N
 20   IF N = 0 THEN 100
 30   FOR I = 2 TO SQR(N)
 40   IF INT(N/I) * I = N THEN 80
 50   NEXT I
 60   PRINT "IS . . . . . . ."
 70   GO TO 10
 80   PRINT "IS . . . . . . ."
 90   GO TO 10
100   END
```

24. The following program has been tampered with in the following manner: With the exception of the first and last statements the program has been arranged in alphabetical order and most of the statement numbers omitted. Study the instructions

carefully and try to reconstruct the original program. Once the program has been unscrambled check it out on the computer.

```
100   LET K = 0
170   IF ABS (N-1) >= .000001 THEN 150
      INPUT G
      INPUT N
      LET D = ABS (G - K)
      LET K = K + 1
150   LET N = SQR (N)
      PRINT "GUESS";
      PRINT "IT ACTUALLY TOOK"; K; "TIMES, SO"
      PRINT "NUMBER";
      PRINT "YOU WERE OFF BY"; D
      PRINT "YOUR GUESS WAS -"; G
230   END
```

25. Indicate whether the following BASIC statements are invalid (I) or valid (V):

    (a)   4   LET X = SQR (X)
    (b)   21   IF X↑2 < SQR (X) THEN 23
    (c)   33   INPUT A, B,
    (d) 107   LET J = SQR (ABS (SIN (J)))
    (e) 147   LET X = INT (SQR (INT (L))
    (f) 243   IF INT (SIN (X) - TAN (X)) = ABS (SIN (2X)) THEN 40
    (g) 444   PRINT X, SQR (X), SIN (X)
    (h) 502   INPUT SQR (X)
    (i)   7   IF SQR (INT (ABS (W))) < 0 THEN 3
    (j)   63   LET Y = SQRT (ABS (X))

26. Evaluate the following BASIC program segments:

    (a) 100   LET Y = 2 * SQR (144)
         110   LET X = SQR ((Y - 4) * 5)

    (b)   50   LET A = INT (SQR (170))
          60   LET X = 2 * A + 4 - 16 / 2

    (c)   10   LET J = 4
          20   LET K = 6
          30   LET X = SQR (INT (K/J))

    (d) 440   LET X = 2 * INT (3.14159)
         450   LET X = X ↑ 2
         460   LET X = SQR (X) + INT (SQR (X))

    (e) 200   LET A = 2 * 3 - 2 ↑ 3
         210   LET B = A * ABS (A)
         220   LET X = A + SQR (ABS (B))

(f) 10 LET J = 7
    20 LET M = J ↑ 2
    30 LET X = ABS (J - M)

(g) 300 LET A = 12
    310 LET X = A ↑ 2 - SGN(A ↑ 2 - A)

(h) 100 LET A = INT (2 * 1.3) ↑ 3
    110 LET B = A + 7.5
    120 LET X = INT ((A + INT(B))/A)

(i) 490 LET X = SGN(- 34) ↑ 3

(j) 780 LET P = INT (SQR (75))
    790 LET P = (P / 4 + 3) ↑ 2
    800 LET X = SQR (P)

27. Indicate whether the following statements are true (T) or false (F).

(a) All standard functions in BASIC consist of three letters.

(b) When using the SQR function the arguments must always be nonnegative.

(c) Both parts of an OR expression must be true for the entire expression to be true.

(d) When the instruction INPUT A,B,C is executed three question marks are printed out to inform the user that three values are required.

(e) Random numbers are generated by the RAN function.

CHAPTER SEVEN

LOOPS, ARRAYS, AND SUBSCRIPTS

7.1 Arrays

Many of the terms and forms used in computer programming are borrowed from mathematics. For example, if in mathematics we have a long list of numbers, we refer to that list as an *array*. An array is generally assigned a name just like ordinary, simple variables are assigned names. Here is an array, arbitrarily designated array X.

$$\frac{X}{\begin{array}{c} 16 \\ 42 \\ -9 \\ 21 \\ 8 \end{array}}$$

In array X we have five items—in mathematics they are called *elements*. The first is 16, the second is 42, etc. When referring to any particular element of an array in mathematics we use a subscript; for example,

$$X_1 = 16$$
$$X_2 = 42$$
$$X_3 = -9$$
$$X_4 = 21$$
$$X_5 = 8$$

where the subscript is usually written in small type just below the associated variable. In BASIC—and several other programming languages as well—subscripts are enclosed in parentheses and placed immediately to the right of the array name. For example, one could set up an array in BASIC in the following way:

```
LET X(1) = 16
LET X(2) = 42
LET X(3) = -9
LET X(4) = 21
LET X(5) =  8
```

When assigning a name to an array in BASIC we are restricted to a single alphabetic letter, rather than to a choice between a single letter or a single letter followed by a digit 0 through 9.

Suppose we wished to find the average of the five elements of the array X. This may be done quite simply in two different ways without using arrays and subscripts. Here is the first program to accomplish the task. It is quite straightforward—the five numbers are assigned the names A, B, C, D, and E and the average is calculated directly.

Program 7-1

```
100   PRINT "***********************"
110   PRINT "*                     *"
120   PRINT "* FINDING THE AVERAGE *"
130   PRINT "*                     *"
140   PRINT "*    OF FIVE NUMBERS  *"
150   PRINT "*                     *"
160   PRINT "*         METHOD 1    *"
170   PRINT "*                     *"
180   PRINT "***********************"
190   PRINT
200   READ A,B,C,D,E
210   DATA 16,42,-9,21,8
220   LET S=A+B+C+D+E
230   LET M=S/5
240   PRINT "THE AVERAGE =";M
250   END

RUN



***********************
*                     *
* FINDING THE AVERAGE *
*                     *
*    OF FIVE NUMBERS  *
*                     *
*         METHOD 1    *
*                     *
***********************


THE AVERAGE = 15.6

DONE
```

In the next version, Program 7-2, each of the elements is referred to as X. As soon as a value of -99 for X is detected, the average is computed by dividing the sum of the X's by the count of the data elements, C.

Both C and S are initialized to zero by a single *multiple assignment* or *multiple variable replacement* statement, which we have encountered previously. Whatever value is defined at the extreme right is assigned successively to those variables to the left and separated by equals signs.

Here is a slightly longer program to calculate the average of the five numbers, using method 2.

Program 7-2

```
100  PRINT "************************"
110  PRINT "*                      *"
120  PRINT "* FINDING THE AVERAGE *"
130  PRINT "*                      *"
140  PRINT "*    OF FIVE NUMBERS   *"
150  PRINT "*                      *"
160  PRINT "*        METHOD 2      *"
170  PRINT "*                      *"
180  PRINT "************************"
190  PRINT
200  LET C=S=0
210  READ X
220  DATA 16,42,-9,21,8,-99
230  IF X=-99 THEN 270
240  LET C=C+1
250  LET S=S+X
260  GO TO 210
270  LET M=S/C
280  PRINT "THE AVERAGE =" ;M
290  END

RUN


************************
*                      *
* FINDING THE AVERAGE *
*                      *
*    OF FIVE NUMBERS   *
*                      *
*        METHOD 2      *
*                      *
************************


THE AVERAGE = 15.6

DONE
```

Whenever an array consisting of more than 10 elements is used, the program must have an appropriate DIM (dimension) statement that defines the maximum dimension of the array. In an array X of 15 elements, the dimension would be 15 and this number is enclosed in parentheses in the following way:

123   DIM X(15)

The purpose of the dimension statement is to reserve memory space in which to store the array. For this reason, the value enclosed within the parentheses must be a specific positive integer value and cannot be a variable name, despite the sometimes irrepressible urge to write in a symbolic name.

If the array is composed of 10 elements or less it is not necessary to include a DIM statement, although it is considered by many to be good programming practice to do so.

Program 7-3 is a somewhat inelegant way of reading an array. Its purpose is merely to illustrate how arrays can be handled; in this case, the array is handled inefficiently. But we will soon learn how to do this with great ease and elegance.

Notice that although the *round* brackets were used in entering the dimension, that is, DIM X(5), whenever the system lists the program it will print out *square* brackets instead. This proves to be no problem whatever. On the contrary, it helps to distinguish dimensioned variables from variables that are the arguments to functions.

Program 7-3

```
100   PRINT "***********************"
110   PRINT "*                     *"
120   PRINT "*INELEGANT METHOD OF*"
130   PRINT "*                     *"
140   PRINT "*READING   AN   ARRAY*"
150   PRINT "*                     *"
160   PRINT "***********************"
170   PRINT
180   DIM X[5]
190   READ X[1],X[2],X[3],X[4],X[5]
200   DATA 16,42,-9,21,8
210   LET S=X[1]+X[2]+X[3]+X[4]+X[5]
220   LET M=S/5
230   PRINT "THE AVERAGE =";M
240   END
```

RUN

```
***********************
*                     *
*INELEGANT METHOD OF*
*                     *
*READING   AN   ARRAY*
*                     *
***********************
```

THE AVERAGE = 15.6

DONE

7.2 A More Elegant Way to Read an Array

The last program is inelegant because each element of the array is individually entered in both the READ statement and the statement setting the sum of the elements to S.

A much more refined and efficient way to do this is to enclose such statements in a FOR/NEXT loop. Here is an illustration of how such a loop works, omitting statement numbers.

```
FOR I = 1 TO 5
READ X(I)
NEXT I
```

Any valid unsubscripted variable name may be selected as the index of the loop. (For reasons of both traditional mathematics and transference of habits from other computer languages, most BASIC programmers seem to use one of the letters I,J,K,L,M, or N for the index but any valid variable name will do.)

In the loop the READ statement relates to X(I). The value of I within parentheses is the current value of the index which goes from 1 to 5 (in increments of 1, since no other increment is indicated).

The next I instruction raises the value of the index by 1 and I then becomes 2. The loop is then repeated for I equal to 2 and so on until I reaches 5. Once this final pass is concluded, the loop is said to be "satisfied" and control passes to the statement following the NEXT I statement.

In the next program two FOR/NEXT loops have been used, even though only one is really necessary. When examining the program, you might consider how to dispense with one of the loops. Here is the more elegant Program 7-4.

Program 7-4

```
100  PRINT "************************"
110  PRINT "*                      *"
120  PRINT "* A MORE ELEGANT WAY *"
130  PRINT "*                      *"
140  PRINT "*   TO HANDLE ARRAYS   *"
150  PRINT "*                      *"
160  PRINT "************************"
170  PRINT
180  DIM X[5]
190  FOR I=1 TO 5
200  READ X[I]
210  DATA 16,42,-9,21,8
220  NEXT I
230  LET S=0
240  FOR J=1 TO 5
250  LET S=S+X[J]
260  NEXT J
270  LET M=S/5
280  PRINT "THE AVERAGE =" ;M
290  END

RUN


************************
*                      *
* A MORE ELEGANT WAY *
*                      *
*   TO HANDLE ARRAYS   *
*                      *
************************

THE AVERAGE = 15.6

DONE
```

At this juncture it might well be argued that introducing the FOR/NEXT loops into the program has not effectively reduced the length of the program, even though the loops might have lent something positive conceptually. The fact is that we have dealt, so far, with an array of length five only. In real-life arrays are often much longer, going into the hundreds if not thousands. It is when arrays are of such dimensions that the power of the FOR/NEXT loops become apparent.

The sole purpose of Program 7-5 is to illustrate that it is perfectly legal in BASIC to transfer control to a dimension statement, even though one might be hard pressed to give a satisfactory reason for doing so. In any case, this program should be self-explanatory.

Program 7-5

```
100   PRINT "************************"
110   PRINT "*                      *"
120   PRINT "*TRANSFERRING   TO   A*"
130   PRINT "*                      *"
140   PRINT "*DIMENSION STATEMENT*"
150   PRINT "*                      *"
160   PRINT "************************"
170   PRINT
180   LET K=1
190   DIM X[10]
200   LET X[K]=K
210   PRINT X[K],
220   LET K=K+1
230   IF K=11 THEN 250
240   GO TO 190
250   PRINT
260   PRINT "YOU SEE, IT'S LEGAL TO GO TO A DIMENSION STATEMENT."
270   PRINT
280   END
```

```
************************
*                      *
*TRANSFERRING   TO   A*
*                      *
*DIMENSION STATEMENT*
*                      *
************************
```

1	2	3	4	5
6	7	8	9	10

YOU SEE, IT'S LEGAL TO GO TO A DIMENSION STATEMENT.

DONE

Sometimes a variable, be it a string or a numeric variable, is inadvertently dimensioned more than once. Should this occur, the error is not detected until the program is executed. This error was made deliberately in the Program 7-6 and the diagnostic message appearing after the word RUN is self-explanatory.

Program 7-6

```
100  PRINT "*********************"
110  PRINT "*                   *"
120  PRINT "* VARIABLES MAY BE *"
130  PRINT "*                   *"
140  PRINT "* DIMENSIONED ONCE *"
150  PRINT "*                   *"
160  PRINT "*********************"
170  PRINT
180  DIM A[9],A[10]
190  FOR K=1 TO 9
200  READ A[K]
210  NEXT K
220  LET A[7]=A[3]*6.7
230  FOR L=1 TO 9
240  PRINT A[L]
250  NEXT L
260  DATA 9,8,7,6,5,4,3,2,1
270  END
```

```
RUN
VARIABLE DIMENSIONED TWICE IN LINE 180
```

7.3 Out of Bounds Subscripts

Referring to an index of zero in a program has the effect of terminating the program with the diagnostic:

SUBSCRIPT OUT OF BOUNDS IN LINE n

The same diagnostic is obtained with a negative index or one that exceeds the declared dimension for the variable.

If a name such as X is selected for a dimensioned array, BASIC permits the use of the name X (without a subscript) as an independent simple variable.

Once an array has been read into the memory of the computer the whole array can be acted upon directly. Thus if it were necessary to find, say, the smallest element of an array (also called the minimum of the array), it would be advantageous if the array were "sitting" in memory. Then we could find the minimum with electronic speed.

7.4 Finding the Minimum of an Array

Suppose a salesperson had a list of numbers representing her daily commissions over the last 30 days. If she wanted to know what her minimum commission was, she might resort to the following mental procedure. Whatever figure was first on the list could represent the tentative minimum. That would be compared with the next figure and, if the second were smaller than the first, that would become the new minimum. If not, it would be ignored and a comparison made with the third item. This process could be repeated until all the items had been compared, substituting the last minimum for the new minimum each time a smaller item was found. It is our belief that this is the natural method for the human being to tackle such a problem.

Of the several methods by which one can find the minimum of an array on a computer, that described above is probably the best. Any unambiguous, step-by-step procedure such as this that will work with any data at all is sometimes called an *algorithm*. This algorithm is incorporated into the following program, where the first element S of the array X, is set equal to X(1). The reason why S was selected was that L stands for both "little" and "large" and might have created some confusion. The letter S stands for "small" and does not invite ambiguity.

Program 7-7

```
100   PRINT "***********************"
110   PRINT "*                     *"
120   PRINT "* FINDING THE MINIMUM *"
130   PRINT "*                     *"
140   PRINT "*     OF AN ARRAY     *"
150   PRINT "*                     *"
160   PRINT "***********************"
170   PRINT
180   DIM X[30]
190   FOR I=1 TO 30
200   READ X[I]
210   NEXT I
220   DATA 14,18.43,84.28,9.23,8.15,6.2,12.25,10,16.5,17.5
230   DATA 54,72,19.5,16.2,2,6,100,8,10,11
240   DATA 19.1,20.2,6.5,48.75,19.02,28.82,10.1,6,8,48
250   LET S=X[1]
260   FOR I=2 TO 30
270   IF S<X[I] THEN 290
280   LET S=X[I]
290   NEXT I
300   PRINT "THE MINIMUM VALUE =" ;S
310   END


RUN


***********************
*                     *
* FINDING THE MINIMUM *
*                     *
*     OF AN ARRAY     *
*                     *
***********************

THE MINIMUM VALUE = 2

DONE
```

7.5   Finding the Minimum and Maximum

The strategy employed in finding the minimum (i.e., defining the first element to be the minimum and comparing it with every other element of the array) could, of course, be used for finding the maximum of the array. In the next program both the minimum and maximum are found in a single FOR/NEXT loop. Of course, it could be done in two separate FOR/NEXT loops but this way is considered more elegant.

Program 7-8

```
100   PRINT "***********************"
110   PRINT "*                     *"
120   PRINT "*FINDING THE MINIMUM*"
130   PRINT "* AND MAXIMUM OF AN *"
140   PRINT "*ARRAY  IN ONE  LOOP*"
150   PRINT "*                     *"
160   PRINT "***********************"
170   PRINT
180   DIM X[30]
190   FOR I=1 TO 30
200   READ X[I]
210   NEXT I
220   DATA 14,18.43,84.28,9.23,8.15,6.2,12.25,10,16.5,17.5
230   DATA 54,72,19.5,16.2,2,6,100,8,10,11
240   DATA 19.1,20.2,6.5,48.75,19.02,28.82,10.1,6,8,48
250   LET S=X[1]
260   LET B=X[1]
270   FOR I=2 TO 30
280   IF S<X[I] THEN 300
290   LET S=X[I]
300   IF B>X[I] THEN 320
310   LET B=X[I]
320   NEXT I
330   PRINT "THE MINIMUM VALUE =" ;S
340   PRINT "THE MAXIMUM VALUE =" ;B
350   END

RUN


***********************
*                     *
*FINDING THE MINIMUM*
* AND MAXIMUM OF AN *
*ARRAY  IN ONE  LOOP*
*                     *
***********************

THE MINIMUM VALUE = 2
THE MAXIMUM VALUE = 100

DONE
```

7.6 Finding the Minimum and Maximum and Their Locations

As a final embellishment to the program we now consider how to determine not only the minimum and maximum but also their locations. What this means is that as soon as a new minimum or a new maximum is found, the value of the index at that particular moment represents the location of the element being assigned to the memory slot for the new minimum or the new maximum.

What we have to do then is to "capture" the value of the index at that time. This turns out to be simple enough. All we have to do is to define two new memory locations in which to store the value of the indices. Since we have selected S for the minimum why not S1 for the location of the minimum? And similarly for the maximum, B; its location is defined to be B1.

Program 7-9

```
100  PRINT "***********************"
110  PRINT "*                     *"
120  PRINT "* FINDING THE MINIMUM,*"
130  PRINT "* MAXIMUM  AND  THEIR *"
140  PRINT "*       LOCATIONS     *"
150  PRINT "*                     *"
160  PRINT "***********************"
170  PRINT
180  DIM X[30]
190  FOR I=1 TO 30
200  READ X[I]
210  NEXT I
220  DATA 14,18.43,84.28,9.23,8.15,6.2,12.25,10,16.5,17.5
230  DATA 54,72,19.5,16.2,2,6,100,8,10,11
240  DATA 19.1,20.2,6.5,48.75,19.02,28.82,10.1,6,8,48
250  LET S=X[1]
260  LET S1=1
270  LET B=X[1]
280  LET B1=1
290  FOR I=2 TO 30
300  IF S<X[I] THEN 330
310  LET S=X[I]
320  LET S1=I
330  IF B>X[I] THEN 360
340  LET B=X[I]
350  LET B1=I
360  NEXT I
370  PRINT "MINIMUM =" ;S;"ITEM NO." ;S1
380  PRINT "MAXIMUM =" ;B;"ITEM NO." ;B1
390  END
```

```
RUN

***********************
*                     *
* FINDING THE MINIMUM,*
* MAXIMUM  AND  THEIR *
*       LOCATIONS     *
*                     *
***********************


MINIMUM  = 2     ITEM NO. 15
MAXIMUM = 100   ITEM NO. 17

DONE
```

7.7   Generalizing Programs

All the programs in this chapter have used READ and DATA statements. This implies, of course, that the data is known in advance. Whereas this is indeed sometimes the case, it is not always so. A program may be written for a *general* case and users of the program might have access to the completed program at their terminals. It would be very convenient if users could enter their data at the time they are ready, *without changing anything in the program.* In the case of a problem involving arrays, the question of the size of the dimension statement arises. How large should the author of the program make it, when he has no idea at the time of writing who might use the program and how many elements the users' arrays will contain?

This is a standard kind of problem that has to be answered by the programmer when writing useful, generalized programs. He has to pick a dimension size that is as small as possible but large enough to fulfill most "reasonable" requirements. The temptation to make it ridiculously large must be resisted at all costs. One rule-of-thumb method to resolve this conflict might be to select a maximum and to add 100 or 200 to it.

In the next chapter we propose to illustrate some problems that have been solved by generalized programs, enabling the user to type in data at the Teletype console. First, however, we would like to illustrate a most convenient way to control the way that the output is printed.

7.8   The Printer Control Instructions: TAB, LIN, and SPA Functions

There are three space functions that can be very helpful in specifying exactly how and where printed output should appear.

7.8.1   The TAB Function

To print in a certain column, say, column 23, one can begin the PRINT instruction with TAB(23). The argument to the function may also be a variable, enabling some sophisticated manipulation of the output to be done, for example,

100   PRINT TAB(23)
120   PRINT TAB(X)

7.8.2   The LIN Function

In order to skip a certain number of lines one may use the LIN (for "line") function. Suppose we want to skip, say, 12 lines; the PRINT instruction would be:

100   PRINT LIN(12)

Again, the argument may be a variable. If X is less than 0, no carriage return is generated. If X = 0, only a carriage return is generated. Advantage of this may be taken by enclosing a PRINT LIN(0); with a loop. It will overprint whatever else is included in the PRINT and the result will resemble bold type.

7.8.3   The SPA Function

One may use the SPA (for "space") function to skip a specified number of spaces. For example:

100   PRINT SPA(3), X, Y, SPA(5)

Like the other two functions, the argument to the SPA function may be a variable.

As a further illustration of the TAB function, this time with the argument a variable, Program 7-10 prints a large letter X using the symbol X.

Program 7-10

```
100  PRINT "*****************"
110  PRINT "*PRINTING AN 'X'*"
120  PRINT "*    USING THE    *"
130  PRINT "* TAB FUNCTION *"
140  PRINT "*****************"
150  PRINT
160  LET N=0
170  LET T=16
180  LET T=T-1
190  LET N=N+1
200  IF T=0 THEN 290
210  IF N=8 THEN 250
220  IF N>8 THEN 270
230  PRINT TAB(N) ;"X";TAB(T) ;"X"
240  GO TO 180
250  PRINT TAB(N) ;"X"
260  GO TO 180
270  PRINT TAB(T) ;"X" ; TAB(N) ;"X"
280  GO TO 180
290  END

RUN


*****************
*PRINTING AN 'X'*
*    USING THE    *
* TAB FUNCTION *
*****************

X                 X
 X               X
  X             X
   X           X
    X         X
     X       X
      X     X
       X   X
        X X
         X
        X X
       X   X
      X     X
     X       X
    X         X
   X           X
  X             X
 X               X
X                 X

DONE
```

7.9 Plotting on the Teletype

Using the TAB function it is possible to use the Teletype terminal to plot graphs of functions, including the sine curve.

There are two principles involved here. They are:

1. Since one cannot backspace the carriage of the teletype one may prefer to choose the x and y axes such that the x axis goes downward along the length of the paper and the y axis at a right angle to it, across the width of the paper.
2. Knowledge of the range of values that the function will produce is necessary in order to scale appropriately.

Our example of the plotting of the sine curve is shown in Program 7-11. It is clear that for each X value there is one Y value and only one asterisk per line is printed.

Scaling for the X axis is accomplished by means of the FOR/NEXT loop in which the index I goes from zero to 2π in steps of 0.3. This index becomes the argument to the SIN function. Since the sine of an angle varies from -1 to $+1$ it is necessary to rescale it in order that it may be used as the argument to the TAB function. The first transformation is linear and is produced by adding 1 to the sine. Thus we have a value varying from 0 to 2. Multiplying this value by 20 will cause each value to vary from 0 to 40. Hence the computer will space over from 0 to 40 spaces before printing the asterisk.

Program 7-11

```
100  PRINT "**************************"
110  PRINT "*                        *"
120  PRINT "*USING THE TAB FUNCTION*"
130  PRINT "*                        *"
140  PRINT "*TO    PLOT    A    CURVE*"
150  PRINT "*                        *"
160  PRINT "**************************"
170  PRINT
180  FOR I=0 TO 2*3.14159 STEP .3
190  PRINT TAB(20*(1+SIN(I))) ;"*"
200  NEXT I
210  END
```

RUN

```
*************************
*                       *
*USING THE TAB FUNCTION*
*                       *
*TO    PLOT    A    CURVE*
*                       *
*************************


                    *
                       *
                  *
                     *
                        *
                          *
                          *
                       *
                  *
                    *
               *
            *
          *
      *
      *
      *
       *
          *
            *
               *
```

DONE

Quick Reference Guide to Chapter Seven

Item	General Form	Example
1. Subscripted variables	Single letter (index)	X(I) W(3) Z(5*6↑3)
2. Dimension statement	*Line number* DIM *array name(constant)*	100 DIM X(200) 200 DIM W(15), Y(170)
3. Multiple assignment	*Line number* LET *variable name = variable name = . . . = expression*	100 LET A = B = C = 0 200 LET X = Y = Z=P=T=-1
4. Printer control	TAB(*expression*) SPA(*expression*) LIN(*expression*)	TAB(5) TAB(X Y) SPA(15) SPA(A/B) LIN(25) LIN(0)
5. Special PRINT instruction	(See examples)	100 PRINT "A=" ;TAB(16) ;X 200 PRINT "<<<" ;LIN(0); ">>>" 300 PRINT SPA(3) ; SPA(I) ; M

Questions

1. What difference is there in BASIC in the naming of variables that are arrays as opposed to those that are simple variables?

2. What is the role of the DIM statement? Must every subscripted variable be dimensioned?

3. Must the name of the subscript of a dimensioned variable be the same as the index of the FOR/NEXT loop in which it is enclosed?

4. To be sure that the dimension for an array is large enough, it is a good idea to jack it up to 300,000. Comment on this statement.

5. Write a program that sums the integers from 17 to 63.

6. What results would you expect from the following program?
   ```
   10  DIM X(4)
   20  READ X(1), X(2), X(3), X(4)
   30  DATA 5, 3, 4, 6
   40  LET T = X(1) + X(2) + X(3) + X(4)
   50  PRINT T
   60  END
   ```

7. Rewrite the program in Question 7 above, using a FOR/NEXT loop.

8. Which of the following, if any, are illegal for use as a dimension statement? Circle those you believe to be invalid.
   ```
   10  DIM X(50)
   20  DIM Y1(10)
   30  DIM XX(100)
   40  DIM A(3)
   50  DIM B(40)
   60  DIM C(-15)
   70  DIM D(1023)
   ```

9. What does the following program accomplish:
   ```
   10  LET S = 0
   20  FOR I = 1 TO 100
   30  LET S = S+I
   40  NEXT I
   50  PRINT S
   60  END
   ```
   Write a more direct program in BASIC to accomplish the same thing.

10. Using the random number generator create an array of 1000 elements each of which is either a 1 or a 2. Locate and print out:
    (a) The longest string of 1's
    (b) The beginning and ending positions of this string

(c) The longest string of 2's

(d) The beginning and ending positions of this string

11. Write a program that asks the user to type any integer (whole number) between 1 and 1000. If an invalid number is selected (e.g., -1, 3.6, 1009) count the number of times such selections are made. Three and she's out. If she selects more than 10 numbers without including the number 18, she should be told she's a loser.

12. Write a BASIC program that computes the squares of the integers from 1 to 100 into an array and then prints out the first, fourth, twenty-sixth, fifty-ninth, and the ninty-ninth elements of the array.

13. What is the effect of the following program?

```
 10  DIM X(30)
 20  FOR L = 1 TO 10
 30  LET X(L) = 0
 40  NEXT L
 50  FOR L = 11 TO 20
 60  LET X(L) = 1
 70  NEXT L
 80  FOR L = 21 TO 30
 90  LET X(L) = 2
100  NEXT L
110  END
```

14. Write a program to compute and print a table of sine x for $x = 0$ to $x = 360$ degrees, in intervals of 5 degrees.

15. Write a program that will read in two lists A and B, each containing N elements. Compute a third list C that consists of the product of the corresponding elements of A and B.

16. Suppose you are given a variable length list of two-digit positive integers followed by a negative number. (Use a DATA statement.) Write a program that counts the number of positive integers and determines the smallest and largest integers in the list. Print out the given integers (close packing) and the smallest and largest integers. Label your output. Provide your own "typical" data to check your program (use at least 25 integers).

17. What output is produced by the following program?

```
10  DIM X[5], Y[5], Z[5]
20  LET K = 5
30  FOR I = 1 TO K
40  READ X[I], Y[I]
50  NEXT I
60  FOR J = 1 TO K
70  LET Z[J] = 2 * X[J] - Y[J]
80  PRINT X[J], Y[J], Z[J]
```

```
 90  NEXT J
100  DATA 2,1,1,2,0,3,-1,4,-2,5
110  END
```

18. Indicate whether the following statements are true (T) or false (F):

    (a) A DIM statement is necessary in every program that contains an array of more than 10 elements.

    (b) The name of a subscripted variable can be any legal variable name followed by parentheses enclosing the subscript of the array.

    (c) The easiest way to keep a program general is to input a variable in the program, say N, and then use that value in the DIM statement, e.g., DIM X(N).

    (d) Every program that contains a FOR/NEXT loop must also have an appropriate DIM statement.

    (e) The BASIC system can differentiate between a simple variable P and an array P in the same program.

19. Indicate whether the following BASIC statements are invalid (I) or valid (V):

    (a) 190   READ X(1), X(2), X(3)

    (b) 70   DIME(5)

    (c) 108   PRINT TAB(INT(X)) ; X

    (d) 100   DIM X(100), Y(100)

    (e) 307   IF SQR(T) >= SPA(T) THEN 35

20. What will the following program yield?

```
100  FOR I = 1 TO 10
110  PRINT "LIN(0)", LIN(0) ;
120  NEXT I
130  END
```

CHAPTER EIGHT

GENERALIZED PROBLEMS

Whenever possible, programs should be written in a generalized form, so that they can be used in a number of situations. This means that the input might have to be entered by means of an INPUT statement. One must always remember that as soon as an INPUT statement is executed, a question mark is printed automatically and the program comes to a grinding halt. It will recommence only when suitable data has been entered. For this reason, it is always an excellent idea for some suitable message or question to be printed out preceding each question mark. When a question is being printed out, the question mark printed by the INPUT statement can be used as the terminal character of the question. In other words, the question can be written without the question mark. Since the action of the INPUT statement is to print a question mark, the final form of the question would appear with the desired question mark. This is much more difficult to explain than to use, so perhaps an illustration is called for.

8.1   Finding the Average, Minimum, and Maximum of an Array

Program 8-1 allows for an array to be typed in at the terminal. Since the dimension statement is declared to be 100, no more than 100 elements may be stored in that array. The program first calls for the typing in of the number of elements N in the array X. N is tested to ensure that it does not exceed the dimensioned value. Then the array is typed in. According to the form of the INPUT statement, the array must be typed only one element per line. (We shall shortly try other techniques enabling us to type more than one element of an array on a line.)

Once the array is entered, the program will proceed to compute the average, the minimum, and the maximum in the same manner as in the previous chapter. At the conclusion of the program, control is sent to the beginning so that another array can be entered. To terminate the program, a negative value for N is entered. Naturally, it is wise to inform the user of this by means of an appropriate printout, as is done in line 440.

Program 8-1

```
100  PRINT "**********************"
110  PRINT "*                    *"
120  PRINT "*A  PROGRAM  WITH  A*"
130  PRINT "*                    *"
140  PRINT "*VARYING NUMBER OF*"
150  PRINT "*                    *"
160  PRINT "*        ELEMENTS        *"
170  PRINT "*                    *"
180  PRINT "**********************"
190  PRINT
200  DIM X[100]
210  PRINT "WHAT IS THE VALUE OF N" ;
220  INPUT N
230  IF N<0 THEN 490
240  IF N>100 THEN 470
250  PRINT "THANK YOU"
260  PRINT
270  PRINT "NOW TYPE IN YOUR" ;N;"VALUES, ONE PER LINE."
280  PRINT
290  FOR I=1 TO N
300  INPUT X[I]
310  NEXT I
320  PRINT
330  LET S=X[1]
340  LET B=X[1]
350  FOR J=2 TO N
360  IF S<X[J] THEN 380
370  LET S=X[J]
380  IF B>X[J] THEN 400
390  LET B=X[J]
400  NEXT J
410  PRINT "MINIMUM=" ;S
420  PRINT "MAXIMUM=" ;B
430  PRINT
440  PRINT "TO STOP THE PROGRAM, ENTER A NEGATIVE VALUE FOR N."
450  PRINT
460  GO TO 210
470  PRINT "PLEASE NOTE THAT THE MAXIMUM ALLOWED IS 100."
480  GO TO 210
490  END
```

RUN

```
* * * * * * * * * * * * * * * * * * * *
*                    *
*A  PROGRAM  WITH  A*
*                    *
*VARYING NUMBER OF*
*                    *
*       ELEMENTS       *
*                    *
* * * * * * * * * * * * * * * * * * * *
```

WHAT IS THE VALUE OF N?6
THANK YOU

NOW TYPE IN YOUR 6   VALUES, ONE PER LINE.

?5
?3
?8
?4
?-1
?7

MINIMUM=-1
MAXIMUM= 8

TO STOP THE PROGRAM, ENTER A NEGATIVE VALUE FOR N.

WHAT IS THE VALUE OF N?111
PLEASE NOTE THAT THE MAXIMUM ALLOWED IS 1ØØ.
WHAT IS THE VALUE OF N?11
THANK YOU

NOW TYPE IN YOUR 11   VALUES, ONE PER LINE.

?5
?19
?21
?-3
?14
?83
?11
?96
?1Ø4
?22
?8Ø

MINIMUM=-3
MAXIMUM= 104

TO STOP THE PROGRAM, ENTER A NEGATIVE VALUE FOR N.

WHAT IS THE VALUE OF N?-1

DONE

8.2   Pearson's Correlation Coefficient

The next program concerns an important statistic known as Pearson's correlation coefficient. It is a value between -1 and +1 that reflects the linear relationship between two sets of variables. A positive coefficient implies a positive correlation and a negative coefficient a negative relationship.

Suppose we are interested in the relationship between height (in feet) and weight (in pounds). Calling these X and Y, respectively, we set up a data table. For convenience, we keep the table small but in practice it could run into the hundreds or even the thousands.

X	Y
5.3	104
6.0	182
3.9	89
4.7	72
5.7	114

We would then make another column composed of the product of X times Y.

X	Y	XY
5.3	104	551.2
6.0	182	1092.0
3.9	89	347.1
4.7	72	338.4
5.7	114	649.8

Next, we have to make a column of X^2 and then one of Y^2. Here is the completed table, together with the totals in each column.

X	Y	XY	X^2	Y^2
5.3	104	551.2	28.09	10816
6.0	182	1092.0	36.00	33124
3.9	89	347.1	15.21	7921
4.7	72	338.4	22.09	5184
5.7	114	649.8	32.49	12996
25.6	561	2978.5	133.88	70041

Let us assign the following names to the five totals:

1. Sum of the X's $\quad\quad\quad\quad$ $\Sigma\,X$
2. Sum of the Y's $\quad\quad\quad\quad$ $\Sigma\,Y$
3. Sum of the X's times Y's $\quad$ $\Sigma\,XY$
4. Sum of the X's squared $\quad$ $\Sigma\,X^2$
5. Sum of the Y's squared $\quad$ $\Sigma\,Y^2$

We can now present the formula for computing the correlation coefficient, R. It is:

$$R = \frac{N\,\Sigma\,XY - \Sigma\,X\,\Sigma\,Y}{\sqrt{[N\,\Sigma\,X^2 - (\Sigma\,X)^2]\,[N\,\Sigma\,Y^2 - (\Sigma\,Y)^2]}}$$

where N is the number of pairs of data items. In our case we have selected an N of 5, but in practice it should never be less than about 30.

The computed result of approximately 0.75 indicates a rather high, positive correlation between height and weight for the sample data tested.

How could we solve such a problem at a computer terminal? Program 8-2 was designed to do precisely that. In this program, the variables have the following meanings: $S1 = \Sigma\,X$, $S2 = \Sigma\,Y$, $S3 = \Sigma\,XY$, $S4 = \Sigma\,X^2$, $S5 = \Sigma\,Y^2$, $S6 =$ numerator, and $S7 =$ denominator.

Program 8-2

```
100   PRINT "**************************"
110   PRINT "*                        *"
120   PRINT "* PEARSON'S CORRELATION  *"
130   PRINT "*                        *"
140   PRINT "*       COEFFICIENT      *"
150   PRINT "*                        *"
160   PRINT "**************************"
170   PRINT
180   DIM X[100], Y[100]
190   PRINT "PLEASE TYPE IN YOUR VALUE FOR N."
200   INPUT N
210   IF N<0 THEN 540
220   IF N>100 THEN 520
230   PRINT "GREAT!"
240   PRINT
250   PRINT "NOW TYPE IN YOUR VALUES FOR X AND Y,";
260   PRINT "SEPARATING THEM BY A COMMA."
270   FOR I=1 TO N
280   INPUT X[I], Y[I]
290   NEXT I
300   REM: INITIALIZING SUMS
310   LET S1=S2=S3=S4=S5=0
320   REM: NOW COMPUTE THE SUMS
330   FOR J=1 TO N
340   LET S1=S1+X[J]
350   LET S2=S2+Y[J]
360   LET S3=S3+X[J] * Y[J]
370   LET S4=S4+X[J] * X[J]
380   LET S5=S5+Y[J] * Y[J]
```

```
390   NEXT J
400   REM: COMPUTE NUMERATOR
410   LET S6=N*S3-S1*S2
420   REM: COMPUTE DENOMINATOR
430   LET S7=SQR((N*S4-S1*S1)*(N*S5-S2*S2))
440   REM: NOW COMPUTE R
450   LET R=S6/S7
460   PRINT
470   PRINT "CORRELATION COEFFICIENT =" ;R
480   PRINT
490   PRINT "TO TERMINATE PROGRAM, ENTER A NEGATIVE VALUE FOR N."
500   PRINT
510   GO TO 190
520   PRINT "PLEASE NOTE THAT N CANNOT EXCEED 100"
530   GO TO 190
540   END
```

RUN

```
*************************
*                       *
*PEARSON'S CORRELATION*
*                       *
*        COEFFICIENT    *
*                       *
*************************
```

PLEASE TYPE IN YOUR VALUE FOR N.
?5
GREAT!

NOW TYPE IN YOUR VALUES FOR X AND Y,SEPARATING THEM BY A COMMA.
?5.3,104
?6.0,182
?3.9,89
?4.7,72
?5.7,114

CORRELATION COEFFICIENT = .752165

TO TERMINATE PROGRAM, ENTER A NEGATIVE VALUE FOR N.

PLEASE TYPE IN YOUR VALUE FOR N.
?410
PLEASE NOTE THAT N CANNOT EXCEED 100
PLEASE TYPE IN YOUR VALUE FOR N.
?10
GREAT!

NOW TYPE IN YOUR VALUES FOR X AND Y, SEPARATING THEM BY A COMMA.
?1,3
?3,4
?4,9
?6,4
?2,1
?0,5
?1,5
?7,8
?8,9
?9,8

CORRELATION COEFFICIENT = .657348

TO TERMINATE PROGRAM, ENTER A NEGATIVE VALUE FOR N.

PLEASE TYPE IN YOUR VALUE FOR N.
?-1

DONE

Note that in Program 8-2 only one DIM statement was used to dimension two different variables. This may be extended to any number of variables, provided that each is separated from the following variable name by a comma.

Note too that in statement 280, the INPUT statement, the two variable names are separated by a comma. Even though the input calls for the typing in of two items, only one question mark is printed out. Typing in two values separated by a comma is necessary to "satisfy" the INPUT statement. This is repeated for N pairs of input.

8.3   The Variance and Standard Deviation

Although it is not our intent to teach statistics, it is important to present another program that illustrates the method of calculating two very commonly used statistics. The *variance* V is defined as:

$$V = \frac{N \Sigma X^2 - (\Sigma X)^2}{N^2}$$

The *standard deviation* is simply the square root of the variance. The flag −99999 is used in Program 8-3 to indicate both the end of the X array of scores and also as a terminator to the program. Since so little additional effort is required, the mean is also computed and printed along with the variance and standard deviation.

Program 8-3

```
100  PRINT "***********************"
110  PRINT "*                      *"
120  PRINT "* THE   VARIANCE   AND *"
130  PRINT "*                      *"
140  PRINT "* STANDARD DEVIATION   *"
150  PRINT "*                      *"
160  PRINT "***********************"
```

```
170   PRINT
180   LET N=S=S2=0
190   PRINT "PLEASE TYPE IN YOUR VALUES ONE AT A TIME"
200   PRINT "(TO TERMINATE PROGRAM, TYPE IN -99999)"
210   INPUT X
220   IF X=-99999. THEN 270
230   LET N=N+1
240   LET S=S+X
250   LET S2=S2+X*X
260   GO TO 210
270   IF N=0 THEN 380
280   LET M=S/N
290   LET V=(N*S2-S*S)/(N*N)
300   LET D=SQR(V)
310   PRINT
320   PRINT "THE MEAN IS:" ;M
330   PRINT
340   PRINT "THE VARIANCE IS:" ;V
350   PRINT
360   PRINT "THE STANDARD DEVIATION IS:" ;D
370   GO TO 170
380   END
```

RUN

```
************************
*                      *
* THE   VARIANCE   AND *
*                      *
* STANDARD DEVIATION   *
*                      *
************************
```

PLEASE TYPE IN YOUR VALUES ONE AT A TIME
(TO TERMINATE PROGRAM, TYPE IN -99999)
?3
?5.1
?4.2
?8
?19
?23
?14
?15
?16.2
?4.8
?9.1
?9.2
?-99999

THE MEAN IS: 1Ø.8833

THE VARIANCE IS: 38.2681

THE STANDARD DEVIATION IS: 6.18612

PLEASE TYPE IN YOUR VALUES ONE AT A TIME
(TO TERMINATE PROGRAM, TYPE IN -99999)
?5
?7
?8
?6
?4
?5
?3
?2
?1
?Ø
?5
?14
?19
?22
?17
?18
?16
?14
?-99999

THE MEAN IS: 9.22222

THE VARIANCE IS: 46.Ø617

THE STANDARD DEVIATION IS: 6.78688

PLEASE TYPE IN YOUR VALUES ONE AT A TIME
(TO TERMINATE PROGRAM, TYPE IN -99999)
?-99999

DONE

8.4 A Data Processing Problem

Suppose we have N students attending a class in computer science. Each student is now required, in turn, to come to a Teletype terminal to type his or her identification number, age as of last birthday, and code for sex (1 = male, 2 = female), in that order.

The problem is to determine how many males and females are in the group, the percentage males and females, the average age of the class, and the number of students aged between 23 and 26 years, inclusive.

We shall assume a maximum of 300 students. The program terminates when any negative value of N is entered.

Several counts have to be kept:

1. the count of students in the group (C)
2. the count of males   (M)
3. the count of females   (F)
4. the count of students between 23 and 26 years of age (T)

Each of these counts must be initialized to zero before any sums are accumulated. This is done by a multiple assignment statement in line 260.

Program 8-4

```
100   PRINT "**********************"
110   PRINT "*                    *"
120   PRINT "* A DATA PROCESSING*"
130   PRINT "*                    *"
140   PRINT "*        PROBLEM     *"
150   PRINT "*                    *"
160   PRINT "**********************"
170   PRINT
180   DIM I[300],A[300],S[300]
190   PRINT "HOW MANY STUDENTS ARE IN THE CLASS" ;
200   INPUT N
210   IF N<0 THEN 610
220   IF N>300 THEN 590
230   PRINT
240   PRINT "EACH STUDENT SHOULD NOW TYPE IN ID, AGE LAST BIRTHDAY,"
250   PRINT "AND SEX CODE (1=MALE, 2=FEMALE),SEPARATED BY COMMAS."
260   LET M=F=T=Y=0
270   FOR K=1 TO N
280   INPUT I[K],A[K],S[K]
290   LET Y=Y+A[K]
300   NEXT K
310   PRINT
320   FOR J=1 TO N
330   IF S[J]=1 THEN 360
340   LET F=F+1
350   GO TO 370
360   LET M=M+1
370   IF A[J]<23 THEN 400
380   IF A[J]>26 THEN 400
390   LET T=T+1
400   NEXT J
410   LET P1=M/N*100
420   LET P2=F/N*100
430   LET X=Y/N
440   PRINT "NUMBER OF STUDENTS IN CLASS" ;N
450   PRINT
460   PRINT "AVERAGE AGE OF STUDENTS=" ;X
470   PRINT.
480   PRINT "NUMBER OF     MALES IN THE CLASS=" ;M
490   PRINT "NUMBER OF FEMALES IN THE CLASS=" ;F
500   PRINT "PERCENTAGE     MALES=" ;P1
```

```
510   PRINT "PERCENTAGE FEMALES=" ;P2
520   PRINT
530   PRINT "NUMBER OF STUDENTS BETWEEN 23 AND 26 YEARS OF AGE=";T
540   PRINT
550   PRINT "THIS CASE IS NOW FINISHED."
560   PRINT
570   PRINT
580   GO TO 190
590   PRINT "SORRY, BUT N CAN'T BE GREATER THAN 300."
600   GO TO 190
610   END
```

```
RUN

* * * * * * * * * * * * * * * * * * * *
*                     *
* A DATA PROCESSING*
*                     *
*        PROBLEM       *
*                     *
* * * * * * * * * * * * * * * * * * * *


HOW MANY STUDENTS ARE IN THE CLASS?10

EACH STUDENT SHOULD NOW TYPE IN ID, AGE LAST BIRTHDAY,
AND SEX CODE (1=MALE, 2=FEMALE) ,SEPARATED BY COMMAS.
?35,17,1
?108,19,2
?100,18,1
?146,19,1
?150,20,2
?160,49,2
?17,21,2
?89,35,1
?133,21,2
?67,17,1

NUMBER OF STUDENTS IN CLASS 10

AVERAGE AGE OF STUDENTS= 23.6

NUMBER OF     MALES IN THE CLASS= 5
NUMBER OF FEMALES IN THE CLASS= 5
PERCENTAGE     MALES= 50
PERCENTAGE FEMALES= 50

NUMBER OF STUDENTS BETWEEN 23 AND 26 YEARS OF AGE = 0

THIS CASE IS NOW FINISHED.
```

HOW MANY STUDENTS ARE IN THE CLASS?3Ø6
SORRY, BUT N CAN'T BE GREATER THAN 3ØØ.
HOW MANY STUDENTS ARE IN THE CLASS?6

EACH STUDENT SHOULD NOW TYPE IN ID, AGE LAST BIRTHDAY,
AND SEX CODE (1=MALE, 2=FEMALE) ,SEPARATED BY COMMAS.
?59,18,2
?224,17,1
?348,19,1
?916,26,2
?444,19,1
?19,19,2

NUMBER OF STUDENTS IN CLASS 6

AVERAGE AGE OF STUDENTS= 19.6667

NUMBER OF   MALES IN THE CLASS= 3
NUMBER OF FEMALES IN THE CLASS= 3
PERCENTAGE   MALES= 5Ø
PERCENTAGE FEMALES= 5Ø

NUMBER OF STUDENTS BETWEEN 23 AND 26 YEARS OF AGE = 1

THIS CASE IS NOW FINISHED.

HOW MANY STUDENTS ARE IN THE CLASS?-1

DONE

8.5   A Mathematics Quiz

Since BASIC provides for the option of the INPUT statement, many programs can
be designed to serve as quizzes for the person sitting at a Teletype terminal. The program can be written to check for the correct response to each question and even to
provide for successive attempts in the event of a wrong response. The total number of
questions answered correctly can be scored, and an alphabetic grade assigned.

What follows is a simple, five-question quiz in elementary arithmetic. If all the questions are answered correctly, a grade of A is scored; 1 wrong is a B, 2 wrong a C, 3
wrong a D, and 4 or 5 wrong, an F.

Program 8-5

```
1ØØ  PRINT "*****************"
11Ø  PRINT "*               *"
12Ø  PRINT "* THIS IS A FIVE *"
13Ø  PRINT "*               *"
14Ø  PRINT "* QUESTION QUIZ *"
15Ø  PRINT "*               *"
16Ø  PRINT "*****************"
17Ø  PRINT
```

```
180   LET C=W=Ø
190   PRINT "THIS IS A FIVE QUESTION QUIZ IN ARITHMETIC."
200   PRINT "TYPE IN THE ANSWER FOLLOWING THE QUESTION MARK."
210   PRINT
220   PRINT "        1.          (7+2)/3 =" ;
230   INPUT Q
240   IF Q=3 THEN 270
250   LET W=W+1
260   GO TO 290
270   LET C=C+1
280   PRINT "VERY GOOD."
290   PRINT
300   PRINT "        2.         7*9 =" ;
310   INPUT Q
320   IF Q=63 THEN 350
330   LET W=W+1
340   GO TO 370
350   LET C=C+1
360   PRINT "VERY GOOD."
370   PRINT
380   PRINT "        3.          100/(3+1) =" ;
390   INPUT Q
400   IF Q=25 THEN 430
410   LET W=W+1
420   GO TO 450
430   LET C=C+1
440   PRINT "VERY GOOD."
450   PRINT
460   PRINT "        4.          100*.1 =" ;
470   INPUT Q
480   IF Q=1Ø THEN 51Ø
490   LET W=W+1
500   GO TO 53Ø
510   LET C=C+1
520   PRINT "VERY GOOD."
530   PRINT
540   PRINT "        5.          1/4 + 2/4 + 4/16 =" ;
550   INPUT Q
560   IF Q=1 THEN 590
570   LET W=W+1
580   GO TO 61Ø
590   LET C=C+1
600   PRINT "VERY GOOD."
610   PRINT
620   PRINT "THE QUIZ IS NOW OVER."
630   PRINT
640   IF C=5 THEN 690
650   IF C=4 THEN 71Ø
660   IF C=3 THEN 73Ø
670   IF C=2 THEN 75Ø
680   GO TO 77Ø
```

```
690  PRINT "CONGRATULATIONS! YOU RECEIVE AN A GRADE."
700  GO TO 780
710  PRINT "CONGRATULATIONS. YOU SCORED A B."
720  GO TO 780
730  PRINT "NOT BAD. YOU SCORED A C."
740  GO TO 780
750  PRINT "WELL, IT WAS A DIFFICULT QUIZ, EVEN SO YOU SCORED A D."
760  GO TO 780
770  PRINT "YOU'RE HOPELESS. YOU GOT AN F GRADE."
780  PRINT
790  PRINT "WOULD YOU LIKE TO TAKE THE QUIZ AGAIN?"
800  PRINT "(TYPE 1 FOR YES, Ø FOR NO)"
810  INPUT M
820  IF M=Ø THEN 840
830  GO TO 170
840  END
```

```
*****************
*               *
* THIS  IS  A  FIVE *
*               *
* QUESTION QUIZ *
*               *
*****************
```

THIS IS A FIVE QUESTION QUIZ IN ARITHMETIC.
TYPE IN THE ANSWER FOLLOWING THE QUESTION MARK.

```
        1.       (7+2)/3 =?3
VERY GOOD.

        2.       7*9 =?56

        3.       100/(3+1) =?34.3

        4.       100*.1 =?1

        5.       1/4 + 2/4 + 4/16 =?1
VERY GOOD.
```

THE QUIZ IS NOW OVER.

WELL, IT WAS A DIFFICULT QUIZ, EVEN SO YOU SCORED A D.

WOULD YOU LIKE TO TAKE THE QUIZ AGAIN?
(TYPE 1 FOR YES, Ø FOR NO)
?1

THIS IS A FIVE QUESTION QUIZ IN ARITHMETIC.
TYPE IN THE ANSWER FOLLOWING THE QUESTION MARK.

      1.   (7+2)/3 =?3
VERY GOOD.

      2.   7*9 =?63
VERY GOOD.

      3.   100/(3+1) =?25
VERY GOOD.

      4.   100*.1 =?12

      5.   1/4 + 2/4 + 4/16 =?1
VERY GOOD.

THE QUIZ IS NOW OVER.

CONGRATULATIONS. YOU SCORED A B.

WOULD YOU LIKE TO TAKE THE QUIZ AGAIN?
(TYPE 1 FOR YES, Ø FOR NO)
?1

THIS IS A FIVE QUESTION QUIZ IN ARITHMETIC.
TYPE IN THE ANSWER FOLLOWING THE QUESTION MARK.

      1.   (7+2)/3 =?3
VERY GOOD.

      2.   7*9 =?63
VERY GOOD.

      3.   100/(3+1) =?25
VERY GOOD.

      4.   100*.1 =?1Ø
VERY GOOD.

      5.   1/4 + 2/4 + 4/16 =?1
VERY GOOD.

THE QUIZ IS NOW OVER.

CONGRATULATIONS. YOU RECEIVE AN A GRADE.

WOULD YOU LIKE TO TAKE THE QUIZ AGAIN?
(TYPE 1 FOR YES, Ø FOR NO)
?Ø

DONE

It is possible to reconstruct this quiz so that it is easier to write and easier to debug. But the method involves a knowledge of *subroutines*, a topic that is covered in Chapter Eleven. At that time, when we present this identical quiz written in subroutine form, we shall refer you to this program. By that time you should have an appreciation of the great utilitarian value of subroutines.

8.6 Another Conditional Transfer—The Computed GO TO

Suppose we needed to categorize a group of N numbers between 0 through 4 inclusive. These numbers could represent the college "grade point average" which is used to assess academic achievement. We would like to know how many are between 0 and less than 1, 1 and less than 2, 2 and less than 3, 3 and less than 4, and, finally, 4, representing a perfect grade point average. A distribution of scores into categories is called a "histogram."

In Program 8-6 users are asked to type in their value of N. Then the N scores are entered using an INPUT statement within a FOR/NEXT loop. By using a logical sequence of five IF statements, the scores are individually listed to see in which category they fall. After each score is tested, 1 is added to the appropriate count. Finally, each of the five counts is printed and the program terminates.

Program 8-6

```
100   PRINT "******************************"
110   PRINT "*                            *"
120   PRINT "* A METHOD  TO  HISTOGRAM *"
130   PRINT "*                            *"
140   PRINT "* THE GRADE POINT AVERAGE *"
150   PRINT "*                            *"
160   PRINT "******************************"
170   PRINT
180   LET X1=X2=X3=X4=X5=0
190   PRINT "PLEASE TYPE IN THE NUMBER OF SCORES TO BE CONSIDERED."
200   PRINT
210   INPUT N
220   PRINT "NOW PLEASE TYPE IN THE SCORES ONE AT A TIME"
230   PRINT "                    (SCORES MUST BE <= 4)"
240   PRINT
250   FOR J=1 TO N
260   INPUT S
270   IF S >= 0 AND S<1 THEN 340
280   IF S >= 1 AND S<2 THEN 360
290   IF S >= 2 AND S<3 THEN 380
300   IF S >= 3 AND S<4 THEN 400
310   IF S=4 THEN 420
320   PRINT "SORRY, TRY AGAIN!"
330   GO TO 260
340   LET X1=X1+1
350   GO TO 430
360   LET X2=X2+1
370   GO TO 430
380   LET X3=X3+1
390   GO TO 430
```

```
400  LET X4=X4+1
410  GO TO 430
420  LET X5=X5+1
430  NEXT J
440  PRINT
450  PRINT "CATEGORY 1: ABOVE 0 AND LESS THAN 1 -";X1
460  PRINT "CATEGORY 2: ABOVE 1 AND LESS THAN 2 -";X2
470  PRINT "CATEGORY 3: ABOVE 2 AND LESS THAN 3 -";X3
480  PRINT "CATEGORY 4: ABOVE 3 AND LESS THAN 4 -";X4
490  PRINT "CATEGORY 5: EXACTLY 4                -";X5
500  END
```

RUN

```
****************************
*                          *
* A  METHOD  TO  HISTOGRAM *
*                          *
* THE GRADE POINT AVERAGE  *
*                          *
****************************
```

PLEASE TYPE IN THE NUMBER OF SCORES TO BE CONSIDERED.

?17
NOW PLEASE TYPE IN THE SCORES ONE AT A TIME
                    (SCORES MUST BE <= 4)

?3.1
?1.2
?0.7
?4
?3.9
?4
?3.8
?0.7
?3.5
?6
SORRY, TRY AGAIN!
?2.6
?2.1
?1
?1.7
?2.3
?3
?1.5
?3.7

```
CATEGORY 1: ABOVE Ø AND LESS THAN 1 - 2
CATEGORY 2: ABOVE 1 AND LESS THAN 2 - 4
CATEGORY 3: ABOVE 2 AND LESS THAN 3 - 3
CATEGORY 4: ABOVE 3 AND LESS THAN 4 - 6
CATEGORY 5: EXACTLY 4                  - 2
```

DONE

Program 8-6 may be criticized for being unnecessarily verbose. Although the sequence of IF statements is logically correct, it may be replaced by a more succinct, single statement, known as the computed GO TO.

The computed GO TO (in the manual referred to as the multibranch GO TO) takes the form:

$$\text{GO TO I OF 10, 20, 30, 40}$$

where transfer of control goes to statement 10 (the first number mentioned) if I is equal to 1, 20 if I = 2, 30 if I = 3, and 40 if I = 4. In other words, the value of the variable or expression between the words TO and OF acts as an index to the appropriate statement number.

In the amended program that follows (Program 8-7) the computed GO TO is found in line 290. If I is not equal to 1, 2, 3, or 4, an error is assumed and control "falls through" to statement 300 which prints out an appropriate message. Otherwise, the program behaves exactly as the previous one, giving the same results.

Should the expression in a computed GO TO be a noninteger quantity, it is automatically *rounded*.

Program 8-7

```
100  PRINT "*******************************"
110  PRINT "*                             *"
120  PRINT "* A  METHOD  TO  HISTOGRAM   *"
130  PRINT "*                             *"
140  PRINT "* USING THE COMPUTED GO TO   *"
150  PRINT "*                             *"
160  PRINT "*******************************"
170  PRINT
180  LET X1=X2=X3=X4=X5=Ø
190  PRINT "PLEASE TYPE IN THE NUMBER OF SCORES TO BE CONSIDERED."
200  PRINT
210  INPUT N
220  PRINT "NOW PLEASE TYPE IN THE SCORES ONE AT A TIME"
230  PRINT "                        (SCORES MUST BE <= 4)"
240  PRINT
250  FOR J=1 TO N
260  INPUT S
270  LET I=INT (S+1)
280  IF S=4 THEN 4ØØ
290  GO TO I OF 32Ø,34Ø,36Ø,38Ø,
300  PRINT "SORRY, TRY AGAIN!"
310  GO TO 26Ø
320  LET X1=X1+1
330  GO TO 41Ø
```

```
340  LET X2=X2+1
350  GO TO 410
360  LET X3=X3+1
370  GO TO 410
380  LET X4 =X4+1
390  GO TO 410
400  LET X5=X5+1
410  NEXT J
420  PRINT
430  PRINT "CATEGORY 1: ABOVE Ø AND LESS THAN 1 -"; X1
440  PRINT "CATEGORY 2: ABOVE 1 AND LESS THAN 2 -"; X2
450  PRINT "CATEGORY 3: ABOVE 2 AND LESS THAN 3 -"; X3
460  PRINT "CATEGORY 4: ABOVE 3 AND LESS THAN 4 -"; X4
470  PRINT "CATEGORY 5: EXACTLY 4           -"; X5
480  END
```

RUN

```
*******************************
*                             *
*  A  METHOD  TO  HISTOGRAM   *
*                             *
*  USING THE COMPUTED GO TO   *
*                             *
*******************************
```

PLEASE TYPE IN THE NUMBER OF SCORES TO BE CONSIDERED.

?17
NOW PLEASE TYPE IN THE SCORES ONE AT A TIME
            (SCORES MUST BE <= 4)

?3.1
?1.2
?Ø.7
?4
?3.9
?4
?3.8
?Ø.7
?3.5
?4.2
SORRY, TRY AGAIN!
?2.6
?2.1 ·
?1
?1.7
?2.3
?3
?1.5
?3.7

CATEGORY 1: ABOVE Ø AND LESS THAN 1 – 2
CATEGORY 2: ABOVE 1 AND LESS THAN 2 – 4
CATEGORY 3: ABOVE 2 AND LESS THAN 3 – 3
CATEGORY 4: ABOVE 3 AND LESS THAN 4 – 6
CATEGORY 5: EXACTLY 4   – 2

DONE

8.7 Calculating the Frequencies of Random Numbers

Since the random number generator RND produces numbers that are uniformly distributed, one would expect 400 such numbers between 1 and 10 to have a frequency of about 40 each.

In Program 8-8 a straightforward approach is used to compute the frequencies of N random numbers, where N is inputted by the user. The numbers generated are all between 1 and 10 inclusive. Each frequency is calculated by means of a separate IF test and the appropriate counter is incremented each time.

The resulting program, although logical in structure and simple to understand, is long and tedious to write. In the absence of any better method this will have to do. However, there is a somewhat sophisticated method that accomplishes this exact task more efficiently and with considerably less effort expended by the programmer. Now it is quite true that we could have shortened the program slightly by resorting to the computed GO TO to replace lines 250 to 340 with the statement:

GO TO R OF 350, 370, 390, 410, 430, 450, 470, 490, 510, 530

The principle behind the elegant way of calculating the frequencies of each of the numbers 1 through 10 is to set up an array of 10 locations in which to store the frequencies. *As each of the numbers 1 through 10 is generated it is used as an index.* For example, if the generated number is 3, then $K(3)$ is incremented by 1. By using this technique one can considerably reduce the size of a program.

In Program 8-8, the frequencies are calculated inefficiently. This program was run twice, once for an N of 400 and then for an N of 20. It will be seen that the higher the value of N, the closer the frequencies tend to the expected.

Program 8-9 uses the same two N's but computes the frequencies in a much more efficient manner.

Program 8-8

```
100  PRINT "****************************"
110  PRINT "*                          *"
120  PRINT "* AN  INEFFICIENT  WAY  TO *"
130  PRINT "*                          *"
140  PRINT "* CALCULATE FREQUENCIES *"
150  PRINT "*                          *"
160  PRINT "****************************"
170  PRINT
180  LET K1=K2=K3=K4=K5=K6=K7=K8=K9=K=Ø
190  PRINT "HOW MANY RANDOM NUMBERS DO YOU WANT GENERATED
         (TO TERMINATE"
200  PRINT "PROGRAM, TYPE A NEGATIVE NUMBER)";
210  INPUT N
```

```
220  IF N<Ø THEN 71Ø
230  FOR I=1 TO N
240  LET R=INT (RND(Ø)*1Ø)+1
250  IF R=1 THEN 35Ø
260  IF R=2 THEN 37Ø
270  IF R=3 THEN 39Ø
280  IF R=4 THEN 41Ø
290  IF R=5 THEN 43Ø
300  IF R=6 THEN 45Ø
310  IF R=7 THEN 47Ø
320  IF R=8 THEN 49Ø
330  IF R=9 THEN 51Ø
340  IF R=1Ø THEN 53Ø
350  LET K1=K1+1
360  GO TO 55Ø
370  LET K2=K2+1
380  GO TO 55Ø
390  LET K3=K3+1
400  GO TO 55Ø
410  LET K4=K4+1
420  GO TO 55Ø
430  LET K5=K5+1
440  GO TO 55Ø
450  LET K6=K6+1
460  GO TO 55Ø
470  LET K7=K7+1
480  GO TO 55Ø
490  LET K8=K8+1
500  GO TO 55Ø
510  LET K9=K9+1
520  GO TO 55Ø
530  LET K=K+1
540  GO TO 55Ø
550  NEXT I
560  PRINT LIN(2)
570  PRINT "NO."; SPA(8); "FREQUENCY"
580  PRINT "---"; SPA(8); "---------"
590  PRINT "1", K1
600  PRINT "2", K2
610  PRINT "3", K3
620  PRINT "4", K4
630  PRINT "5", K5
640  PRINT "6", K6
650  PRINT "7", K7
660  PRINT "8", K8
670  PRINT "9", K9
680  PRINT "1Ø", K
690  PRINT
700  GO TO 17Ø
710  END
```

```
***************************
*                         *
* AN  INEFFICIENT  WAY  TO *
*                         *
* CALCULATE FREQUENCIES *
*                         *
***************************
```

HOW MANY RANDOM NUMBERS DO YOU WANT GENERATED (TO TERMINATE PROGRAM, TYPE A NEGATIVE NUMBER)? 400

NO.	FREQUENCY
1	37
2	40
3	34
4	38
5	41
6	51
7	44
8	37
9	39
10	39

HOW MANY RANDOM NUMBERS DO YOU WANT GENERATED (TO TERMINATE PROGRAM, TYPE A NEGATIVE NUMBER)? 20

NO.	FREQUENCY
1	1
2	2
3	2
4	3
5	1
6	2
7	3
8	2
9	2
10	2

HOW MANY RANDOM NUMBERS DO YOU WANT GENERATED (TO TERMINATE PROGRAM, TYPE A NEGATIVE NUMBER)? -9

DONE

8.8 An Efficient Method for Calculating Frequencies

Program 8-9

```
100  PRINT "****************************"
110  PRINT "*                          *"
120  PRINT "* AN   EFFICIENT   WAY  TO *"
130  PRINT "*                          *"
140  PRINT "* CALCULATE FREQUENCIES *"
150  PRINT "*                          *"
160  PRINT "****************************"
170  PRINT
180  PRINT "HOW MANY RANDOM NUMBERS DO YOU WANT GENERATED
         (TO TERMINATE"
190  PRINT "PROGRAM, TYPE A NEGATIVE NUMBER)";
200  INPUT N
210  IF N<Ø THEN 380
220  DIM K[10]
230  FOR I=1 TO 10
240  LET K[I]=Ø
250  NEXT I
260  FOR I=1 TO N
270  LET R=INT(RND(Ø)*1Ø)+1
280  LET K[R]=K[R]+1
290  NEXT I
300  PRINT LIN(2)
310  PRINT "NO."; SPA(8); "FREQUENCY"
320  PRINT "---"; SPA(8); "---------"
330  FOR I=1 TO 10
340  PRINT I,K[I]
350  NEXT I
360  PRINT
370  GO TO 170
380  END
```

```
RUN



****************************
*                          *
* AN   EFFICIENT   WAY  TO *
*                          *
* CALCULATE FREQUENCIES *
*                          *
****************************


HOW MANY RANDOM NUMBERS DO YOU WANT GENERATED (TO
TERMINATE PROGRAM, TYPE A NEGATIVE NUMBER)?4ØØ
```

NO.	FREQUENCY
1	39
2	5Ø
3	38
4	39
5	37
6	32
7	31
8	47
9	47
1Ø	4Ø

HOW MANY RANDOM NUMBERS DO YOU WANT GENERATED (TO TERMINATE PROGRAM, TYPE A NEGATIVE NUMBER)?2Ø

NO.	FREQUENCY
1	2
2	3
3	3
4	1
5	1
6	4
7	2
8	Ø
9	Ø
1Ø	4

HOW MANY RANDOM NUMBERS DO YOU WANT GENERATED (TO TERMINATE PROGRAM, TYPE A NEGATIVE NUMBER)?-9

DONE

8.9 The Random Function with a Negative Argument

When using the random number generator to compute frequencies one has to be sure that the argument is not negative; if it is, the same random number will be generated each time—this would hardly be random. This is done deliberately in the next program where the argument to the random number generator is -5. As a result, all of the 400 numbers in the first case and then all 20 numbers in the second case fall into category 3.

Program 8-10

```
100  PRINT "*******************************"
110  PRINT "*                             *"
120  PRINT "*  COMPUTING THE FREQUENCY  *"
130  PRINT "*                             *"
140  PRINT "* USING   A   NEGATIVE   SEED *"
150  PRINT "*                             *"
160  PRINT "*******************************"
170  PRINT
180  PRINT "HOW MANY RANDOM NUMBERS DO YOU WANT GENERATED
        (TO TERMINATE"
190  PRINT "PROGRAM, TYPE A NEGATIVE NUMBER)";
200  INPUT N
210  IF N<0 THEN 380
220  DIM K[10]
230  FOR I=1 TO 10
240  LET K[I]=0
250  NEXT I
260  FOR I=1 TO N
270  LET R=INT RND (-5) * 10) +1
280  LET K[R]=K[R]+1
290  NEXT I
300  PRINT LIN(2)
310  PRINT "NO."; SPA(8); "FREQUENCY"
320  PRINT "---"; SPA(8); "---------"
330  FOR I=1 TO 10
340  PRINT I,K[I]
350  NEXT I
360  PRINT
370  GO TO 170
380  END


RUN



*******************************
*                             *
*  COMPUTING THE FREQUENCY  *
*                             *
* USING   A   NEGATIVE   SEED *
*                             *
*******************************

HOW MANY RANDOM NUMBERS DO YOU WANT GENERATED (TO
TERMINATE PROGRAM, TYPE A NEGATIVE NUMBER)?400
```

```
NO.        FREQUENCY
---        - - - - - - - - -
1              Ø
2              Ø
3             4ØØ
4              Ø
5              Ø
6              Ø
7              Ø
8              Ø
9              Ø
1Ø             Ø
```

HOW MANY RANDOM NUMBERS DO YOU WANT GENERATED (TO
TERMINATE PROGRAM, TYPE A NEGATIVE NUMBER)?2Ø

```
NO.        FREQUENCY
---        - - - - - - - - -
1              Ø
2              Ø
3             2Ø
4              Ø
5              Ø
6              Ø
7              Ø
8              Ø
9              Ø
1Ø             Ø
```

HOW MANY RANDOM NUMBERS DO YOU WANT GENERATED (TO
TERMINATE PROGRAM, TYPE A NEGATIVE NUMBER)?-9

DONE

8.10 Playing the Game Buzz

As children we often played the game Buzz. In this game a player starts out at 1 and
this number is always incremented in turn by the other players by 1. When a number
containing a 7 is reached the player says "buzz" rather than the number. In fact, one
says "buzz" for each occurrence of the digit 7 in the current number. Any number di-
visible by 7 is also substituted by a "buzz."

This game, though intriguing, is somewhat taxing for the human brain. Letting a
computer program do the thinking might possibly increase one's enjoyment of the
game even if it atrophies the brain. (We have programmed the game of Buzz in Program 8-11.)

Program 8-11

```
100   PRINT "*********************"
110   PRINT "*                   *"
120   PRINT "*  THE GAME OF BUZZ  *"
130   PRINT "*                   *"
140   PRINT "*********************"
150   PRINT
160   PRINT "PLEASE TYPE IN YOUR NUMBER FOR THE GAME OF BUZZ"
170   PRINT "(TO TERMINATE THE GAME, TYPE IN Ø)"
180   PRINT
190   INPUT N
200   IF N=Ø THEN 450
210   LET N1=N
220   LET K=Ø
230   LET N1=N1/1Ø
240   LET N2=N1 – INT (N1)
250   IF INT (N2*1Ø+.1)=7 THEN 280
260   IF INT (N1)=Ø THEN 300
270   GO TO 230
280   LET K=K+1
290   GO TO 230
300   IF N/7 < > INT (N/7) THEN 320
310   LET K=K+1
320   IF K=Ø THEN 410
330   PRINT
340   PRINT "THE NUMBER IS ";
350   FOR L=1 TO K
360   PRINT "BUZZ ";
370   NEXT L
380   PRINT
390   PRINT
400   GO TO 160
410   PRINT
420   PRINT "THE NUMBER IS "; N
430   PRINT
440   GO TO 160
450   END
```

RUN


```
*********************
*                   *
*  THE GAME OF BUZZ  *
*                   *
*********************
```

PLEASE TYPE IN YOUR NUMBER FOR THE GAME OF BUZZ
(TO TERMINATE THE GAME, TYPE IN Ø)

?6

THE NUMBER IS   6

PLEASE TYPE IN YOUR NUMBER FOR THE GAME OF BUZZ
(TO TERMINATE THE GAME, TYPE IN Ø)

?8

THE NUMBER IS   8

PLEASE TYPE IN YOUR NUMBER FOR THE GAME OF BUZZ
(TO TERMINATE THE GAME, TYPE IN Ø)

?7

THE NUMBER IS BUZZ BUZZ

PLEASE TYPE IN YOUR NUMBER FOR THE GAME OF BUZZ
(TO TERMINATE THE GAME, TYPE IN Ø)

?14.2

THE NUMBER IS   14.2

PLEASE TYPE IN YOUR NUMBER FOR THE GAME OF BUZZ
(TO TERMINATE THE GAME, TYPE IN Ø)

?126

THE NUMBER IS BUZZ

PLEASE TYPE IN YOUR NUMBER FOR THE GAME OF BUZZ
(TO TERMINATE THE GAME, TYPE IN Ø)

?77

THE NUMBER IS BUZZ BUZZ BUZZ

PLEASE TYPE IN YOUR NUMBER FOR THE GAME OF BUZZ
(TO TERMINATE THE GAME, TYPE IN Ø)

?777

THE NUMBER IS BUZZ BUZZ BUZZ BUZZ

PLEASE TYPE IN YOUR NUMBER FOR THE GAME OF BUZZ
(TO TERMINATE THE GAME, TYPE IN Ø)

?1824

THE NUMBER IS   1824

PLEASE TYPE IN YOUR NUMBER FOR THE GAME OF BUZZ
(TO TERMINATE THE GAME, TYPE IN Ø)

?3Ø84

THE NUMBER IS   3Ø84

PLEASE TYPE IN YOUR NUMBER FOR THE GAME OF BUZZ
(TO TERMINATE THE GAME, TYPE IN Ø)

?Ø

DONE

8.11 Making Change

One can simulate the role of a cashier on a computer. In Program 8-12 the user is asked to input, in dollars and cents, the cost of the item being purchased and then enter the amount given to the cashier. A test is made to ensure that both inputted values are not negative and that the purchaser hands over sufficient money to cover the cost of the item. One tenth of a cent is added to the charge (in line 300) to take care of any rounding problems that would inevitably arise.

The program then proceeds to compute the exact number of ten dollar bills, fives, singles, quarters, dimes, nickels, and pennies to make the necessary change.

Program 8-12

```
100   PRINT "********************"
110   PRINT "*                  *"
120   PRINT "*  MAKING CHANGE  *"
130   PRINT "*                  *"
140   PRINT "********************"
150   PRINT
160   PRINT "PLEASE TYPE IN THE COST OF THE ITEM."
170   INPUT C
180   IF C<Ø THEN 59Ø
190   PRINT LIN (2), "HOW MUCH ARE YOU PAYING";
200   INPUT P
210   IF P<Ø THEN 59Ø
220   IF P >C THEN 27Ø
230   LET C=C-P
240   IF C<.ØØ5 THEN 61Ø
250   PRINT LIN (2), "YOUR PAYMENT IS SHORT BY"; C
260   GO TO 15Ø
270   LET R=P-C
280   IF R<.ØØ5 THEN 61Ø
290   PRINT LIN (2), "YOU HAVE OVERPAID; HERE IS YOUR CHANGE."
300   LET R=R+.ØØ1
310   LET Y=INT (R/1Ø)
```

```
320  IF Y=Ø THEN 350
330  PRINT LIN (2), Y, "TENS"
340  LET R=R-10*Y
350  LET Y=INT (R/5)
360  IF Y=Ø THEN 390
370  PRINT Y, "FIVES"
380  LET R=R-5
390  LET Y=INT (R)
400  IF Y=Ø THEN 430
410  PRINT Y, "ONES"
420  LET R=R-Y
430  LET Y=INT (4*R)
440  IF Y=Ø THEN 470
450  PRINT Y, "QUARTERS"
460  LET R=R-.25*Y
470  LET Y=INT (10*R)
480  IF Y=Ø THEN 510
490  PRINT Y, "DIMES"
500  LET R=R-.1*Y
510  LET Y=INT (20*R)
520  IF Y=Ø THEN 550
530  PRINT Y, "NICKELS"
540  LET R=R-.05
550  LET Y=INT (100*R)
560  IF Y=Ø THEN 610
570  PRINT Y, "PENNIES"
580  GO TO 610
590  PRINT LIN (2), "OOPS, THERE SEEMS TO BE SOME MISTAKE!"
600  GO TO 150
610  PRINT LIN (2), "THANK YOU SO MUCH; HAVE A NICE DAY."
620  PRINT LIN(3), "DO YOU WANT TO CONTINUE? TYPE 1 FOR YES, Ø FOR NO."
630  INPUT Z
640  IF Z=1 THEN 150
650  END


RUN


* * * * * * * * * * * * * * * * * *
*                                 *
*  MAKING CHANGE  *
*                                 *
* * * * * * * * * * * * * * * * * *

PLEASE TYPE IN THE COST OF THE ITEM.
?3.15


HOW MUCH ARE YOU PAYING?5.ØØ
```

YOU HAVE OVERPAID; HERE IS YOUR CHANGE.

1	ONES
3	QUARTERS
1	DIMES

THANK YOU SO MUCH; HAVE A NICE DAY.

DO YOU WANT TO CONTINUE? TYPE 1 FOR YES, Ø FOR NO.
?1

PLEASE TYPE IN THE COST OF THE ITEM.
?-2.16

OOPS, THERE SEEMS TO BE SOME MISTAKE!

PLEASE TYPE IN THE COST OF THE ITEM.
?2.16

HOW MUCH ARE YOU PAYING?1Ø.ØØ

YOU HAVE OVERPAID; HERE IS YOUR CHANGE.

1	FIVES
2	ONES
3	QUARTERS
1	NICKELS
4	PENNIES

THANK YOU SO MUCH; HAVE A NICE DAY.

DO YOU WANT TO CONTINUE? TYPE 1 FOR YES, Ø FOR NO.
?1

PLEASE TYPE IN THE COST OF THE ITEM.
?.1Ø

HOW MUCH ARE YOU PAYING?-1.ØØ

OOPS, THERE SEEMS TO BE SOME MISTAKE!

PLEASE TYPE IN THE COST OF THE ITEM.
?.1Ø

HOW MUCH ARE YOU PAYING?1.ØØ

YOU HAVE OVERPAID; HERE IS YOUR CHANGE.
    3   QUARTERS
    1   DIMES
    1   NICKELS

THANK YOU SO MUCH; HAVE A NICE DAY.

DO YOU WANT TO CONTINUE? TYPE 1 FOR YES, Ø FOR NO.
?1

PLEASE TYPE IN THE COST OF THE ITEM.
?7Ø.ØØ

HOW MUCH ARE YOU PAYING?5Ø.ØØ

YOUR PAYMENT IS SHORT BY 2Ø

PLEASE TYPE IN THE COST OF THE ITEM.
?7Ø.ØØ

HOW MUCH ARE YOU PAYING?1ØØ.ØØ

YOU HAVE OVERPAID; HERE IS YOUR CHANGE.

    3   TENS

THANK YOU SO MUCH; HAVE A NICE DAY.

DO YOU WANT TO CONTINUE? TYPE 1 FOR YES, Ø FOR NO.
?1

PLEASE TYPE IN THE COST OF THE ITEM.
?2Ø.ØØ

HOW MUCH ARE YOU PAYING?2Ø.ØØ

THANK YOU SO MUCH; HAVE A NICE DAY.

DO YOU WANT TO CONTINUE? TYPE 1 FOR YES, Ø FOR NO.
?Ø

DONE

8.12   Balancing a Checkbook

We had the computer act as a cashier in the previous program, and we would now like to show how a simplified checkbook operation may also be simulated on a computer.

The user is asked to initiate the simulation by typing in the previous month's closing balance B. The user then types in a 1 if she wishes to make a deposit to the account, and a 2 to draw a check. (If the amount of a check exceeds the balance the user is charged $3.00.) If 3 is entered the computer prints out the end-of-month balance, the number of deposits made, and the number of checks drawn, and the program comes to a halt.

If, in response to the question, anything other than a 1, 2, or 3 is entered, control "falls through" to line 280 where a printout advises the user that she has made an error and permits her to rectify it after a repeated printing of the instructions.

Program 8-13

```
100  PRINT "************************"
110  PRINT "*                      *"
120  PRINT "*  CHECKBOOK BALANCE  *"
130  PRINT "*                      *"
140  PRINT "************************"
150  PRINT
160  LET C=D=Ø
170  PRINT "PLEASE TYPE IN LAST MONTH'S CLOSING BALANCE."
180  INPUT B
190  PRINT LIN (2), "THANK YOU.  NOW TYPE:"
200  PRINT "1 FOR A DEPOSIT"
210  PRINT "2 FOR A DRAWN CHECK"
220  PRINT "(REMEMBER, IF YOUR CHECK BOUNCES, YOU ARE CHARGED $3.ØØ)"
230  PRINT "3 TERMINATES THE PROGRAM"
240  INPUT T
250  IF T=3 THEN 45Ø
260  IF T=2 THEN 35Ø
270  IF T=1 THEN 3ØØ
280  PRINT LIN (2), "SORRY, READ THE INSTRUCTIONS AGAIN."
290  GO TO 2ØØ
300  PRINT LIN (2), "HOW MUCH IS YOUR DEPOSIT";
310  INPUT A
320  LET D=D+1
```

```
330  LET B=B+A
340  GO TO 400
350  PRINT LIN (2), "HOW MUCH IS THE CHECK DRAWN FOR";
360  INPUT A
370  IF B<A THEN 420
380  LET C=C+1
390  LET B=B-A
400  PRINT LIN (2), "YOUR BALANCE IS NOW"; B
410  GO TO 200
420  PRINT LIN (2), "YOUR CHECK BOUNCED; $3.00 SERVICE CHARGE."
430  LET B=B-3
440  GO TO 400
450  PRINT LIN (2), "DEPOSITS "; D, "CHECKS "; C
460  PRINT LIN (3), "END OF MONTH BALANCE IS ", B
470  END
```

RUN

```
*************************
*                       *
*  CHECKBOOK BALANCE  *
*                       *
*************************
```

PLEASE TYPE IN LAST MONTH'S CLOSING BALANCE.
?500.00

THANK YOU. NOW TYPE:
1 FOR A DEPOSIT
2 FOR A DRAWN CHECK
(REMEMBER, IF YOUR CHECK BOUNCES, YOU ARE CHARGED $3.00)
3 TERMINATES THE PROGRAM
?1

HOW MUCH IS YOUR DEPOSIT?10.00

YOUR BALANCE IS NOW   510
1 FOR A DEPOSIT
2 FOR A DRAWN CHECK
(REMEMBER, IF YOUR CHECK BOUNCES, YOU ARE CHARGED $3.00)
3 TERMINATES THE PROGRAM
?1

HOW MUCH IS YOUR DEPOSIT?600.00
```
```

```
YOUR BALANCE IS NOW                1110
1  FOR A DEPOSIT
2  FOR A DRAWN CHECK
(REMEMBER, IF YOUR CHECK BOUNCES, YOU ARE CHARGED $3.00)
3  TERMINATES THE PROGRAM
?200


SORRY, READ THE INSTRUCTIONS AGAIN.
1  FOR A DEPOSIT
2  FOR A DRAWN CHECK
(REMEMBER, IF YOUR CHECK BOUNCES, YOU ARE CHARGED $3.00)
3  TERMINATES THE PROGRAM
?2


HOW MUCH IS THE CHECK DRAWN FOR?610


YOUR BALANCE IS NOW                500
1  FOR A DEPOSIT
2  FOR A DRAWN CHECK
(REMEMBER, IF YOUR CHECK BOUNCES, YOU ARE CHARGED $3.00)
3  TERMINATES THE PROGRAM
?2


HOW MUCH IS THE CHECK DRAWN FOR?500


YOUR BALANCE IS NOW                0
1  FOR A DEPOSIT
2  FOR A DRAWN CHECK
(REMEMBER, IF YOUR CHECK BOUNCES, YOU ARE CHARGED $3.00)
3  TERMINATES THE PROGRAM
?1


HOW MUCH IS YOUR DEPOSIT?350.00


YOUR BALANCE IS NOW                350
1  FOR A DEPOSIT
2  FOR A DRAWN CHECK
(REMEMBER, IF YOUR CHECK BOUNCES, YOU ARE CHARGED $3.00)
3  TERMINATES THE PROGRAM
?2


HOW MUCH IS THE CHECK DRAWN FOR?400.00
```

YOUR CHECK BOUNCED: $3.ØØ SERVICE CHARGE.

YOUR BALANCE IS NOW   347
1 FOR A DEPOSIT
2 FOR A DRAWN CHECK
(REMEMBER, IF YOUR CHECK BOUNCES, YOU ARE CHARGED $3.ØØ)
3 TERMINATES THE PROGRAM
?2

HOW MUCH IS THE CHECK DRAWN FOR?1ØØØ.75

YOUR CHECK BOUNCED; $3.ØØ SERVICE CHARGE.

YOUR BALANCE IS NOW   344
1 FOR A DEPOSIT
2 FOR A DRAWN CHECK
(REMEMBER, IF YOUR CHECK BOUNCES, YOU ARE CHARGED $3.ØØ)
3 TERMINATES THE PROGRAM
?3

DEPOSITS 3   CHECKS 2

END OF MONTH BALANCE IS   344

DONE

QUICK REFERENCE GUIDE TO CHAPTER EIGHT

Item	General Form	Example
1. Computed GO TO	*Line number* GO TO *expression* OF *line number,* *line number, . . .*	100 GO TO J OF 123,246,398 200 GO TO SQR(X↑3) OF 6,7,8

Questions

1. Set three arrays, W, D, and G, in which to store the weight, distance traveled, and the number of gallons of fuel consumed by a series of new automobiles during a test run. Generate a fourth array R in which is stored the miles per gallon. Find the correlation coefficient between the W and the R arrays. If it is greater than 0.1 find the minimum and maximum number of gallons used in the G array. If it is less than −0.1 find the minimum and maximum of the distances traveled in the D array. If R is between −0.1 and +0.1. The program should print out the W array, together with its range.

2. What output would be printed by the following program?

```
10   DIM A[10], B[10], C[10], D[10]
20   FOR I = 1 TO 10
30   LET A[I] = 2 * I - 1
40   LET B[11 - I] = 2 * I
50   NEXT I
60   FOR J = 1 TO 9 STEP 2
70   READ C[J], C[J+1]
80   NEXT J
90   DATA 1,2,3,4,5
100  DATA 6,7,8,9,10
110  FOR K = 1 TO 10
120  LET D[K] = A[K] + B[K] + C[K]
130  NEXT K
140  FOR L = 1 TO 4 STEP 3
150  PRINT D[L], D[L+1], D[L+2]
160  NEXT L
170  END
```

3. Write a program that will compute the sum of the squares of a given list of positive numbers. Assume the numbers are READ into an array by DATA statements. The last positive number is followed by a negative number. The maximum number of positive numbers must not exceed 50.

4. Write a program that READS exactly 12 numbers from a DATA statement and places these numbers into an array. Once the numbers are stored in the array, perform the following calculations on them:

   (a) Find the average of the first, second, and third numbers, the average of the second, third, and fourth numbers, and so on up to and including the average of the tenth, eleventh, and twelfth numbers.

   (b) Print out these averages in a column.

5. Examine the following program and determine exactly what will be printed out.

```
10   READ A
20   DATA 1,3,2,5,-1
30   IF A < 0 THEN 140
40   GO TO A OF 60,80,90
50   GO TO 120
60   PRINT "OVER"
70   GO TO 10
80   PRINT "UNDER"
90   PRINT "THE"
100  PRINT "TABLE"
110  GO TO 10
120  PRINT "CLOTH"
130  GO TO 10
140  END
```

6. Write a computerized "test" that asks a student *five* questions about five different countries and their capitals. If the student gives an incorrect answer, give him a second chance. If he fails again, give him the correct answer. At the end of the test, give the student a grade as follows: One point for a correct answer the first time, one-half point for a correct answer the second time; and zero for an incorrect answer. If the student gets a perfect score, compliment him. If he gets a zero, be kind.

7. Write a program to test whether the random number standard function in BASIC really generates random numbers. One reasonable and simple approach would be to use the function perhaps a thousand times, divide the range of possible results into a few small groups of the same size, and see whether the random number falls into each group approximately the same number of times. For example, if five groups are chosen and 1000 trials made, then the output of the desired program might look like this:

RANDOM NUMBER TEST

GROUP	NUMBER OF HITS
1	2009
2	1998
3	1987
4	2003
5	2003

Group 1 would be the number of hits in the first fifth of the range, that is, between 0 and 0.2. It may make your task easier if you change the expression using the random function so that answers are the integers from 1 to 5.

CHAPTER NINE
SORTING

In almost all branches of computing, sorting is a basic procedure. The insurance company sorts policies in order of expiration dates, the accountant sorts accounts in descending order of gross income, the householder may sort expenses in ascending order, and so on. The list is infinite. The need to be able to sort data is universal and a great amount of effort, time, and expense has been invested in devising efficient ways to do this on a computer. Unfortunately, the most efficient methods are fairly complicated. However, we propose to present a sorting technique that is neither terribly inefficient nor particularly difficult to comprehend. For most purposes it will do the job quite satisfactorily. However, in order to understand the algorithm we shall have to discuss in detail what is known as a "nest of loops."

9.1 Nests of Loops

In all of the programs using FOR/NEXT loops that we have encountered so far in this book, each loop was separate, complete unto itself. Even when a program contained several loops, the loops were done in sequence, in the order in which the logic of the program dictated. We could describe the pattern schematically as:

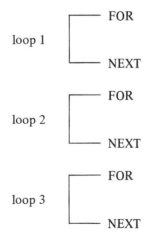

When one loop completely *encloses* another, and this may in turn enclose another, we have what may be regarded as layers of loops, somewhat reminiscent of the method a bird uses in building its nest, layer upon layer. It is for this reason that we speak of *nests of loops.*

A nest of two loops may be represented diagramatically as:

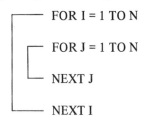

FOR I = 1 TO N

FOR J = 1 TO N

NEXT J

NEXT I

Such a configuration of loops behaves in a very special manner. The outer loop (which uses the index I) begins at 1 and subsequently the inner loop (which contains the index J) is encountered. At this point, the inner loop's index J is set to 1 and the inner loop iterates until its conclusion, going from J = 1 to J = N, but *the value of I remains at 1 for the entire time.* After the inner loop is "satisfied," the NEXT I instruction is encountered and I becomes incremented to 2. Once again, the inner loop is encountered and J goes once more from 1 to N.

This process continues until the outer loop is satisfied, at which point control is passed to the statement *following* the nest of loops. There is no question that, at first exposure, this mechanism of the nest of loops will seem strange and difficult to the novice. However, as is usual with programming practice, familiarity begets understanding.

Great care must be exercised when constructing nests of loops. What must be avoided is the interweaving of individual loops. In other words, the following pattern is not permitted.

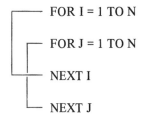

FOR I = 1 TO N

FOR J = 1 TO N

NEXT I

NEXT J

Some useful "don'ts" are:

1. Don't alter the value of the index of a loop.
2. Don't assume anything about the index of the loop once the loop is "satisfied."
3. Don't use any index more than once in a nest of loops.

We now present a series of programs that will illustrate the concept of a nest of loops.

9.2   The Multiplication Tables

To begin, we shall have the computer print out the multiplication tables for us. Program 9-1 will do it, and it will permit the user to type in his own value of N.

Program 9-1

```
100  PRINT "***********************"
110  PRINT "*                     *"
120  PRINT "* THE MULTIPLICATION *"
130  PRINT "*    TABLE PROBLEM    *"
140  PRINT "*                     *"
150  PRINT "***********************"
160  PRINT
```

```
170   PRINT "PLEASE TYPE IN THE VALUE FOR N."
180   INPUT N
190   PRINT "YOU'RE MOST OBLIGING."
200   PRINT
210   PRINT "MULTIPLICATION TABLE"
220   PRINT "-------------- -----"
230   PRINT
240   FOR I=1 TO N
250   PRINT
260   FOR J=1 TO N
270   LET P=I*J
280   PRINT I;"X";J;"=";P
290   NEXT J
300   NEXT I
310   END


RUN


*********************
*                   *
*THE MULTIPLICATION*
*   TABLE PROBLEM   *
*                   *
*********************


PLEASE TYPE IN THE VALUE FOR N.
?5
YOU'RE MOST OBLIGING.

MULTIPLICATION TABLE
-------------- -----


 1        X 1        = 1
 1        X 2        = 2
 1        X 3        = 3
 1        X 4        = 4
 1        X 5        = 5

 2        X 1        = 2
 2        X 2        = 4
 2        X 3        = 6
 2        X 4        = 8
 2        X 5        = 10

 3        X 1        = 3
 3        X 2        = 6
 3        X 3        = 9
 3        X 4        = 12
 3        X 5        = 15
```

4	X 1	= 4
4	X 2	= 8
4	X 3	= 12
4	X 4	= 16
4	X 5	= 20
5	X 1	= 5
5	X 2	= 10
5	X 3	= 15
5	X 4	= 20
5	X 5	= 25

DONE

9.3 The Four Arithmetic Tables

We can make the same nest of loops do even more for us. For instance, it is possible to write a program that will compute and print for a given N the tables of multiplication, division, addition, and subtraction. As with the last program, however, we shall restrict the value of N to 5 to conserve space. To further save space we shall have Program 9-2 print the multiplication and division tables side by side.

Program 9-2

```
100  PRINT "************************"
110  PRINT "*                      *"
120  PRINT "* THE FOUR ARITHMETIC *"
130  PRINT "*                      *"
140  PRINT "*         TABLES        *"
150  PRINT "*                      *"
160  PRINT "************************"
170  PRINT
180  PRINT "PLEASE TYPE IN YOUR VALUE FOR N."
190  INPUT N
200  PRINT "MULTIPLICATION TABLE              DIVISION TABLE"
210  PRINT "-------------- -----            -------- -----"
220  PRINT
230  FOR I=1 TO N
240  PRINT
250  FOR J=1 TO N
260  LET P=I*J
270  LET Q=I/J
280  PRINT I;"X";J;"=";P,I;"/";J;"=";Q
290  NEXT J
300  NEXT I
310  PRINT
320  PRINT "ADDITION TABLE                 SUBTRACTION TABLE"
330  PRINT "--------- -----               ----------- -----"
340  FOR K=1 TO N
350  PRINT
360  FOR L=1 TO N
370  LET A=K+L
380  LET D=K-L
```

```
390   PRINT K;"+";L;"=";A,K;"–";L;"=";D
400   NEXT L
410   NEXT K
420   END
```

END

```
* * * * * * * * * * * * * * * * * * * * * * * *
*                                             *
* THE FOUR ARITHMETIC *
*                                             *
*              TABLES                         *
*                                             *
* * * * * * * * * * * * * * * * * * * * * * * *
```

PLEASE TYPE IN YOUR VALUE FOR N.
?5

MULTIPLICATION TABLE			DIVISION TABLE		
– – – – – – – – – – – – – – – –			– – – – – – – – – – –		
1	X 1	= 1	1	/ 1	= 1
1	X 2	= 2	1	/ 2	= .5
1	X 3	= 3	1	/ 3	= .333333
1	X 4	= 4	1	/ 4	= .25
1	X 5	= 5	1	/ 5	= .2
2	X 1	= 2	2	/ 1	= 2
2	X 2	= 4	2	/ 2	= 1
2	X 3	= 6	2	/ 3	= .666667
2	X 4	= 8	2	/ 4	= .5
2	X 5	= 10	2	/ 5	= .4
3	X 1	= 3	3	/ 1	= 3
3	X 2	= 6	3	/ 2	= 1.5
3	X 3	= 9	3	/ 3	= 1
3	X 4	= 12	3	/ 4	= .75
3	X 5	= 15	3	/ 5	= .6
4	X 1	= 4	4	/ 1	= 4
4	X 2	= 8	4	/ 2	= 2
4	X 3	= 12	4	/ 3	= 1.33333
4	X 4	= 16	4	/ 4	= 1
4	X 5	= 20	4	/ 5	= .8
5	X 1	= 5	5	/ 1	= 5
5	X 2	= 10	5	/ 2	= 2.5
5	X 3	= 15	5	/ 3	= 1.66667
5	X 4	= 20	5	/ 4	= 1.25
5	X 5	= 25	5	/ 5	= 1

ADDITION TABLE   SUBTRACTION TABLE
- - - - - - - - - - - - -   - - - - - - - - - - - - - -

1	+ 1	= 2		1	- 1	= 0
1	+ 2	= 3		1	- 2	=-1
1	+ 3	= 4		1	- 3	=-2
1	+ 4	= 5		1	- 4	=-3
1	+ 5	= 6		1	- 5	=-4
2	+ 1	= 3		2	- 1	= 1
2	+ 2	= 4		2	- 2	= 0
2	+ 3	= 5		2	- 3	=-1
2	+ 4	= 6		2	- 4	=-2
2	+ 5	= 7		2	- 5	=-3
3	+ 1	= 4		3	- 1	= 2
3	+ 2	= 5		3	- 2	= 1
3	+ 3	= 6		3	- 3	= 0
3	+ 4	= 7		3	- 4	=-1
3	+ 5	= 8		3	- 5	=-2
4	+ 1	= 5		4	- 1	= 3
4	+ 2	= 6		4	- 2	= 2
4	+ 3	= 7		4	- 3	= 1
4	+ 4	= 8		4	- 4	= 0
4	+ 5	= 9		4	- 5	=-1
5	+ 1	= 6		5	- 1	= 4
5	+ 2	= 7		5	- 2	= 3
5	+ 3	= 8		5	- 3	= 2
5	+ 4	= 9		5	- 4	= 1
5	+ 5	= 10		5	- 5	= 0

9.4 Sorting an Array

We are now ready to discuss a method for sorting numbers in say, ascending order. The method we devise—the algorithm—will have to work for a small list of numbers just as for a long list. To illustrate the technique let us assume a list of only five numbers, each of which has been read into memory, using an appropriate dimension statement:

33   14   -2   4   19

For the sake of convenience let us list these five numbers in a vertical manner:

33
14
-2
4
19

The technique now is to compare the first number with the second number. Since the second number is smaller we want to "switch" the first and the second numbers. The list now becomes:

$$14$$
$$33$$
$$-2$$
$$4$$
$$19$$

The first item is now compared with the third. Again we want to switch:

$$-2$$
$$33$$
$$14$$
$$4$$
$$19$$

Comparing the first with the fourth, we find there's no change to be made since these two numbers are already in ascending order and, similarly, when comparing the first with the fifth item. We have now "isolated" the smallest number and sent it to the top of the list. Now we want to leave it there, ignore it, in a manner of speaking, and compare the second item with the third, etc. Here are the changes that now take place.

-2	-2
14	4
33	33
4	14
19	19

Now comparing the third with the fourth and fifth:

$$-2$$
$$4$$
$$14$$
$$33$$
$$19$$

Finally, comparing the fourth with the fifth:

$$-2$$
$$4$$
$$14$$
$$19$$
$$33$$

At last, the sorting into ascending order is accomplished.

The question now raised is how to do it in BASIC. The easiest way to do it is to set up a nest of FOR/NEXT loops. Each time a switch must be made, a temporary memory location must be used to store one of the numbers to be switched. But this is not new; we encountered precisely the same problem in Chapter Six. Here is a program that will not only read in the elements of the array *five* per line but, after sorting the numbers in ascending order, will print them out in *ten* elements per line. (Pay close attention to the manner in which this is done.) The program allows for a maximum of 100 elements for the array. The program may be used again for any number of sorts. To terminate it any negative value for N is entered.

Program 9-3

```
100  PRINT "*********************"
110  PRINT "*                    *"
120  PRINT "* SORTING AN ARRAY *"
130  PRINT "*                    *"
140  PRINT "*      OF NUMBERS     *"
150  PRINT "*                    *"
160  PRINT "*********************"
170  PRINT
180  DIM X[100]
190  PRINT "PLEASE TYPE IN YOUR VALUE FOR N."
200  INPUT N
210  IF N<0 THEN 510
220  IF N>100 THEN 490
230  PRINT
240  PRINT "WE'RE IN BUSINESS!"
250  PRINT
260  PRINT "NOW TYPE IN YOUR ARRAY, TYPING 5 NUMBERS PER LINE, EACH"
270  PRINT "NUMBER SEPARATED BY A COMMA."
280  PRINT
290  FOR I=1 TO N STEP 5
300  INPUT X[I],X[I+1],X[I+2],X[I+3],X[I+4]
310  NEXT I
320  PRINT
330  REM: NOW SORT THE NUMBERS IN ASCENDING ORDER
340  FOR I=1 TO N-1
350  FOR J=I+1 TO N
360  IF X[I]<X[J] THEN 400
370  LET S=X[I]
380  LET X[I]=X[J]
390  LET X[J]=S
400  NEXT J
410  NEXT I
420  PRINT "HERE ARE THE SORTED NUMBERS"
430  PRINT
440  FOR I=1 TO N STEP 10
450  PRINT X[I];X[I+1];X[I+2];X[I+3];X[I+4];X[I+5];X[I+6];X[I+7];X[I+8];
460  PRINT X[I+9]
470  NEXT I
480  GO TO 170
490  PRINT "PLEASE NOTE THAN N MAY NOT EXCEED 100."
500  GO TO 190
510  END
```

RUN

```
********************
*                  *
* SORTING AN ARRAY *
*                  *
*     OF NUMBERS   *
*                  *
********************
```

PLEASE TYPE IN YOUR VALUE FOR N.
?1Ø

WE'RE IN BUSINESS!

NOW TYPE IN YOUR ARRAY, TYPING 5 NUMBERS PER LINE, EACH
NUMBER SEPARATED BY A COMMA.

?35,19,-42,16,21
?14,18,26,3,Ø

HERE ARE THE SORTED NUMBERS

-42   Ø   3   14   16   18   19   21   26   35

PLEASE TYPE IN YOUR VALUE FOR N.
?152
PLEASE NOTE THAT N MAY NOT EXCEED 1ØØ.
PLEASE TYPE IN YOUR VALUE FOR N.
?26

WE'RE IN BUSINESS!

NOW TYPE IN YOUR ARRAY, TYPING 5 NUMBERS PER LINE, EACH
NUMBER SEPARATED BY A COMMA.

?5,9,-22,-17,8
?49,1Ø6,72,3,19
?4,99,2,1,43
?59,58,1Ø1,7,8
?5Ø,6Ø,7Ø,8Ø,71
?34,Ø,Ø,Ø,Ø

HERE ARE THE SORTED NUMBERS

-22   -17   1   2   3   4   5   7   8   8
  9   19   34   43   49   5Ø   58   59   6Ø   7Ø
 71   72   8Ø   99 1Ø1 1Ø6   Ø   Ø   Ø   Ø
```
```

PLEASE TYPE IN YOUR VALUE FOR N.
?-99

DONE

Very careful attention should be paid to lines 340 to 410 in the Program 9-3, for they contain the mechanism for the sorting of the numbers into ascending order. These lines hold a nest of two loops, the inner loop having as its initial value of J the value of I + 1, from the outer loop. The only way to clearly understand how such a nest of loops works is to take an array of numbers and go through the loop, step by step.

You should also examine lines 290 to 310 and 440 to 470, where provision is made to deal with more than one number per line.

If, when using this input technique, the value of N is not an exact multiple of 5, any numbers at all may be inserted to pad out the last line of numbers entered.

It is pointed out that every time a sort is completed, the values of the minimum and the maximum are readily available. If the numbers were sorted into ascending order, the minimum is the first element and the maximum is the last element. Of course, if the numbers were sorted into descending order the reverse would be true.

Now that we are familiar with sorting we can tackle another problem in statistics, namely the finding of the *median* of an array. There are various ways to do this but we shall use the method that necessitates the sorting of the array into either ascending or descending order. It makes no difference which order is selected.

9.5   Finding the Median

A most useful statistic is that called the *median*. It is defined as the point (or score) above which and below which are an equal number of scores. In this sense it represents, to some extent, all of the scores.

Suppose a class of seven children is tested in some skill or other and it is determined that their skills, rated from 1 to 100, are as follows:

$$17 \quad 49 \quad 99 \quad 17 \quad 88 \quad 46 \quad 78$$

In order to see more clearly what the median is, let us now rearrange the scores into ascending order.

$$16 \quad 17 \quad 46 \quad 49 \quad 78 \quad 88 \quad 99$$

Now that the numbers are in ascending order we can see at a glance that there are three scores to the left of the number 49 and three scores to the right. Thus 49 is the median score. If there are an *even* number of scores, the median is the average of the two middle scores after sorting.

It is clear then that we have to be able to get the compiler to differentiate between an even number and an odd number. This may easily be done by using the INT function, which we have already used in Chapter Six.

Program 9-4 allows for an array containing a maximum of 30 elements. It will compute the median, whether N is odd or even. A negative value for N terminates the program. The array X, which is sorted in descending order, is printed for its documentation value, enabling the programmer to be sure the sort was correctly performed.

If N is not an even multiple of 5, the balance of the last line of input data can contain any numbers at all. They will be ignored.

Program 9-4

```
100   PRINT "*********************"
110   PRINT "*                   *"
120   PRINT "* FINDING THE MEDIAN*"
130   PRINT "*                   *"
140   PRINT "*********************"
150   PRINT
160   DIM X[200]
170   PRINT "HOW MANY ELEMENTS ARE IN YOUR ARRAY";
180   INPUT N
190   IF N<0 THEN 590
200   IF N>200 THEN 570
210   PRINT
220   PRINT "FINE!"
230   PRINT
240   PRINT "PLEASE TYPE IN YOUR ARRAY, 5 NUMBERS PER LINE."
250   PRINT "(DON'T FORGET TO SEPARATE THEM BY A COMMA!)"
260   PRINT
270   FOR I=1 TO N STEP 5
280   INPUT X[I],X[I+1],X[I+2],X[I+3],X[I+4]
290   NEXT I
300   PRINT
310   REM: SORTING THE NUMBERS INTO DESCENDING ORDER
320   PRINT
330   FOR I=1 TO N-1
340   FOR J=I+1 TO N
350   IF X[I]>X[J] THEN 390
360   LET T=X[I]
370   LET X[I]=X[J]
380   LET X[J]=T
390   NEXT J
400   NEXT I
410   PRINT
420   PRINT "HERE ARE THE NUMBERS IN DESCENDING ORDER"
430   PRINT "---- --- --- ------- -- ---------- -----"
440   PRINT
450   FOR I=1 TO N
460   PRINT X[I];
470   NEXT I
480   PRINT
490   PRINT
500   REM: NOW TEST WHETHER N IS ODD OR EVEN
510   IF INT(N/2)*2=N THEN 540
520   LET M=X[N/2+.5]
530   GO TO 550
540   LET M=(X[N/2]+X[N/2+1])/2
550   PRINT "THE MEDIAN = ";M
560   GO TO 150
570   PRINT "SORRY, 200 IS THE MAXIMUM!  TRY AGAIN."
580   GO TO 150
590   END
```

RUN

```
* * * * * * * * * * * * * * * * * * * * *
*                               *
* FINDING THE MEDIAN*
*                               *
* * * * * * * * * * * * * * * * * * * * *
```

HOW MANY ELEMENTS ARE IN YOUR ARRAY?5

FINE!

PLEASE TYPE IN YOUR ARRAY, 5 NUMBERS PER LINE.
(DON'T FORGET TO SEPARATE THEM BY A COMMA!)

?1,2,3,4,5

HERE ARE THE NUMBERS IN DESCENDING ORDER
 ---- --- --- ------- -- ---------- -----

    5   4   3   2   1

THE MEDIAN = 3

HOW MANY ELEMENTS ARE IN YOUR ARRAY?1Ø

FINE!

PLEASE TYPE IN YOUR ARRAY, 5 NUMBERS PER LINE.
(DON'T FORGET TO SEPARATE THEM BY A COMMA!)

?35,19,-42,16,21
?14,18,26,3,Ø

HERE ARE THE NUMBERS IN DESCENDING ORDER
 ---- --- --- ------- -- ---------- -----

    35   26   21   19   18   16   14   3   Ø   -42

THE MEDIAN = 17

HOW MANY ELEMENTS ARE IN YOUR ARRAY?15

FINE!

PLEASE TYPE IN YOUR ARRAY, 5 NUMBERS PER LINE.
(DON'T FORGET TO SEPARATE THEM BY A COMMA!)

?5,9,-22,-17,8
?49,1Ø6,72,3,19
?4,99,2,1,43

HERE ARE THE NUMBERS IN DESCENDING ORDER

---- --- --- ------- -- ---------- -----

| 1Ø6 | 99 | 72 | 49 | 43 | 19 | 9 | 8 | 5 | 4 | 3 | 2 |
| 1 | -17 | -22 |

THE MEDIAN = 8

HOW MANY ELEMENTS ARE IN YOUR ARRAY?215
SORRY, 2ØØ IS THE MAXIMUM! TRY AGAIN.

HOW MANY ELEMENTS ARE IN YOUR ARRAY?-1

DONE

9.6 Sorting in Tandem

Examine the following table of ID numbers and corresponding IQs:

ID	IQ
731	135
286	161
489	78
334	96
542	129

It is sometimes necessary to sort one of the columns, say, ID numbers, and print them out such that *its corresponding* IQ is printed alongside. At first blush, this might seem to be a difficult task, which it most certainly is not.

Upon examining the matter closely, it becomes clear that whenever two elements of the ID array are switched, the corresponding elements, that is, the elements of the IQ array with exactly the same subscripts as those of the ID array, must also be switched. The following program is designed to read in N ID numbers and corresponding IQ scores.

The problem is to sort the ID numbers in *descending* order, printing out the corresponding IQ scores alongside them. When this is done, the IQs are to be sorted in *ascending* order, printing out the associated ID number, together with its IQ.

In order to accomplish this task, both variables should be read into two separate arrays, say, D and Q. This can be done with a single FOR/NEXT loop, as indeed, is done in Program 9-5, which allows for a maximum of 250 elements in each array.

Program 9-5

```
100   PRINT "*************"
110   PRINT "*           *"
120   PRINT "*SORTING IN *"
130   PRINT "*  TANDEM   *"
140   PRINT "*           *"
150   PRINT "*************"
160   PRINT
170   DIM D[250],Q[250]
180   PRINT "WHAT IS THE VALUE OF N";
190   INPUT N
```

```
200  IF N<0 THEN 820
210  IF N>250 THEN 800
220  PRINT "O.K., LET'S GO!"
230  PRINT
240  PRINT "PLEASE TYPE IN EACH ID AND IQ SEPARATED BY A COMMA."
250  PRINT
260  FOR I=1 TO N
270  INPUT D[I],Q[I]
280  NEXT I
290  PRINT
300  REM: NOW SORT THE ID NUMBERS INTO DESCENDING ORDER
310  FOR I=1 TO N-1
320  FOR J=I+1 TO N
330  IF D[I]>D[J] THEN 400
340  LET T=D[I]
350  LET D[I]=D[J]
360  LET D[J]=T
370  LET T=Q[I]
380  LET Q[I]=Q[J]
390  LET Q[J]=T
400  NEXT J
410  NEXT I
420  PRINT
430  PRINT "SORTED IN DESCENDING ORDER OF ID"
440  PRINT "------ -- ---------- ----- -- --"
450  PRINT
460  PRINT "   ID            IQ"
470  PRINT "   --            --"
480  FOR I=1 TO N
490  PRINT D[I],Q[I]
500  NEXT I
510  FOR I=1 TO 5
520  PRINT
530  NEXT I
540  PRINT "SORTED IN ASCENDING ORDER OF IQ"
550  PRINT "------ -- ---------- ----- -- --"
560  FOR I=1 TO N-1
570  FOR J=I+1 TO N
580  IF Q[I]<Q[J] THEN 650
590  LET T=Q[I]
600  LET Q[I]=Q[J]
610  LET Q[J]=T
620  LET T=D[I]
630  LET D[I]=D[J]
640  LET D[J]=T
650  NEXT J
660  NEXT I
670  PRINT
680  PRINT "  ID            IQ"
690  PRINT "  --            --"
```

```
700  FOR I=1 TO N
710  PRINT D[I],Q[I]
720  NEXT I
730  PRINT
740  PRINT
750  PRINT "THIS IS THE END OF THE RUN."
760  PRINT
770  PRINT
780  PRINT "(TO TERMINATE THE PROGRAM, TYPE IN A NEGATIVE
         NUMBER FOR N)"
790  GO TO 160
800  PRINT "THE MAXIMUM IS 250; SORRY ABOUT THAT!"
810  GO TO 160
820  END
```

```
*************
*           *
*SORTING IN *
*  TANDEM   *
*           *
*************


WHAT IS THE VALUE OF N?260
THE MAXIMUM IS 250; SORRY ABOUT THAT!

WHAT IS THE VALUE OF N?5
O.K., LET'S GO!

PLEASE TYPE IN EACH ID AND IQ SEPARATED BY A COMMA.

?731,135
?286,161
?489,78
?334,96
?542,129


SORTED IN DESCENDING ORDER OF ID
------ -- ---------- ----- -- --

    ID           IQ
    --           --
    731          135
    542          129
    489          78
    334          96
    286          161
```

SORTED IN ASCENDING ORDER OF IQ

```
–– –– –– ––   –– ––   –––––––––   ––––– –– ––
```

ID	IQ
--	--
489	78
334	96
542	129
731	135
286	161

THIS IS THE END OF THE RUN.

(TO TERMINATE THE PROGRAM, TYPE IN A NEGATIVE NUMBER FOR N)

WHAT IS THE VALUE OF N?–1

DONE

Questions

1. Write a program to input 100 numbers into an array X. The numbers should be entered *five elements at a time* by means of an INPUT statement. Sort the array into descending order and print out the sorted array 10 elements per line. Print out also the minimum, the maximum, and the median.

2. What changes have to be made in Program 9-3 in order that the array X is sorted in descending rather than ascending order.

3. Write a BASIC program that computes and prints out the following statistical quantities for a given list of data: (a) mean, (b) median, (c) range, (d) standard deviation. Also, print out the given data in the original order and then in ascending order. Assume (1) all data is read into an array by means of an INPUT statement; (2) the first number read is the number of data items in the list; and (3) the maximum number of data items must not exceed 100. (Note: The first number is *not* read into the array—only the actual data items in the list are read in. Prepare a heading and label your output.)
   Run your program for the following data:
   (i) 12, 30, 45, 50, 60, 40, 35, 50, 65, 55, 55, 45, 60

   (ii) 15, 30, 20, 45, 60, 70, 65, 35, 50, 40, 55, 65, 30, 25, 60, 50

4. Nests of loops have been used in both of the following programs, which are designed to produce prime numbers. Discuss the relative merits of both programs.

```
100  INPUT N                    100  INPUT N
110  IF N<0 THEN 200            110  IF N<0 THEN 200
120  FOR I = 1 TO N             120  FOR I = 1 TO N
130  FOR J = 2 TO I-1           130  FOR J = 2 TO SQR(I)
```

```
140  IF INT(I/J)*J = I THEN 170        140  IF INT(I/J)*J = I THEN 170
150  NEXT J                            150  NEXT J
160  PRINT I;                          160  PRINT I;
170  NEXT I                            170  NEXT I
180  PRINT                             180  PRINT
190  GO TO 100                         190  GO TO 100
200  END                               200  END
```

5. Weather forecasts sometimes quote "wind chill temperatures" which are based not only on the temperature, but also on the velocity of the wind, in order to give a clearer indication of the degree of "coldness." Assume that the relationship,

$$C = 91.4 - (.288\sqrt{V} + .45 - .019V)(91.4 - T)$$

is used to determine the chill temperature C from the temperature T and the wind velocity V. Write a program for evaluating the chill temperatures for several velocities and temperatures. The output should look like this:

TEMP		WIND VELOCITIES			
	0	10	20	30	40
− 20					
− 10					
0					
10					
20					

6. Study this program and answer the multiple choice questions below.

```
100  DIM X[200]
110  PRINT "WHAT IS YOUR VALUE FOR N";
120  INPUT N
130  IF N<0 THEN 380
140  IF N>200 THEN 360
150  PRINT "PLEASE TYPE IN YOUR ARRAY."
160  FOR I = 1 TO N
170  INPUT X[I]
180  NEXT I
190  FOR I = 1 TO N-1
200  FOR J = I+1 TO N
210  IF X[I]<X[J] THEN 250
220  LET K = X[I].
230  LET X[I] = X[J]
240  LET X[J] = K
250  NEXT J
260  NEXT I
270  FOR J = 1 TO N
280  PRINT X[J]
290  NEXT J
```

300 IF INT(N/2)=N/2 THEN 330

310 LET M = X[(N+1)/2]

320 GO TO 340

330 LET M = (X[N/2+1]+X[N/2])/2

340 PRINT "MEDIAN =" ;M

350 GO TO 110

360 PRINT "THE MAXIMUM N IS 200. TRY AGAIN."

370 GO TO 110

380 END

(1) In order to terminate this program the user must:
    (a) input a zero for each value of X
    (b) input a negative number for the first value of X
    (c) input a value of N over 200
    (d) input any negative value for N

(2) The variable N is:
    (a) the minimum number of elements in the array
    (b) the minimum value of the array
    (c) the exact number of elements in the array
    (d) the appropriate maximum number of arrays

(3) In statements 190 to 260 this program sorts the elements of the array
    (a) into random order
    (b) into descending order
    (c) into ascending order
    (d) into reverse order

(4) The index J in statement 200 is not in conflict with the index J in line 270 because:
    (a) the two loops are not nested together
    (b) the two loops are nested together
    (c) X(J) is a standard acceptable array name
    (d) the same index is not used in consecutive FOR/NEXT loops

(5) In lines 270 to 290 the values of the array X are printed out
    (a) 10 numbers per line
    (b) J numbers per line
    (c) 1 number per line
    (d) an indeterminate number of numbers per line

(6) The removal of statement 320 would cause the median to be computed:
    (a) incorrectly, only when the value of N is even
    (b) incorrectly, only when the value of N is odd
    (c) incorrectly, every time the program is run
    (d) correctly, regardless of the removal of the statement.

(7) Indicate which of the following statements are true (T) or false (F):
    (a) The FOR/NEXT loop is an example of conditional transfer of control.
    (b) Layers of FOR/NEXT loops, each of which encloses the inner one, is known as a "nest of loops."

(c) A nest of loops differs from consecutive FOR/NEXT loops in that the inside loop is completely satisfied for each iteration of the outside loop.

(d) It is possible to have two loops in a nest with the same indexes so that only one NEXT rather than two, would be needed.

CHAPTER TEN

MATRICES

We have already encountered arrays, which were merely lists of numbers. The advantage of dealing with arrays was that we could give all the elements the same name and operate efficiently on the array as a single unit.

A matrix (plural, matrices) resembles an extended array. It is, in general, composed of rows and columns, even though it can be a single row, or a single column, or even a single element. Here are some typical matrices. Notice they are either square or rectangular. There is no such thing as a circular matrix.

$$A = \begin{pmatrix} 3 & 4 & 2 \\ 1 & 9 & 6 \end{pmatrix} \qquad B = \begin{pmatrix} 3 & -1 & 4 \\ 0 & 9 & 6 \\ 4 & 2 & 1 \end{pmatrix}$$

$$C = \begin{pmatrix} 3 & 5 \\ 2 & 3 \end{pmatrix} \qquad D = \begin{pmatrix} 5 & 4 & 3 & 2 & 1 \\ 5 & -1 & -2 & -3 & 0 \\ 0 & 1 & 2 & 3 & 3 \\ 4 & 1 & 2 & 3 & 4 \end{pmatrix}$$

Matrices are variously written in textbooks with brackets around them, or braces, or double lines. Matrix arithmetic is an extremely useful technique; it is used in such divergent fields as finance and psychology.

10.1 Matrix Statements in BASIC

The BASIC language is fairly richly endowed with provisions for matrices, making matrices both easy to understand and to use. Indeed, it is probably the most powerful aspect of the BASIC language. First, each matrix (like an array) must be accompanied by an appropriate dimension statement, which reflects the fact that it has a certain number of *rows* and a certain number of *columns, in that order.*

Matrix A above, for example, has two rows and three columns, so its dimension statement would be:

DIM A (2,3)

172

where the numbers specifying the rows and columns are separated by a comma. The dimension statements for matrices B, C, and D would be, respectively:

$$DIM\ B\ (3,3)$$
$$DIM\ C\ (2,2)$$
$$DIM\ D\ (4,5)$$

Matrix A is called a 2 × 3 (read, two by three) matrix, B a 3 × 3, C a 2 × 2, and D a 4 × 5 matrix.

As with arrays, names for matrices must be only one of the 26 letters of the alphabet. However, the same name can be used to represent a simple variable.

Matrices of 10 × 10 or less do not need dimension statements but, as pointed out when explaining arrays, it is highly recommended that dimension statements be used.

10.2 Reading and Printing a Matrix

The elements of a matrix may be included in a DATA statement and read by means of the now familiar READ statement. However, if the entire matrix is to be READ in at once, the abbreviation MAT must precede the READ instruction.

When printing a matrix, the PRINT instruction is used, and, if the whole matrix is to be printed, the instruction PRINT must also be preceded by MAT.

We are now ready to follow Program 10-1, which reads in and immediately prints out a 5 × 4 matrix which we call M. It is printed out in three different formats. In the first, the matrix M is printed out without any further punctuation. In the second, "M," is printed, where the M is followed by a comma. In the last format "M;" is printed.

It will be seen that there is no difference between the first and second printouts, which demonstrates that the comma may be omitted, but the third printout clearly illustrates that the semicolon has the effect of printing out the elements of the matrix closer together.

Program 10-1

```
100  PRINT "****************************"
110  PRINT "*                          *"
120  PRINT "*  READING AND PRINTING    *"
130  PRINT "*         A MATRIX         *"
140  PRINT "*                          *"
150  PRINT "****************************"
160  PRINT
170  DIM M[5,4]
180  MAT  READ M
190  DATA 5,4,3,2,1,5,-1,-2,-3,0,0,1,2,3,3,4,1,2,3,4
200  MAT  PRINT M
210  PRINT
220  PRINT
230  MAT  PRINT M,
240  PRINT
250  PRINT
260  MAT  PRINT M;
270  END
```

RUN

```
****************************
*                          *
*  READING AND PRINTING    *
*         A MATRIX         *
*                          *
****************************
```

5	4	3	2
1	5	-1	-2
-3	Ø	Ø	1
2	3	3	4
1	2	3	4

5	4	3	2
1	5	-1	-2
-3	Ø	Ø	1
2	3	3	4
1	2	3	4

5	4	3	2
1	5	-1	-2
-3	Ø	Ø	1
2	3	3	4
1	2	3	4

DONE

One can operate on matrices and one can also construct several standard kinds of matrices by means of special matrix statements.

10.3 The ZERO Matrix

If all of the elements in a matrix are zero, it is called a *zero matrix*. This is an example of a zero matrix:

$$\begin{pmatrix} 0 & 0 & 0 \\ 0 & 0 & 0 \end{pmatrix}$$

In BASIC one can replace the elements of a matrix by zeros by using the simple MAT function ZER. For example, in Program 10-2 the elements of a 3 × 4 matrix X are replaced by zeros as is confirmed by the output.

Program 10-2

```
100  PRINT "********************"
110  PRINT "*                  *"
120  PRINT "*  THE ZER MATRIX  *"
130  PRINT "*                  *"
140  PRINT "*     STATEMENT     *"
150  PRINT "*                  *"
160  PRINT "********************"
170  PRINT
180  DIM X[3,4]
190  MAT   READ X
200  DATA 1,2,3,2,3,4,3,4,5,7,-2,2
210  MAT   PRINT X;
220  PRINT
230  PRINT
240  REM: NOW RESET ALL ELEMENTS TO ZERO
250  MAT   X=ZER
260  MAT   PRINT X;
270  END
```

```
RUN


********************
*                  *
*  THE ZER MATRIX  *
*                  *
*     STATEMENT     *
*                  *
********************

 1      2      3      2
 3      4      3      4
 5      7     -2      2


 Ø      Ø      Ø      Ø
 Ø      Ø      Ø      Ø
 Ø      Ø      Ø      Ø


DONE
```

10.4 The Identity Matrix

An *identity matrix* is a square matrix of special form. All of the elements are zero, except those of the main diagonal (top left to bottom right) which are 1.

In Program 10-3, a 4 × 4 matrix X is defined and printed. It is then replaced by the identity matrix by invoking the BASIC MAT IDN function. The output is a 4 × 4 identity matrix, composed of zeros, except for the main diagonal which consists of 1's.

Program 10-3

```
100  PRINT "*******************"
110  PRINT "*                 *"
120  PRINT "*  THE IDN MATRIX *"
130  PRINT "*                 *"
140  PRINT "*    STATEMENT    *"
150  PRINT "*                 *"
160  PRINT "*******************"
170  PRINT
180  DIM X[4,4]
190  MAT  READ X
200  DATA 1,2,3,2,3,4,3,4,5,7,-2,2,3,4,5,6
210  MAT  PRINT X;
220  PRINT
230  PRINT
240  REM: NOW REPLACE ALL ELEMENTS WITH Ø; DIAGONAL ELEMENTS WITH 1
250  MAT X=IDN
260  MAT  PRINT X
270  END

RUN
```

```
*******************
*                 *
*  THE IDN MATRIX *
*                 *
*    STATEMENT    *
*                 *
*******************


   1     2     3     2
   3     4     3     4
   5     7    -2     2
   3     4     5     6


   1     Ø     Ø     Ø
   Ø     1     Ø     Ø
   Ø     Ø     1     Ø
   Ø     Ø     Ø     1


DONE
```

10.5 The Constant Matrix

A matrix in which all of the elements are equal to 1 is known as the *constant matrix*. In BASIC such a matrix may be generated by the MAT function CON, as shown in Program 10-4.

Program 10-4

```
100  PRINT "*******************"
110  PRINT "*                 *"
120  PRINT "*  THE CON MATRIX *"
130  PRINT "*                 *"
140  PRINT "*    STATEMENT     *"
150  PRINT "*                 *"
160  PRINT "*******************"
170  PRINT
180  DIM X[4,4]
190  MAT  READ X
200  DATA 1,2,3,2,3,4,3,4,5,7,-2,2,3,4,5,6
210  MAT  PRINT X;
220  PRINT
230  PRINT
240  REM: NOW REPLACE ALL THE ELEMENTS WITH 1
250  MAT X=CON
260  MAT  PRINT X;
270  END

RUN


*******************
*                 *
*  THE CON MATRIX *
*                 *
*    STATEMENT     *
*                 *
*******************

1       2       3       2
3       4       3       4
5       7      -2       2
3       4       5       6


1       1       1       1
1       1       1       1
1       1       1       1
1       1       1       1


DONE
```

10.6 The Addition of Matrices

Only when two matrices **A** and **B** are of the same order (i.e., they have the same number of rows and columns) does adding them together have any meaning. Matrix addition is ordinarily accomplished by adding the elements of one matrix to the corresponding elements of the other. The resulting matrix is of the same order as A and B.

Once two matrices have been defined, the sum matrix, C, may be calculated directly in BASIC by the instruction

$$\text{MAT C} = \text{A} + \text{B}$$

as shown in Program 10-5, where two 3 X 4 matrices are added. Naturally, an appropriate dimension statement for the sum matrix, C, must also be supplied.

Program 10-5

```
100  PRINT "***********************"
110  PRINT "*                     *"
120  PRINT "* SUMMING MATRICES *"
130  PRINT "*                     *"
140  PRINT "***********************"
150  PRINT
160  DIM A[3,4] , B[3,4] , C[3,4]
170  MAT   READ A,B
180  DATA 3,1,4,4,17,5,28,4,3,0,-1,3
190  DATA 6,7,3,2,1,-4,-5,3,6,2,9,-3
200  PRINT "MATRIX A"
210  PRINT "- - - - - - -"
220  PRINT
230  MAT   PRINT A
240  PRINT
250  PRINT "MATRIX B"
260  PRINT "- - - - - - -"
270  PRINT
280  MAT   PRINT B
290  PRINT
300  REM:  NOW ADD A TO B TO CREATE C
310  MAT C=A+B
320  PRINT "THE SUM MATRIX C"
330  PRINT "- - - - - - - - - - - -"
340  PRINT
350  MAT   PRINT C
360  END

RUN

***********************
*                     *
* SUMMING MATRICES *
*                     *
***********************

MATRIX A
- - - - - - -

   3         1         4         4
  17         5        28         4
   3         0        -1         3
```

MATRIX B
- - - - - - -

6	7	3	2
1	-4	-5	3
6	2	9	-3

THE SUM MATRIX C
- - - - - - - - - - - - - - -

9	8	7	6
18	1	23	7
9	2	8	Ø

DONE

10.7   The Subtraction of Matrices

If two matrices A and B are of the same order, one may be substracted from the other. To find the matrix C = A - B, the elements of matrix B are subtracted from the corresponding elements of matrix A.

In BASIC this may be done directly by the statement:

$$MAT \ C = A - B$$

as is illustrated in Program 10-6, where the matrices A and B are again 3 X 4.

Program 10-6

```
100  PRINT "*****************"
110  PRINT "*               *"
120  PRINT "*  SUBTRACTING  *"
130  PRINT "*    MATRICES   *"
140  PRINT "*               *"
150  PRINT "*****************"
160  PRINT
170  DIM A[3,4] , B[3,4] , C[3,4]
180  MAT   READ A,B
190  DATA 3,1,4,4,17,5,28,4,3,Ø,-1,3
200  DATA 6,7,3,2,1,-4,-5,3,6,2,9,-3
210  PRINT "MATRIX A"
220  PRINT "- - - - - -"
230  PRINT
240  MAT   PRINT A
250  PRINT
260  PRINT "MATRIX B"
270  PRINT "- - - - - -"
280  PRINT
290  MAT  PRINT B
300  PRINT
310  REM:  NOW SUBTRACT B FROM A TO CREATE C
320  MAT C=A-B
```

```
330  PRINT "THE DIFFERENCE MATRIX C"
340  PRINT "--- ---------- ------ -"
350  PRINT
360  MAT  PRINT C
370  END

RUN
```

```
****************
*              *
*  SUBTRACTING *
*    MATRICES  *
*              *
****************
```

MATRIX A
- - - - - -

3	1	4	4
17	5	28	4
3	Ø	-1	3

MATRIX B
- - - - - -

6	7	3	2
1	-4	-5	3
6	2	9	-3

THE DIFFERENCE MATRIX C
--- ---------- ------ -

-3	-6	1	2
16	9	33	1
-3	-2	-1Ø	6

DONE

10.8 Scalar Multiplication

A matrix may be multiplied by a scalar. Such is the case when each element of a matrix is multiplied by the same factor, as in the following example, where the scalar is equal ro 4:

$$4 \begin{pmatrix} 2 & 3 & 2 \\ 1 & 0 & 1 \\ 2 & -1 & 2 \\ 5 & 2 & 1 \end{pmatrix} = \begin{pmatrix} 8 & 12 & 8 \\ 4 & 0 & 4 \\ 8 & -4 & 8 \\ 20 & 8 & 4 \end{pmatrix}$$

Such an operation is possible in BASIC by simply enclosing the scalar in parentheses, following it with the asterisk for multiplication, and then the name of the matrix to be multiplied. The scalar may take the form of a constant, a variable, or an expression, as is done in Program 10-7.

Program 10-7

```
100  PRINT "****************************"
110  PRINT "*                          *"
120  PRINT "*  SCALAR MULTIPLICATION   *"
130  PRINT "*                          *"
140  PRINT "****************************"
150  PRINT
160  DIM  A[4,3] , B[4,3] , C[4,3] , D[4,3]
170  MAT   READ A
180  DATA 2,3,2,1,0,1,2,-1,2,5,2,1
190  PRINT "MATRIX A"
200  PRINT "- - - - - - -"
210  PRINT
220  MAT  PRINT A
230  REM: NOW MULTIPLY MATRIX A BY 4
240  MAT B=(4)*A
250  PRINT
260  PRINT "MATRIX A MULTIPLIED BY THE SCALAR 4"
270  PRINT "- - - - - - - - - - - - - - - - - - - - - -"
280  PRINT
290  MAT  PRINT B
300  PRINT
310  REM: NOW DEFINE N=6 AND MULTIPLY MATRIX A BY THE SCALAR N*2
320  LET N=6
330  MAT C=(N*2)*A
340  PRINT "MATRIX A MULTIPLIED BY THE SCALAR N*2"
350  PRINT "- - - - - - - - - - - - - - - - - - - - - - -"
360  PRINT
370  MAT  PRINT C
380  PRINT
390  REM: NOW MULTIPLY MATRIX A BY SQR (10)+1
400  MAT D=(SQR(10)+1)*A
410  PRINT "MATRIX A MULTIPLIED BY THE SCALAR (SQR(10)+1)"
420  PRINT "- - - - - - - - - - - - - - - - - - - - - - - - - - - -"
430  PRINT
440  MAT  PRINT D
450  END
```

RUN

```
***************************
*                         *
*  SCALAR MULTIPLICATION  *
*                         *
***************************
```

MATRIX A
- - - - - - -

```
2               3               2
1               Ø               1
2              -1               2
5               2               1
```

MATRIX A MULTIPLIED BY THE SCALAR 4
- -

```
8              12               8
4               Ø               4
8              -4               8
2Ø              8               4
```

MATRIX A MULTIPLIED BY THE SCALAR N*2
- -

```
24             36              24
12              Ø              12
24            -12              24
6Ø             24              12
```

MATRIX A MULTIPLIED BY THE SCALAR (SQR(1Ø)+1)
- -

```
8.32456        12.4868         8.32456
4.16228         Ø              4.16228
8.32456        -4.16228        8.32456
2Ø.8114         8.32456        4.16228
```

DONE

10.9 Matrix Multiplication

Matrix multiplication is not to be confused with scalar multiplication, the subject of the previous section. Two matrices may be multiplied if the number of columns of the first is equal to the number of rows of the second. One cannot multiply a 5 X 3 by a 4 X 4 matrix but one can multiply a 6 X 2 by a 2 X 3 matrix.

But what does multiplication of matrices mean? The easiest way to answer this important question is with an illustration. Let us, in fact, multiply a 6×2 by a 2×3 matrix.

$$A = \begin{pmatrix} 2 & 3 \\ 1 & -2 \\ 0 & 1 \\ -1 & 2 \\ 3 & 2 \\ 1 & 2 \end{pmatrix} \qquad B = \begin{pmatrix} 4 & 2 & 1 \\ 5 & 1 & 1 \end{pmatrix}$$

First we take the first *row* of matrix A and line it up against the first *column* of matrix B. The corresponding elements are *multiplied* and the results are *added*. The result becomes the element of the product matrix, occupying the position first row, first column. Next, the second row of A is ranged against the first column of B, the process repeated, and so on until each of the six rows of A has been matched against the first column of matrix B. The whole process is repeated with the second and third columns of matrix B. When the process is completed, we have the following result for the product matrix:

$$\begin{pmatrix} 8+15 & 4+3 & 2+3 \\ 4-10 & 2-2 & 1-2 \\ 0+5 & 0+1 & 0+1 \\ -4+10 & -2+2 & -1+2 \\ 12+10 & 6+2 & 3+2 \\ 4+10 & 2+2 & 1+2 \end{pmatrix} = \begin{pmatrix} 23 & 7 & 5 \\ -6 & 0 & -1 \\ 5 & 1 & 1 \\ 6 & 0 & 1 \\ 22 & 8 & 5 \\ 14 & 4 & 3 \end{pmatrix}$$

Note that multiplying a 6×2 by a 2×3 matrix results in a product matrix with six rows and three columns. It is as if the 2's on the inside "cancel" each other, while the remaining numbers 6 and 3 represent the dimensions of the product matrix.

This somewhat complex operation may be performed quite simply in BASIC by using the matrix multiplication feature provided. As in the scalar multiplication the asterisk is used but this time that to the left of the asterisk is *not* parenthesized. Program 10-8, operates on the two matrices A and B as defined above, and the product matrix C, is printed. As will be seen from the output, the product matrix C checks out correctly with the hand-worked product shown above.

Program 10-8

```
100  PRINT "********************"
110  PRINT "*                  *"
120  PRINT "*       MATRIX      *"
130  PRINT "*                  *"
140  PRINT "* MULTIPLICATION   *"
150  PRINT "*                  *"
160  PRINT "********************"
170  PRINT
180  DIM A[6,2], B[2,3], C[6,3]
190  MAT  READ A
200  DATA 2,3,1,-2,0,1,-1,2,3,2,1,2
```

```
210  MAT  READ B
220  DATA 4,2,1,5,1,1
230  PRINT "MATRIX A"
240  PRINT "- - - - - - -"
250  PRINT
260  MAT  PRINT A
270  PRINT
280  PRINT "MATRIX B"
290  PRINT "- - - - - - -"
300  PRINT
310  MAT  PRINT B
320  PRINT
330  REM: NOW MULTIPLY MATRIX A BY MATRIX B
340  MAT  C=A*B
350  PRINT "THE PRODUCT MATRIX C"
360  PRINT "--- - - - - - - - - - - - - -"
370  PRINT
380  MAT  PRINT C
390  END
```

RUN

```
*******************
*      MATRIX      *
*                  *
*  MULTIPLICATION  *
*                  *
*******************
```

MATRIX A
- - - - - -

2	3
1	-2
0	1
-1	2
3	2
1	2

MATRIX B
- - - - - -

4	2	1
5	1	1

THE PRODUCT MATRIX C

--- ------- ------ -

23	7	5
-6	Ø	-1
5	1	1
6	Ø	1
22	8	5
14	4	3

DONE

10.10 Matrix Transposition

Substituting the rows for the columns of a matrix and *vice versa* has the effect of *transposing* the matrix. Thus a 3 × 4 matrix becomes a 4 × 3 matrix when transposed.

$$
\begin{pmatrix} 2 & 4 & 3 & -1 \\ 3 & 1 & 1 & 0 \\ 4 & 2 & 1 & 2 \end{pmatrix} \longrightarrow \begin{pmatrix} 2 & 3 & 4 \\ 4 & 1 & 2 \\ 3 & 1 & 1 \\ -1 & 0 & 2 \end{pmatrix}
$$

Original matrix   Transposed matrix

Of course, two appropriate dimension statements must be present in the program in order to accommodate both the original and the transposed matrices.

In BASIC a matrix A may be transposed to a matrix B by means of a statement of the type:

$$\text{MAT B} = \text{TRN (A)}$$

as is done in Program 10-9.

Program 10-9

```
100   PRINT "******************"
110   PRINT "*                *"
120   PRINT "*  TRANSPOSE OF  *"
130   PRINT "*                *"
140   PRINT "*    A    MATRIX *"
150   PRINT "*                *"
160   PRINT "******************"
170   PRINT
180   DIM A[3,4] , B[4,3]
190   MAT  READ A
200   DATA 2,4,3,-1,3,1,1,Ø,4,2,1,2
210   PRINT "MATRIX A"
220   PRINT "------ -"
```

```
230  PRINT
240  MAT  PRINT A
250  PRINT
260  REM: NOW TRANSPOSE MATRIX A
270  MAT B=TRN(A)
280  PRINT "TRANSPOSED MATRIX B"
290  PRINT "---------- ------ -"
300  PRINT
310  MAT  PRINT B
320  END
```

RUN

```
*****************
*               *
*  TRANSPOSE OF  *
*               *
*    A   MATRIX  *
*               *
*****************
```

MATRIX A
- - - - - - -

2	4	3	-1
3	1	1	0
4	2	1	2

TRANSPOSED MATRIX B
- - - - - - - - - - - - - - - -

2	3	4
4	1	2
3	1	1
-1	0	2

DONE

10.11 Matrix Inversion

Just a brief description of what is known as the *inverse of a matrix* will now be given. Any square matrix, A, when multiplied by the identity matrix (see Section 10.4) will yield the identical matrix A. (It is for this reason that a square matrix containing 1's in the main diagonal and 0's everywhere else is called the identity matrix.)

Now, for every (nonsingular)* square matrix there exists an inverse. The product of the matrix and its inverse is the identity matrix.

*For a discussion of singular and nonsingular matrices please refer to any of the standard college textbooks on matrix algebra.

In BASIC the inverse of a matrix is found by using a statement of the type:

$$MAT\ B = INV\ (A)$$

Computing the inverse of a matrix can be most helpful in solving simultaneous equations.

Let us take a pair of simultaneous equations and solve them.

$$x - 2y = -4$$
$$3x + y = -5$$

These equations may be written in an equivalent mathematical form in matrix notation, as follows:

$$\begin{pmatrix} 1 & -2 \\ 3 & 1 \end{pmatrix} \cdot \begin{pmatrix} x \\ y \end{pmatrix} = \begin{pmatrix} -4 \\ -5 \end{pmatrix}$$

If the *inverse* of the 2 X 2 matrix on the left is multiplied by the vector $\begin{pmatrix} -4 \\ -5 \end{pmatrix}$, we obtain a vector containing the values for x and y. Program 10-10 is a BASIC program that will do just that. It will be noticed that once the inverse of matrix A is computed, it is stored in C and is printed out. Next, this inverse matrix and matrix B are multiplied together giving matrix D. The solutions -2 and 1 to the original simultaneous equations are contained in matrix D and are printed.

Program 10-10

```
100  PRINT "***************************"
110  PRINT "*                         *"
120  PRINT "* SOLVING SIMULTANEOUS    *"
130  PRINT "*                         *"
140  PRINT "*          EQUATIONS      *"
150  PRINT "*                         *"
160  PRINT "***************************"
170  PRINT
180  DIM A[2,2], B[2,1], C[2,2], D[2,1]
190  MAT  READ A
200  DATA 1,-2,3,1
210  MAT  READ B
220  DATA -4,-5
230  REM: COMPUTE INVERSE OF MATRIX A
240  MAT C=INV(A)
250  MAT  PRINT C
260  PRINT
270  REM: NOW MULTIPLY INVERSE MATRIX BY B
280  MAT D=C*B
290  PRINT "THESE ARE THE SOLUTIONS FOR X AND Y"
300  PRINT
310  MAT  PRINT D
320  END
```

RUN

```
***************************
*                         *
*  SOLVING SIMULTANEOUS   *
*                         *
*       EQUATIONS         *
*                         *
***************************
```

```
  .142857           .285714
 -.428571           .142857
```

THESE ARE THE SOLUTIONS FOR X AND Y

```
 -2
  1.
```

DONE

Before leaving the subject of matrices it should be said that BASIC is very useful for finding the inverse of a matrix and solving simultaneous equations. BASIC solves these problems with ease and implements the technique in a particularly elegant fashion. However, it should also be noted that there are still serious limitations when dealing with matrices. For example, one cannot hope to accomplish a correct result by writing:

$$MAT\ D = A + B + C$$

even if A, B, and C are defined to be matrices. One is restricted to the addition of two matrices only.

By the same token one is not permitted to resort to other desirable forms of matrix manipulation such as:

$$MAT\ D = A + (2) * B$$

Such formulations would considerably enhance the usefulness of the language. Perhaps future versions of the language will permit these forms.

However, advantage of the matrix features may be taken when dealing with arrays. For example to zero out array A of dimension 100 one could write:

```
DIM A (100)
MAT A = ZER
```

Other acceptable manipulations on one-dimensional arrays are:

```
(1)                          MAT A = CON
(2)                          MAT PRINT A
(3)                          MAT READ A
(4)                          MAT A = B + C
```

where A, B, and C are arrays of equal dimension. And similarly for subtraction where we can write:

(5)   MAT A = B − C

(6)   MAT A = (5) * A

where each element of A is multiplied by 5 and is stored back into A.

(7)   MAT A = B

On the other hand, it is meaningless to attempt to multiply two arrays, or to get their inverse, or a transpose.

QUICK REFERENCE GUIDE TO CHAPTER TEN

Item	General Form	Example
1. Matrix dimension	*Line number matrix name (constant, constant)*	100 DIM X(5,3) 200 DIM V(6,4), U(9,3), B(8,8), C(3)
2. Matrix initialization	*Line number* MAT *matrix* $name = \begin{Bmatrix} ZER \\ IDN \\ CON \end{Bmatrix}$	100 MAT M = ZER 200 MAT H = IDN 300 MAT D = CON
3. Scalar multiplication	*Line number* MAT *matrix name = (expression) * matrix name*	100 MAT A = (3.14159) * B 200 MAT C = (D) * E
4. Matrix arithmetic	*Line number* MAT *matrix name = matrix name* $\begin{Bmatrix} + \\ - \\ * \end{Bmatrix}$ *matrix name*	100 MAT A = B * C 200 MAT D = E − F 300 MAT G = H + I
5. Matrix functions	*Line number* MAT *matrix* $name = \begin{Bmatrix} TRN \\ INV \end{Bmatrix}$ *(matrix name)*	100 MAT A = TRN(B) 200 MAT C = INV(D)
6. Matrix input/output	*Line number* MAT $\begin{Bmatrix} READ \\ PRINT \end{Bmatrix}$ *matrix list*	100 MAT READ A 200 MAT PRINT B

Questions

1. In the matrix indicated locate the appropriate elements:

Matrix X

$$\begin{pmatrix} 7 & 4 & 9 & 2 \\ 15 & 10 & 16 & 8 \\ 12 & 14 & 18 & 3 \\ 5 & 1 & 6 & 11 \\ 13 & 17 & 20 & 19 \end{pmatrix}$$

(a) X(4,4)

(b) X(2,3)

(c) X(3,2)

(d) X(1,3)

(e) X(4,2)

2. Write a program to solve the following system of equations:

$$x + 3y - 8 = 0 \qquad x - y + 3z - 1 = 0 \qquad 2x - 5z + 3 = 0$$

3. Solve the following systems of simultaneous equations:

(a) $x + 2y + 4z = 2$

$8x + 2y - \ z = -4$

$4x + 6y + \ z = 12$

(b) $x - 13y + \ 6z + \ 2w = \ 14$

$x + \ 2y - 31z + \quad w = - \ 4$

$3x - \quad y + 43z + \ 2w = \quad 8$

$3x - \ 8y - 11z + 10w = \ 12$

CHAPTER ELEVEN

SUBROUTINES AND FUNCTIONS

11.1 Subroutines

On occasion, it is necessary to repeat a certain sequence of instructions many times. Of course, the sequence can simply be included each time it is needed, but this leads to an unnecessarily long and repetitious program. A much better approach—and one that leads to more efficient programs—is to take advantage of the subroutine facility that BASIC provides.

Any sequence of instructions that is to be executed repeatedly may be written in the subroutine form. A subroutine is characterized by the presence of a RETURN statement. When a subroutine is invoked by means of a GOSUB statement, control is sent to that subroutine, just as if the GOSUB were a regular GO TO statement.

Suppose the GOSUB statement appears in line 200. The computer automatically stores the *subsequent* line number. When the RETURN statement of the subroutine is executed, it too behaves like a GO TO statement, sending control back to the line number stored by the computer. The efficacy of such an arrangement lies in the fact that the subroutine may be invoked *any number of times* and it will always return to the appropriate line number.

A simple example will help to clarify the way in which this powerful feature operates.

Program 11-1

```
100  PRINT "*******************"
110  PRINT "*               *"
120  PRINT "* ILLUSTRATION OF *"
130  PRINT "*               *"
140  PRINT "* A     SUBROUTINE *"
150  PRINT "*               *"
160  PRINT "*******************"
170  PRINT
180  READ A,B
190  DATA 13,5,57,18,9,7,164,73,-1,-3
200  IF A<0 THEN 1050
210  LET X=A+B
220  GOSUB 1000
230  LET X=A-B
240  GOSUB 1000
```

```
250  LET X=A*B
260  GOSUB 1000
270  LET X=A/B
280  GOSUB 1000
290  GO TO 180
300  REM: THIS IS THE SUBROUTINE BEGINNING IN LINE 1000
1000  LET Y=SQR(X)
1010  PRINT
1020  PRINT "X = ";X,"SQUARE ROOT OF X = ";Y
1030  PRINT
1040  RETURN
1050  END
```

RUN

```
*******************
*                 *
*ILLUSTRATION OF*
*                 *
*A     SUBROUTINE*
*                 *
*******************
```

X = 18   SQUARE ROOT OF X = 4.24264

X = 8   SQUARE ROOT OF X = 2.82843

X = 65   SQUARE ROOT OF X = 8.06226

X = 2.6   SQUARE ROOT OF X = 1.61245

X = 75   SQUARE ROOT OF X = 8.66026

X = 39   SQUARE ROOT OF X = 6.245

X = 1026   SQUARE ROOT OF X = 32.0312

X = 3.16667   SQUARE ROOT OF X = 1.77951

X = 16   SQUARE ROOT OF X = 4

X = 2   SQUARE ROOT OF X = 1.41421

X = 63   SQUARE ROOT OF X = 7.93725

X = 1.28571   SQUARE ROOT OF X = 1.13389

X = 237   SQUARE ROOT OF X = 15.3948

X = 91   SQUARE ROOT OF X = 9.53939

X = 11972   SQUARE ROOT OF X = 109.417

X = 2.24658   SQUARE ROOT OF X = 1.49886

In Program 11-1, a succession of values for A and B is read. The sum X of A and B is computed and control is sent to the subroutine at line 1000 where the square root of X is computed and printed out. Upon executing the RETURN statement, control is sent to line 230, which is the line *following* line 220, in which the subroutine was invoked. At line 230 the difference of A and B is calculated and once again the subroutine is invoked. Executing the RETURN statement this time sends control back to line 250, where the product is computed and the subroutine again invoked. This time the RETURN statement sends control to line 270 for the final calculation of A/B. On this occasion, control is sent to line 290, which goes back to the READ statement to read the next values of A and B.

It is customary to place all subroutines at the end of a program. One can "fall through" the subroutine by executing the RETURN statement without entering the subroutine by means of a GOSUB statement. This may be prevented by preceding the subroutine with an appropriate GO TO statement or by placing a STOP statement there. Executing the STOP statement causes the program to terminate just as if the END statement had been executed.

11.2   A Quiz Using Subroutines

We would now like to remind the reader of the five-question quiz program that we presented in Chapter Eight. In that program we tackled the problem in what was then a perfectly logical manner.

Now that you have some understanding of subroutines, you will probably agree that in retrospect it was a rather inelegant program. Many identical steps that were repeated for each question could have been neatly packaged in subroutines. This is what we have done in Program 11-2, which contains the identical questions but is easier to write, easier to follow, and lends itself to a more elegant approach and printout.

Program 11-2

```
100  PRINT "***************************"
110  PRINT "*                         *"
120  PRINT "* THE FIVE QUESTION QUIZ *"
130  PRINT "*                         *"
140  PRINT "* IN   SUBROUTINE   FORM *"
150  PRINT "*                         *"
160  PRINT "***************************"
170  PRINT
180  LET C=W=0
190  PRINT "THIS IS A FIVE QUESTION QUIZ IN ARITHMETIC."
200  PRINT "TYPE IN THE ANSWER FOLLOWING THE QUESTION MARK."
210  GOSUB 1000
220  PRINT "      1.        (7+2)/3 =";
230  INPUT Q
240  IF Q=3 THEN 270
250  GOSUB 2000
260  GO TO 290
270  GOSUB 3000
280  GOSUB 1000
290  PRINT "      2.        7*9 =";
300  INPUT Q
310  IF Q=63 THEN 340
320  GOSUB 2000
330  GO TO 360
340  GOSUB 3000
350  GOSUB 1000
360  PRINT "      3.        100/(3+1) =";
370  INPUT Q
380  IF Q=25 THEN 410
390  GOSUB 2000
400  GO TO 430
410  GOSUB 3000
420  GOSUB 1000
430  PRINT "      4.        100*.1 =";
440  INPUT Q
450  IF Q=10 THEN 480
460  GOSUB 2000
470  GO TO 500
480  GOSUB 3000
490  GOSUB 1000
500  PRINT "      5.        1/4 + 2/4 + 4/16 =";
510  INPUT Q
520  IF Q=1 THEN 550
530  GOSUB 2000
540  GO TO 570
550  GOSUB 3000
560  GOSUB 1000
570  GOSUB 1000
580  PRINT "THE QUIZ IS NOW OVER (RELIEVED?)."
590  GOSUB 1000
600  IF C=5 THEN 650
```

```
610  IF C=4 THEN 670
620  IF C=3 THEN 690
630  IF C=2 THEN 710
640  GO TO 730
650  PRINT "CONGRATULATIONS.  YOU RECEIVE AN A GRADE."
660  GO TO 740
670  PRINT "CONGRATULATIONS.  YOU SCORED A B."
680  GO TO 740
690  PRINT "NOT BAD.  YOU SCORED A C."
700  GO TO 740
710  PRINT "WELL, IT WAS A DIFFICULT QUIZ, EVEN SO YOU SCORED A D."
720  GO TO 740
730  PRINT "YOU'RE HOPELESS.  YOU GOT AN F GRADE."
740  GOSUB 1000
750  PRINT "ANSWERS RIGHT = ";C
760  PRINT "ANSWERS WRONG = ";W
770  GOSUB 1000
780  GOSUB 1000
790  PRINT "WOULD YOU LIKE TO TAKE THE QUIZ AGAIN?"
800  PRINT "(TYPE 1 FOR YES, Ø FOR NO)"
810  GOSUB 1000
820  INPUT M
830  IF M=Ø THEN 3040
840  GO TO 170
1000  PRINT
1010  RETURN
2000  LET W=W+1
2010  PRINT "OH WELL, . . . "
2020  PRINT
2030  RETURN
3000  LET C=C+1
3010  PRINT "VERY GOOD."
3020  PRINT
3030  RETURN
3040  END


RUN


*************************
*                       *
* THE FIVE QUESTION QUIZ *
*                       *
* IN   SUBROUTINE   FORM *
*                       *
*************************


THIS IS A FIVE QUESTION QUIZ IN ARITHMETIC.
TYPE IN THE ANSWER FOLLOWING THE QUESTION MARK.

        1.       (7+2)/3 =?3
VERY GOOD.
```

```
        2.        7*9 =?56
OH WELL, . . .

        3.        100/(3+1) =?34.3
OH WELL, . . .

        4.        100*.1 =?1
OH WELL, . . .

        5.        1/4 + 2/4 + 4/16 =?0.487
OH WELL, . . .

THE QUIZ IS NOW OVER (RELIEVED?).

YOU'RE HOPELESS.  YOU GOT AN F GRADE.

ANSWERS RIGHT =  1
ANSWERS WRONG =  4

WOULD YOU LIKE TO TAKE THE QUIZ AGAIN?
(TYPE 1 FOR YES, 0 FOR NO)

?1

THIS IS A FIVE QUESTION QUIZ IN ARITHMETIC.
TYPE IN THE ANSWER FOLLOWING THE QUESTION MARK.

        1.        (7+2)/3 =?3
VERY GOOD.

        2.        7*9 =?63
VERY GOOD.

        3.        100/(3+1) =?25
VERY GOOD.

        4.        100*.1 =?10
VERY GOOD.

        5.        1/4 + 2/4 + 4/16 =?1
VERY GOOD.

THE QUIZ IS NOW OVER (RELIEVED?).

CONGRATULATIONS.  YOU RECEIVE AN A GRADE.

ANSWERS RIGHT = 5
ANSWERS WRONG = 0

WOULD YOU LIKE TO TAKE THE QUIZ AGAIN?
(TYPE 1 FOR YES, 0 FOR NO)

?0

DONE
```

11.3   A Quiz in BASIC Using Subroutines

The following program was written to test one's knowledge of BASIC. The user answers each question with a T or an F.

There is a subroutine to check for the validity of the answer, one to keep track of the number of questions answered correctly and to print some encouraging blurb, one to print out an appropriate message if an incorrect answer is given, and, finally, a subroutine to skip four lines.

Question 4 could possibly be criticized as being ambiguous but it has been retained because it deserves some attention. Normally, every subroutine has a RETURN statement. However, if a RETURN statement is not present, the chances are quite good that it will not function as it is supposed to. However, if the purpose of the subroutine is to terminate the program, it could well do so without a RETURN. Execution of an included END statement would terminate the program.

Program 11-3

```
100   PRINT "***************************"
110   PRINT "*                         *"
120   PRINT "* A 5 QUESTION TRUE-FALSE *"
130   PRINT "*                         *"
140   PRINT "* QUIZ IN BASIC USING FIVE*"
150   PRINT "*                         *"
160   PRINT "*        SUBROUTINES      *"
170   PRINT "*                         *"
180   PRINT "***************************"
190   PRINT
210   LET C=W=Ø
220   LET B$="T"
230   LET C$="F"
240   PRINT "THIS IS A TRUE-FALSE QUIZ."
250   PRINT
260   GOSUB 5ØØØ
270   GOSUB 4ØØØ
280   PRINT "1. EVERY BASIC PROGRAM MUST HAVE AN END STATEMENT. ";
290   INPUT A$
300   IF A$=B$ THEN 35Ø
310   IF A$=C$ THEN 37Ø
320   GOSUB 1Ø6Ø
330   GOSUB 5ØØØ
340   GO TO 280
350   GOSUB 2ØØØ
360   GO TO 38Ø
370   GOSUB 3ØØØ
380   GOSUB 4ØØØ
390   PRINT "2. ANY PROGRAM CONTAINING A FOR/NEXT LOOP MUST HAVE"
400   PRINT "   A DIM STATEMENT. ";
410   INPUT A$
420   IF A$=B$ THEN 49Ø
430   IF A$=C$ THEN 47Ø
440   GOSUB 1Ø6Ø
450   GOSUB 5ØØØ
460   GO TO 39Ø
```

```
470   GOSUB 2000
480   GO TO 500
490   GOSUB 3000
500   GOSUB 4000
510   PRINT "3. ALL BASIC STATEMENTS MUST HAVE A LINE NUMBER. ";
520   INPUT A$
530   IF A$=B$ THEN 580
540   IF A$=C$ THEN 600
550   GOSUB 1060
560   GOSUB 5000
570   GO TO 510
580   GOSUB 2000
590   GO TO 610
600   GOSUB 3000
610   GOSUB 4000
620   "4. EVERY SUBROUTINE MUST HAVE A RETURN STATEMENT. ";
630   INPUT A$
640   IF A$=B$ THEN 710
650   IF A$=C$ THEN 690
660   GOSUB 1060
670   GOSUB 5000
680   GO TO 620
690   GOSUB 2000
700   GO TO 720
710   GOSUB 3000
720   GOSUB 4000
730   PRINT "5. ALL BASIC STANDARD FUNCTION NAMES HAVE 3 LETTERS.";
740   INPUT A$
750   IF A$=B$ THEN 800
760   IF A$=C$ THEN 820
770   GOSUB 1060
780   GOSUB 5000
790   GO TO 730
800   GOSUB 2000
810   GO TO 830
820   GOSUB 3000
830   GOSUB 4000
840   IF C=5 THEN 890
850   IF C=4 THEN 910
860   IF C=3 THEN 930
870   IF C=2 THEN 950
880   IF C<-1 THEN 970
890   PRINT "YOU GOT EVERY QUESTION CORRECT — GOOD SHOW!"
900   GO TO 980
910   PRINT "YOU GOT 4 CORRECT AND ONLY 1 WRONG — VERY GOOD."
920   GO TO 980
930   PRINT "YOU GOT 3 CORRECT AND 2 WRONG — NOT BAD AT ALL."
940   GO TO 980
950   PRINT "YOU GOT 2 CORRECT AND 3 WRONG — TOO BAD."
960   GO TO 980
970   PRINT "LOOKS LIKE YOU'RE GOING TO HAVE TO STUDY HARDER — SORRY!"
```

```
 980   GOSUB 4000
 990   PRINT "DO YOU WANT TO TAKE THE QUIZ AGAIN?"
1000   PRINT "IF SO, TYPE 1, IF NOT, TYPE 2."
1010   INPUT Q
1020   IF Q=1 THEN 190
1030   IF Q=2 THEN 5030
1040   PRINT "OOPS, YOU SEEM TO HAVE GOOFED!"
1050   GO TO 980
1060   PRINT "LOOKS LIKE YOU WEREN'T CONCENTRATING."
1070   PRINT "PLEASE TYPE IN EITHER TRUE OR FALSE."
1080   RETURN
2000   LET C=C+1
2010   PRINT "KEEP IT UP!  YOU'RE DOING FINE."
2020   RETURN
3000   PRINT "NOT QUITE RIGHT.  BETTER LUCK NEXT TIME."
3010   RETURN
4000   FOR I=1 TO 4
4010   PRINT
4020   NEXT I
4030   RETURN
5000   PRINT "WHEN YOU SEE THE QUESTION MARK, ANSWER THE QUESTION:"
5010   PRINT "EITHER 'TRUE' OR 'FALSE'."
5020   RETURN
5030   END


RUN


* * * * * * * * * * * * * * * * * * * * * * * * * *
*                                 *
* A 5 QUESTION TRUE-FALSE*
*                                 *
* QUIZ IN BASIC USING FIVE*
*                                 *
*        SUBROUTINES        *
*                                 *
* * * * * * * * * * * * * * * * * * * * * * * * * *


THIS IS A TRUE-FALSE QUIZ.

WHEN YOU SEE THE QUESTION MARK, ANSWER THE QUESTION:
EITHER 'TRUE' OR 'FALSE'.




 1. EVERY BASIC PROGRAM MUST HAVE AN END STATEMENT.  ?T
KEEP IT UP!  YOU'RE DOING FINE.
```

2. ANY PROGRAM CONTAINING A FOR/NEXT LOOP MUST HAVE
   A DIM STATEMENT. ?F
KEEP IT UP! YOU'RE DOING FINE.

3. ALL BASIC STATEMENTS MUST HAVE A LINE NUMBER. ?Y
LOOKS LIKE YOU WEREN'T CONCENTRATING.
PLEASE TYPE IN EITHER TRUE OR FALSE.
WHEN YOU SEE THE QUESTION MARK, ANSWER THE QUESTION:
EITHER 'TRUE' OR 'FALSE'.
3. ALL BASIC STATEMENTS MUST HAVE A LINE NUMBER. ?T
KEEP IT UP! YOU'RE DOING FINE.

4. EVERY SUBROUTINE MUST HAVE A RETURN STATEMENT. ?F
KEEP IT UP! YOU'RE DOING FINE.

5. ALL BASIC STANDARD FUNCTION NAMES HAVE 3 LETTERS. ?F
NOT QUITE RIGHT. BETTER LUCK NEXT TIME.

YOU GOT 4 CORRECT AND ONLY 1 WRONG — VERY GOOD.

DO YOU WANT TO TAKE THE QUIZ AGAIN?
IF SO, TYPE 1, IF NOT, TYPE 2.
?Ø
OOPS, YOU SEEM TO HAVE GOOFED!

DO YOU WANT TO TAKE THE QUIZ AGAIN?
IF SO, TYPE 1, IF NOT, TYPE 2.
?1

THIS IS A TRUE-FALSE QUIZ.

WHEN YOU SEE THE QUESTION MARK, ANSWER THE QUESTION:
EITHER 'TRUE' OR 'FALSE'.

1. EVERY BASIC PROGRAM MUST HAVE AN END STATEMENT. ?T
KEEP IT UP! YOU'RE DOING FINE.

2. ANY PROGRAM CONTAINING A FOR/NEXT LOOP MUST HAVE
   A DIM STATEMENT. ?F
KEEP IT UP! YOU'RE DOING FINE.

3. ALL BASIC STATEMENTS MUST HAVE A LINE NUMBER. ?T
KEEP IT UP! YOU'RE DOING FINE.

4. EVERY SUBROUTINE MUST HAVE A RETURN STATEMENT. ?F
KEEP IT UP! YOU'RE DOING FINE.

5. ALL BASIC STANDARD FUNCTION NAMES HAVE 3 LETTERS. ?T
KEEP IT UP! YOU'RE DOING FINE.

YOU GOT EVERY QUESTION CORRECT — GOOD SHOW!

DO YOU WANT TO TAKE THE QUIZ AGAIN?
IF SO, TYPE 1, IF NOT, TYPE 2.
?2

DONE

11.4 Nested GOSUBs

It is perfectly in order for a subroutine to invoke yet another subroutine. This may be continued to a maximum depth of nine on the HP-2000C. However, it should be understood that each time the RETURN statement in a particular subroutine is executed, control is sent to the preceding level.

11.5 User-Defined Functions

We have already encountered several of the standard functions such as SQR, INT, SIN, COS, and TAN. These are supplied to the user who has to do little work, if any at all, to take complete advantage of them. In certain situations, however, none of these standard functions is suitable for solving a particular problem. For such situations, the programmer is free to define her own functions. These user-defined functions must be written in a special format.

One is permitted a maximum of 26 user-defined functions, named FNA, FNB, FNC, . . . , FNZ. For each user-defined function, a definition statement, denoted by the letters DEF, must appear somewhere in the program. This statement defines the specific name of the function, shows the dummy argument enclosed in parentheses (any legal, simple variable name), and is followed by an equals sign which in turn is followed by the expression of the function.

Admittedly, this might seem complex to the novice but an example or two should clarify the concept. First, here are some simple, single-line function definitions:

(1)	100	DEF FNR(X) = INT(X + 0.5)
(2)	101	DEF FNC(Y) = -INT(-Y)
(3)	102	DEF FNN(N) = INT(N*RND(0)) + 1
(4)	103	DEF FNQ(X) = 5 * X ↑ 3 - 2 * X + 14
(5)	104	DEF FNA(Z9) = B + Q/P - 12

The first definition, FNR above, is a rounding function that behaves in the following manner. When the function is invoked, the argument is inserted into the expression on the right-hand side of the equals sign in the definition, replacing the dummy variable X. Thus a statement invoking the function, for example,

LET Q = FNR(13.2 + 17.4)

is evaluated as

LET Q = INT((13.2 + 17.4) + 0.5)

Since the argument in the definition statement is a dummy argument (its name is of no consequence), any appearance of this same name elsewhere in the program has no connection with the dummy argument.

In the last example shown above (5), the dummy argument does not appear anywhere on the right-hand side. When the function is invoked, the argument is ignored and, instead, the expression on the right-hand side is evaluated using the values of the variables at the time the function is invoked.

It might interest the reader to note that the second function listed produces the so-called ceiling of a number. That means that if the number has a fractional part, the number itself is raised to the next integer value. The function in (3) above will generate a random *integer* between 1 and the argument.

QUICK REFERENCE GUIDE TO CHAPTER ELEVEN

Item	General Form	Example	
1. GO SUB	*Line number* GOSUB *line number*	100	GOSUB 150
		200	GOSUB 250
2. RETURN	*Line number* RETURN	100	RETURN
		200	RETURN
3. Function Definition	*Line number* DEF FN *letter* *(variable name) = expression*	100	DEF FNC(X)=3*SQR(X)
		200	DEF FNZ(Q1) = X↑2 + Y↑2
4. STOP	*Line number* STOP	100	STOP
		200	STOP

Questions

1. Write a program that evaluates and prints out the function

$$F(X) = X^3 - 3X^2 - 9X + 11$$

for values of X ranging from -2 to +4 in steps of 0.1. Also determine and print out the maximum and minimum values of the function and the corresponding values of X. There is exactly one maximum and one minimum in the interval.

2. What output would you expect from the following program?

```
 10  DEF FNB(X) = (X-1) * (X+3)
 20  DEF FND(X) = (X-2) * (X+4)
 30  READ X
 40  DATA 1,2,-1,4,0
 50  IF X = 0 THEN 300
 60  LET A = FNB(X)
 70  LET B = FND(X)
 80  GOSUB 200
 90  PRINT "S= ", S
100  GO TO 30
200  LET S = A + B
210  IF S < 0 THEN 240
220  PRINT "S IS POSITIVE OR ZERO"
230  GO TO 250
240  PRINT "S IS NEGATIVE"
250  RETURN
300  END
```

3. Deduce what output would be produced by the following program:

```
 10  READ A,B
 20  DATA 1,3,2,4,1,2,-1,3
 30  IF A < 0 THEN 190
 40  IF A = 1 THEN 60
 50  GO TO 70
 60  GOSUB 130
 70  IF B = 3 THEN 100
 80  PRINT A, B
 90  GO TO 10
100  GOSUB 160
110  PRINT A, B
120  GO TO 10
130  LET A = A + B
140  LET B = B + 1
150  RETURN
160  LET A = A + 1
```

170   LET B = B + 2

180   RETURN

190   END

4. Examine the following program carefully and deduce what output could be expected:

     10   READ A

     20   DATA 1,4,-1

     30   IF A < 0 THEN 120

     40   FOR B = 1 TO 3

     50   LET X = A + B

     60   LET D = A * FNC(X)

     70   LET E = B * FNC(X)

     80   PRINT A,B,X,D,E

     90   NEXT B

     100 GO TO 10

     110 DEF FNC(X) = X * X+1

     120 END

5. Prepare a table for the following functions of X if X ranges from -2 to +2 in steps of 0.25:

$$f(x) = \frac{x^4 - 3x^2 + 1}{\sqrt{x^2 - 4}} \qquad g(x) = \frac{1 + 4\cos^2 x}{\sin x} \qquad h(x) = \frac{e^{-1/2x} + e^{1/2x}}{4(1 - e^x)}$$

If any of the functions are undefined for a particular value of X, print UNDEFINED. Label your output. [Hint: Test that each denominator is not equal to zero.]

6. Write a subroutine that finds the maximum of an array X with N elements. The maximum should be returned in the variable B.

7. Define a function FNR(M,N) that returns a random integer between M and N inclusive.

CHAPTER TWELVE

CHARACTER STRINGS

So far we have dealt primarily with numerical aspects of BASIC programming. However, one is not confined to numerical processing when using this language. One may wish to deal with data in the form of typewriter or keypunch characters. Such data are known as *character strings* or, alternatively, just *strings*.

12.1 The Naming of String Variables

There are 26 special variables provided in BASIC for the purpose of containing character string data. These are called *string variables*. They are symbolized by a single letter of the alphabet followed by a dollar sign. They are referred to as A-string, B-string, . . . , Z-string and are written as A$, B$, . . . , Z$ (It is quite possible that the dollar sign was selected because it resembles the letter S, the first letter of the word "string.") Just as there are numeric constants, so there are string constants. In fact, we have been using string constants regularly beginning in Chapter Three. Each message printed by a PRINT statement was a string constant.

We have already encountered programs where string variables contained only single characters. However, if a string variable is to contain more than one character, a dimension statement must be present. The size of the dimension statement must be greater than or equal to the maximum number of characters that the string will contain, but cannot exceed 72. The program:

```
DIM X$ (5)
LET X$ = "HELLO"
PRINT X$
END
```

will print out the word HELLO without the quotation marks.

12.2 The Length Function LEN

The only function available on the HP-2000 system that can take a string as its argument is the length function LEN, which returns as its value the logical length of the string in its argument. The logical length of a string is the total number of characters *including spaces* that make up the string, as opposed to the dimensioned value, which is the physical length.

The length function is of the form:

LEN (X$)

where X$ is a string.

In Program 12-1, character strings A$, B$, C$, and D$ are dimensioned 72, 13, 15, and 5, respectively. They are the *physical* lengths of the strings. However, A$, B$, and C$ are defined in the program to be the strings "HI," "JOE," and "TABLE," respectively, each one considerably shorter than the dimensions allow for. Nevertheless, when the LENgth function is applied to them, the correct lengths of 2, 3, and 5, respectively are printed out. These are therefore known as the *logical* lengths.

Notice that D$ is not defined. If a numeric variable were not defined, attempting an operation upon it would result in an error termination. However, this is not true for character strings. All character strings are initially assigned to what is known as the *null* string, which has a length of zero. It is for this reason that taking the length of D$, which was not defined anywhere in the program, gives a result of zero.

It should also be clear that because the string E$ (it's an exclamation mark) has a length of 1, it does not need to be dimensioned.

Program 12-1

```
100  PRINT "************************"
110  PRINT "*                      *"
120  PRINT "*  CHARACTER STRING    *"
130  PRINT "*                      *"
140  PRINT "*    MANIPULATION       *"
150  PRINT "*                      *"
160  PRINT "************************"
170  PRINT
180  DIM A$[72],B$[13],C$[15],D$[5]
190  LET A$="HI"
200  LET B$="JOE"
210  LET C$="TABLE"
220  LET E$="!"
230  PRINT LEN(A$),LEN(B$),LEN(C$),LEN(D$),LEN(E$)
240  END


RUN


************************
*                      *
*  CHARACTER STRING    *
*                      *
*    MANIPULATION      *
*                      *
************************


   2         3         5         0         1

DONE
```

12.3 Numeric Strings

Since a string may contain any of the available characters it can also be composed of numeric characters. However, once a numeric string is defined to be a string by virtue of the $ attached to its name, it cannot be processed arithmetically as was attempted in Program 12-2. Two numeric strings are "added" but setting the result equal to a string C$ or a simple variable C resulted in the diagnostic messages shown.

Program 12-2

```
100  PRINT "****************************"
110  PRINT "*                          *"
120  PRINT "* ATTEMPTING ARITHMETIC *"
130  PRINT "*                          *"
140  PRINT "* ON    NUMERIC    STRINGS *"
150  PRINT "*                          *"
160  PRINT "****************************"
170  PRINT
180  DIM A$[72],B$[72]
190  READ A$,B$
200  DATA "123", "406"
210  LET C=A$+B$
ERROR: STRING VARIABLE NOT LEGAL HERE
210  LET C$=A$+B$
ERROR: CHARACTERS AFTER STATEMENT END
```

12.4 Substrings

It is possible to refer to continuous sequences of characters within a string by means of an operation called substringing. This is done in Program 12-3 where the fourth through the sixth characters of a string are assigned to a different variable.

Program 12-3

```
100  PRINT "****************************"
110  PRINT "*                          *"
120  PRINT "*   MORE CHARACTER STRING  *"
130  PRINT "*                          *"
140  PRINT "*        MANIPULATION      *"
150  PRINT "*                          *"
160  PRINT "****************************"
170  PRINT
180  DIM X$[20],Y$[3]
190  LET X$="OPERATION"
200  LET Y$=X$[4,6]
210  PRINT X$,LEN(X$)
220  PRINT
230  PRINT Y$,LEN(Y$)
240  END
```

RUN

```
*****************************
*                           *
*  MORE CHARACTER STRING  *
*                           *
*        MANIPULATION       *
*                           *
*****************************
```

OPERATION   9

RAT   3

DONE

In Program 12-3 we access the fourth through sixth characters of X$ by writing X$(4,6). This *substring* becomes the string Y$.

If the instruction X$(4,6) were written X$(4), omitting the second parameter, the sequence of characters beginning with the fourth until the *end of the string* would have been accessed.

The distinction must now be made between such forms as:

$$X\$(4,6)$$
$$X\$(5)$$
$$X(4,6)$$
$$X(5)$$

In the first case X$(4,6), as stated above, refers to the substring of X$ beginning with the fourth character and ending with the sixth. The second case, X$(5) also refers to a substring, namely the fifth character of X$ through to its end. X(4,6) and X(5) refer to completely different entities, namely a matrix of four rows and six columns and an array of five elements, respectively. It follows that it is not possible to have arrays of strings in BASIC because of the ambiguities that would arise.

12.5 Counting Words in a String

If a sentence is typed into a string, it is possible to distinguish one word from another by the presence of a blank, or, for the final word, the presence of a period.

In Program 12-4, the sentence is contained in M$. Using a FOR/NEXT loop, each character of the string is tested for the presence of a blank or a period. When either is found, 1 is added to the word count W.

Program 12-4

```
100  PRINT "*****************************"
110  PRINT "*                           *"
120  PRINT "*  COUNTING   THE   NUMBER  *"
130  PRINT "*                           *"
140  PRINT "*  OF WORDS IN A SENTENCE   *"
150  PRINT "*                           *"
160  PRINT "*****************************"
170  PRINT
```

```
180  DIM M$[72]
190  LET W=0
200  PRINT "PLEASE TYPE IN YOUR STRING OF WORDS."
210  INPUT M$
220  PRINT LIN(20),"THANKS!",LIN(2)
230  FOR I=1 TO LEN(M$)
240  IF M$[I,I]=" " THEN 270
250  IF M$[I,I]="." THEN 290
260  GO TO 310
270  LET W=W+1
280  GO TO 310
290  LET W=W+1
300  GO TO 320
310  NEXT I
320  PRINT "THE NUMBER OF WORDS IN THIS STRING IS ";W
330  END
```

RUN

```
*******************************
*                             *
*   COUNTING  THE  NUMBER     *
*                             *
*   OF WORDS IN A SENTENCE    *
*                             *
*******************************
```

PLEASE TYPE IN YOUR STRING OF WORDS.
?ROLL OUT THE BARREL; WE'LL HAVE A BARREL OF FUN.

THANKS!

THE NUMBER OF WORDS IN THIS STRING IS 10

DONE

The purpose of Program 12-5 is to show the various ways strings may be formed. For example, A$ is explicitly defined in the program, while B$ is a substring of A$. The string C$ is entered at the terminal by the user, and D$, E$, F$, and G$ are elements of the DATA statement.

Program 12-5

```
100  PRINT "**********************"
110  PRINT "*                    *"
120  PRINT "*   VARIOUS FORMS OF *"
130  PRINT "*                    *"
140  PRINT "*        STRINGS     *"
150  PRINT "*                    *"
160  PRINT "**********************"
```

```
170  PRINT
180  DIM A$[60],B$[60],C$[60],D$[60],E$[60],F$[60],G$[60]
190  LET A$="OPTIMISM"
200  LET B$=A$[3,5]
210  INPUT C$
220  READ D$,E$,F$,G$
230  DATA "HENRY", "STEVE", "ROBERT", "JIMMY"
240  PRINT A$,B$,C$
250  PRINT
260  PRINT D$,E$,F$,G$
270  END


RUN


***********************
*                     *
*  VARIOUS FORMS OF   *
*                     *
*       STRINGS       *
*                     *
***********************

?TIKVA
OPTIMISM            TIM              TIKVA

HENRY               STEVE            ROBERT          JIMMY

DONE
```

12.6 Concatenation of Strings

In Program 12-6 the string HELLO THERE is typed in by the user. The string becomes the argument of the LEN function and the length of the string, 11, is determined and printed out.

Next the substring from the first to the seventh character, that is, HELLO T, is "concatenated" to the two string constants ED. COME HERE to form a new string HELLO TED. COME HERE, which is printed out.

Program 12-6

```
100  PRINT "*****************************************"
110  PRINT "*                                       *"
120  PRINT "* CHARACTER STRING CONCATENATION        *"
130  PRINT "*                                       *"
140  PRINT "*****************************************"
150  PRINT
160  PRINT "PLEASE TYPE IN A CHARACTER STRING."
170  PRINT "(TO TERMINATE PROGRAM, TYPE IN 'NOMORE')"
180  DIM A$[72]
190  PRINT
```

```
200   INPUT A$
210   IF A$="NOMORE" THEN 260
220   LET L=LEN (A$)
230   PRINT LIN (2),"THE STRING ";A$;" HAS ";L;" CHARACTERS'"
240   PRINT LIN (2),A$[1,7] ;"ED. COME ";A$[8]
250   GO TO 150
260   END
```

RUN

```
*******************************************
*                                         *
*   CHARACTER STRING CONCATENATION         *
*                                         *
*******************************************
```

PLEASE TYPE IN A CHARACTER STRING.
(TO TERMINATE PROGRAM, TYPE IN 'NOMORE')

?HELLO THERE

THE STRING HELLO THERE HAS 11   CHARACTERS.

HELLO TED. COME HERE

PLEASE TYPE IN A CHARACTER STRING.
(TO TERMINATE PROGRAM, TYPE IN 'NOMORE')

?NOMORE

DONE

12.7   Reversing a String

Program 12-7 allows for a string of up to 72 characters to be typed in at the Teletype. The program will reverse the string and print it out.

Program 12-7

```
100   PRINT "*****************************"
110   PRINT "*                           *"
120   PRINT "*   REVERSING A CHARACTER   *"
130   PRINT "*                           *"
140   PRINT "*           STRING          *"
150   PRINT "*                           *"
160   PRINT "*****************************"
170   PRINT
180   DIM A$[72]
190   PRINT "PLEASE TYPE IN YOUR STRING TO BE REVERSED."
```

```
200  INPUT A$
210  PRINT
220  PRINT "THANK YOU."
230  PRINT LIN (2), A$,LIN (2)
240  FOR I=LEN (A$) TO 1 STEP -1
250  PRINT A$[I,I] ;
260  NEXT I
270  PRINT
280  END


RUN


******************************
*                            *
*   REVERSING A CHARACTER    *
*                            *
*            STRING          *
*                            *
******************************


PLEASE TYPE IN YOUR STRING TO BE REVERSED.
?TURN THIS AROUND

THANK YOU.


TURN THIS AROUND


DNUORA SIHT NRUT

DONE
```

When two string variables are separated by a semicolon in a PRINT statement, no spaces whatever are inserted between the printouts. For this reason, the reverse form of the string prints out as a string identical in length to the inputted string. This is the effect of the semicolon in line 250.

12.8 String Relational Operators

The six relational operators:

$$= \quad <> \quad <= \quad >= \quad < \quad >$$

that were so useful in dealing with numeric data can also be used effectively with string data.

In order for two strings A$ and B$ to be "equal" they must be equal in all respects. That is, they must contain the same number of characters and the same sequence of characters in the same order. Any two strings that do not satisfy these requirements will satisfy the requirements for "not equal."

When the remaining four relational operators are used, the strings are compared, character by character, until an inequality is found. When an inequality is found, the character's ASCII values are compared and the one with the lower ASCII value (see Chapter Sixteen for a list of characters and their ASCII codes) is considered the "smaller."

Program 12-8 illustrates some string comparisons.

Program 12-8

```
100   PRINT "*****************************"
110   PRINT "*                           *"
120   PRINT "*   ILLUSTRATIONS OF SOME   *"
130   PRINT "*                           *"
140   PRINT "*   STRING     COMPARISONS  *"
150   PRINT "*                           *"
160   PRINT "*****************************"
170   PRINT
180   DIM B$[5],C$[5],D$[5],E$[5]
190   LET A$-"I"
200   LET B$-"BINGO"
210   LET C$="CAST"
220   LET D$="CASTE"
230   LET E$="TASTE"
240   IF A$=B$ THEN 320
250   PRINT "A$ IS NOT EQUAL TO B$."
260   IF D$<C$ THEN 320
270   PRINT "D$ IS NOT SMALLER THAN C$."
280   IF A$ >= D$ THEN 320
290   PRINT "A$ IS LESS THAN D$."
300   IF D$ <> E$ THEN 320
310   PRINT "D$ IS EQUAL TO E$."
320   END
```

```
RUN


*****************************
*                           *
*  ILLUSTRATIONS OF SOME    *
*                           *
*  STRING      COMPARISONS  *
*                           *
*****************************

A$ IS NOT EQUAL TO B$.
D$ IS NOT SMALLER THAN C$.

DONE
```

When the string "CAST" is compared with the string "CASTE" the matching is done from left to right. The letters C, A, S, and T match but the former word is then packed with a trailing null character* so that the lengths of the two words are the same. When the trailing null character is matched with the E, the test, of course, fails.

The word CAST is lexically smaller than CASTE—the word CAST appears in a dictionary *before* the word CASTE.

It should be clear that any of the characters on the Teletype may be included in a string and each character has its own binary value, enabling a test for equality to be made.

Strings also may be read in by means of a READ statement, by an INPUT statement, or may be created as substrings.

A word of caution: the reader may be tempted to construct a compound IF statement when comparing strings. Although the syntax of the language allows for this when comparing numeric values, it does not permit one to compare more than one character string at a time. Attempting to type the statement:

IF A$ = "YES" OR A$ = "NO" THEN 180

will result in the error message:

ERROR MISSING OR ILLEGAL 'THEN'

12.9 The ENTER Statement

An interesting and equally useful version of the INPUT statement is the ENTER statement, which permits the user to enter (input) a response. It differs from the INPUT statement in that:

1. No question mark is printed
2. No line feed is effected after returning the carriage
3. The time permitted for a response is controlled by the programmer
4. A record is maintained internally of the elapsed time in seconds
5. Only a single variable or string may be inputted
6. If the time limit for a response is exceeded, the program resumes execution beginning with the next instruction
7. Permits the interrogation of the terminal number of the terminal on which the user is logged
8. If a character string is ENTERed it may include quotes as embedded characters. The string itself should not be enclosed in quotes.

Typical uses for the ENTER statement are in timed responses such as those encountered in quizzes, games, and reaction tests.

There are three forms of the ENTER instruction. The first form is used only for determining the current user's terminal number. It is:

100   ENTER #X

When this instruction is executed the program does *not* stop. It sets the variable X equal to the user terminal number (between 0 and 31 inclusive). This implies, of course, that the HP-2000C can accommodate up to 32 terminals.

The second version of the ENTER statement, which is of far greater interest to the programmer, has the form:

200 ENTER *time limit, expression, variable name for response time, input variable name*

For instance:

300   ENTER 60,T1,I

*The null character as opposed to the null string, is a nonprinting character that has the lowest ASCII value.

This instruction has the effect of making the computer wait up to 60 seconds for the response. The actual time taken for the response is stored in T1, and the response itself is stored in I. Naturally, a suitable PRINT statement should precede the execution of each ENTER instruction advising the user of the expected kind of response. In the above example, where I is the response variable, a numeric response is expected. The reader is reminded that no line feed is effected when using the ENTER statement so that it might be advisable to use a PRINT instruction to skip a line.

Here is another example of the second form:

400   ENTER P*Q,T2,A$

This example shows that the allotted time may be a computed value such as P*Q. The response time is stored in T2. The input variable name A$ clearly indicates that a string input is expected.

The third and final version of the ENTER statement is actually a combination of the first two versions. For example:

500   ENTER #L, (RND(0)*100) + 20, T3, Z$

The terminal number is stored in L; the computer then waits for the random period between 20 and 120 seconds, the actual lapsed time is stored in T3 and the string response is stored in Z$.

Exceeding the Time Limit

If the time limit associated with an ENTER statement is exceeded, the number -256 is stored as the response time (in the examples shown, response time would be stored in T1, T2, and T3, respectively). The maximum time permitted is 255 seconds. Timing begins as soon as the execution of the preceding statement is completed.

In Program 12-9 the user is invited to become familiar with the ENTER statement. The user is asked to type in his or her name within 20 seconds of the ENTER instruction being executed. The actual time taken is stored in T as an integer number of seconds. The program was run twice, once with the author at the terminal and then with his assistant and friend.

If the response is typed in within the 20-second time limit specified, the user is advised of the actual time it took. If the time limit is exceeded, the value of T is automatically set to -256. If T is found to have this value in line 230, an appropriate uncomplimentary printout is typed by the machine.

Program 12-9

```
100  PRINT "****************************"
110  PRINT "*                          *"
120  PRINT "*  ILLUSTRATION OF THE     *"
130  PRINT "*                          *"
140  PRINT "*  ENTER    STATEMENT      *"
150  PRINT "*                          *"
160  PRINT "****************************"
170  PRINT
180  DIM N$[72]
190  PRINT "YOU HAVE 20 SECONDS TO TYPE IN YOUR FULL NAME."
200  PRINT "READY OR NOT . . . START TYPING: ";
210  ENTER 20,T,N$
220  PRINT
230  IF T=-256 THEN 260
```

```
240  PRINT "IT TOOK YOU "T"SECONDS TO RESPOND."
250  GO TO 280
260  PRINT "YOU LOSE! NEXT TIME TRY TAKING YOUR HANDS"
270  PRINT "OUT OF YOUR POCKETS."
280  END


RUN


*************************
*                       *
*  ILLUSTRATION OF THE   *
*                       *
*  ENTER     STATEMENT   *
*                       *
*************************

YOU HAVE 20 SECONDS TO TYPE IN YOUR FULL NAME.
READY OR NOT . . . START TYPING: HENRY MULLISH
IT TOOK YOU 5    SECONDS TO RESPOND.

DONE
RUN


*************************
*                       *
*  ILLUSTRATION OF THE   *
*                       *
*  ENTER     STATEMENT   *
*                       *
*************************

YOU HAVE 20 SECONDS TO TYPE IN YOUR FULL NAME.
READY OR NOT . . . START TYPING: MICHAEL DENNIS EDWARD POMPA
THE FIRST
YOU LOSE! NEXT TIME TRY TAKING YOUR HANDS
OUT OF YOUR POCKETS.

DONE
```

In Program 12-10, a string A$ is inputted by means of an ENTER statement. The maximum possible time limit of 255 seconds is allowed for the response.

The idea of the program is to scan the string A$ for each of the 14 words contained in the passage that begins: "I know you all . . . ." The string A$ is searched for each of these words and if a word is not found an error is recorded.

Line 370 computes the typing speed that the user demonstrates when responding to the computer's request to type in the passage. Line 380 merely subtracts the number of errors detected from the gross typing speed.

This program is not comprehensive in scope nor is it foolproof. There are many errors that would go undetected but we leave the finding of these errors to the diligent students. Perhaps such students would like to improve the program.

Program 12-10

```
100   PRINT "***********************"
110   PRINT "*                     *"
120   PRINT "*  SPEED TYPING TEST  *"
130   PRINT "*                     *"
140   PRINT "***********************"
150   PRINT
160   DIM A$[72] , W$[15]
170   PRINT "THIS IS A TEST FOR TYPING SPEED AND ACCURACY."
180   PRINT "TYPE THE FOLLOWING PASSAGE:"LIN(1)
190   PRINT "I KNOW YOU ALL BUT WILL AWHILE ";
200   PRINT "UPHOLD THE UNYOKED HUMOR OF YOUR IDLENESS"; LIN(3)
210   ENTER 255,T,A$
220   PRINT
230   LET E=0
240   LET P=1
250   FOR W=1 TO 14
260   READ W$
270   DATA "I","KNOW","YOU","ALL","BUT","WILL","AWHILE","UPHOLD","THE"
280   DATA "UNYOKED","HUMOR","OF","YOUR","IDLENESS"
290   LET L=LEN(W$)
300   FOR I=P TO LEN(A$)-L+1
310   IF A$[I,I+L-1] =W$ THEN 350
320   NEXT I
330   LET E=E+1
340   GO TO 360
350   LET P=I+L
360   NEXT W
370   LET G=INT(14/T*60+.5)
380   LET N=C-E
390   PRINT LIN(2);"YOUR GROSS TYPING SPEED IS "C" WORDS PER MINUTE"
400   PRINT "AND YOUR NET SPEED AFTER DEDUCTING FOR ERRORS IS "N
410   END


***********************
*                     *
*  SPEED TYPING TEST  *
*                     *
***********************


THIS IS A TEST FOR TYPING SPEED AND ACCURACY.
TYPE THE FOLLOWING PASSAGE:

*I KNOW YOU ALL BUT WILL AWHILE UPHOLD THE UNYOKED HUMOR
   OF YOUR IDLENESS
```

*For technical reasons of publication this line is shown as two separate lines. In actuality it is printed as a single line at the terminal.

*I KNOW YOU ALL BUT WILL AWHILE UPHOLD THE UNYOKED HUMOR
OF YOUR IDLENESS

YOUR GROSS TYPING SPEED IS 3Ø WORDS PER MINUTE
AND YOUR NET SPEED AFTER DEDUCTING FOR ERRORS IS 29

DONE

Entering a String Response Instead of Numeric

If the computer detects a character string response when it "expects" a numeric
value to be typed in at the terminal, it indicates this error condition by setting the
response time to the *negative* value of the actual response time.

QUICK REFERENCE GUIDE TO CHAPTER TWELVE

Item	General Form	Examples
1. String dimension statement	*Line number* DIM *letter* $ *(integer constant)*	100 DIM A$ (15) 200 DIM B$ (63), T$ (19), X (21)
2. Explicit substrings	*String variable (beginning characters, ending character)*	A$ (6,6) B$ (1,1) C$ (3,11) D$ (X1,Y2) E$ (X1, X1+6)
3. Implicit substring	*String variable (beginning character)*	A$ (1) B$ (3) C$ (I↑2)
4. Substring assignment	*Line number* LET *substring* = *string* or *substring*	100 LET A$ (4,6)=B$ (7,9) 200 LET C$ (X,Y)= D$
5. LEN function	LEN *(string* or *substring)*	LEN (A$) LEN (B$ (5))
6. String compare	*Line number* IF *string* or *substring relational operator string* or *substring* THEN *line number*	100 IF A$ = B$ THEN 150 200 IF C$ = D$ (3,5) THEN 250 300 IF E$ (6,9) <"MIKE" THEN 350
7. ENTER statement	*Line number* ENTER *variable name*	100 ENTER # N
	Line number ENTER *expression, variable name, string* or *variable name*	200 ENTER 60,X,Y
	Line number ENTER# *variable name, expression, variable name, string* or *variable name*	300 ENTER #Z, 3*C,X,Y$

Questions

1. A police department has a list of license plate numbers of the form ABC-123
   (three alphabetic letters followed by a dash, followed by three digits).
   Write a program that READs a list of license plate numbers and counts the total
   plates whose first three letters are FBI and whose three numeric digits are greater
   than 007. Assume the list is terminated by the number "ZZZ-999."

---

*For technical reasons of publication this line is shown as two separate lines. In actuality it is
printed as a single line at the terminal.

2. Write a program that reads in, prints out, and counts the number of words contained in the first sentence of the Bible. Assume that the sentence is terminated by a period.

3. What output would you expect from the following program?
```
10   DIM A$[72], B$[10], C$[10], D$[10]
20   READ A$, B$, C$, D$
30   DATA "NEW YORK STATE", "ABCDE"
40   DATA "FGHIJ", "KLM"
50   FOR I=LEN(A$) TO 1 STEP -1
60   PRINT A$[I,I]
70   NEXT I
80   PRINT C$; B$; D$; A$; "NOPQR"
90   PRINT "BE CAREFUL"
100  END
```

4. What follows is the beginning and end of a program designed to analyze the answer given in response to a question printed by the computer. The answer should then be examined to determine whether it corresponds to the correct answer. Provision has to be made, however, for possible variations on the correct answer. In other words, a key phrase must be searched for. The program should go to statement 9998 for any input that contains mention of the words WHITE HOUSE, such as IN THE WHITE HOUSE or AT THE WHITE HOUSE.
Complete the program, inserting the appropriate instructions to accomplish the task of searching A$ for the presence of B$.
```
100   DIM A$(72), B$(72)
110   PRINT "THE PRESIDENT OF THE U.S. OFFICIALLY STAYS";
120   INPUT A$
130   LET B$ = "WHITE HOUSE"
          .
          .
          .
9996  PRINT "NO"
9997  GO TO 9999
9998  PRINT "YES"
9999  END
```

5. Without running the following program deduce what output will be produced.
```
100   DIM X$(72)
110   LET X$ = "MY NAME IS RICHARD KESTENBAUM."
120   FOR I = 1 TO LEN(X$)
130   PRINT X$(I)
140   NEXT I
150   END
```

6. The following program reads in a character string that is stored as X$. The string is reversed and stored into Y$. Amend the program so that it allows for repeated inputting of strings. The computer should print out whether the string read in is a

palindrome or not. (A palindrome is a word or phrase that reads the same backward and forward.) Ignoring spaces and punctuation, the following are palindromes:

(a) LEVEL

(b) MADAM I'M ADAM

(c) A MAN, A PLAN, A CANAL, PANAMA

(d) ABLE WAS I ERE I SAW ELBA

```
100   DIM X$[72], Y$[72]
110   INPUT X$
120   LET J = 1
130   LET Y$ = " "
140   FOR I = LEN(X$) TO 1 STEP -1
150   LET Y$[J,J] = X$[I,I]
160   LET J = J+1
170   NEXT I
180   PRINT X$, Y$
190   END
```

CHAPTER THIRTEEN

FORMATTED OUTPUT

Thus far each time information whether numeric or literal, was printed in a program advantage was taken of the simple instruction PRINT. For most purposes this was quite satisfactory. The BASIC system printed the data into the standard five fields across the page, or if the semicolon was used, it had the effect of compressing the output—"packing it," so to speak. But this, together with the TAB and SPA functions, represented the total control that the programmer had over the manner in which his output was printed. He had no control whatever over the location of the decimal point nor could he predetermine the number of significant digits by which a number was represented in a printout.

In an attempt to provide the BASIC programmer with the means to improve the format of his output, the HP-2000 BASIC system contains a special feature known as "formatted output."

13.1 Formatting Symbols

Ten symbols may be used to affect the manner in which output is printed. They are:

D	digit	.	decimal point
S	sign	E	exponent form
X	blank space	,	format separator
A	string	" "	literal
/	line advancing	( )	grouping

Each of these will be illustrated in the next series of programs.

13.2 Print Using/Image

In order to implement the formatting symbols listed above, BASIC provides another PRINT instruction, slightly more involved than the regular PRINT instruction with which we are familiar. It is composed of two statements, the PRINT USING and the IMAGE statements. The IMAGE statement reflects the form of the line to be printed and includes the required formatting symbols. The line number of the IMAGE statement is referred to by the PRINT USING statement(s). Here is a typical example:

```
150  PRINT USING 200; N
200  IMAGE DD
```

Note that a semicolon follows the line number that references the IMAGE statement.

In the discussion that follows, various aspects of fixed point formats are illustrated. Numerous references are made to Program 13-1, which deserves very special attention. It is recommended that each paragraph be read slowly and several times if need be.

As mentioned earlier, the IMAGE clause contains the precise specifications to format the associated number. The letter D specifies that a digit should appear in that particular position. The inclusion of a decimal point not only prints the decimal in the desired location but also adjusts the number either left or right to align the decimal points.

It will be noted in the same program that when N is printed in line 190 using the familiar PRINT statement (the first printout of the program) the number N is preceded by a blank space. This is the standard way of printing numbers using the print statement and it is not difficult to understand why this is desirable. When the number is negative, the blank space after "N=" is used to house the minus sign. In the case of a positive number, such as in this example, the plus sign does not normally appear but nevertheless a blank space is reserved for it.

Since the IMAGE in line 210 is specified as DD.DDDD, the number 12.3456 is printed out in full, with no leading space in the second line of the printout.

The second pair of examples, lines 230 to 250, illustrates the fact that the ordinary PRINT statement not only inserts a leading blank but also appends trailing blanks to the number. In this case it will be seen that there are four trailing blanks although the number of blanks will vary for different numbers. By contrast, when the number is printed three times in succession using the IMAGE 3(DD.DDDD) the output becomes a continuous string of digits containing three decimal points. Such a printout is hardly recommended because of the difficulty in reading it.

In an IMAGE statement, if fewer digits are specified after the decimal point than the number actually contains, the rightmost digit is *rounded*. This is illustrated in the third set, lines 270 to 320, where the number 12.3456 is printed according to an IMAGE of DD.DD, printing out the *rounded* result, 12.35.

On the other hand, if the specified fractional part of the field is longer than the fraction itself, the additional positions are filled with zeros. This feature is useful when printing out numbers representing dollars and cents, in which case one would use two D's after the decimal point. Since in the example shown we use the format DD.DDDDDD, the last two digits are printed as zeros.

If the integer portion of an IMAGE decimal specification is wider than the integer part of the number itself, the leading zeros are suppressed, as shown in Program 13-1. Here the IMAGE to print the number 12.3456 is specified to be DDDDDD.DD. Therefore it is printed out as bbbb12.35, where b represents a blank space.

To print out only the integer portion of a number, deleting the decimal point entirely, one can omit the decimal point from the image and include an appropriate number of D's to accommodate the integer portion of the number. See line 350.

It is possible to insert one or more blanks anywhere within a number by including the letter X in the appropriate position in the IMAGE. Thus the number 12.3456, printed using an IMAGE of DXDX.XDXDXDXD, is printed as 1b2b.b3b4b5b6.

The X does not have to be a part of the specific format for a number. It may also be used external to the format in order to force spaces to be printed out between successive numbers. By this means we can now improve the readability of the three numbers printed out in statements 240 to 250. The IMAGE used in line 400 includes the specification for the format XX (for two spaces) separated by a comma.

Ordinarily one does not need to have a plus sign printed in order to identify a positive number. It is always assumed to be there. However, in special cases it is desired that a number be prefixed by a plus sign on a printout; provision for this is made in BASIC. One simply places the letter S (for sign) in front of the format specification. When printed the plus sign will "float" to the immediate left of the first significant digit.

The floating plus sign is not the only option; one may "fix" its position by embedding the S within the D's. In other words at least one D must precede the S. Wherever the S is placed within the field of D's will be the position in which the plus will appear in the printout.

One is not compelled to write out in longhand a string of D's for a specific format, but this will be left for the next illustrative program.

Program 13-1

```
100   PRINT "****************"
110   PRINT "*              *"
120   PRINT "*  FIXED POINT *"
130   PRINT "*              *"
140   PRINT "*    FORMAT    *"
150   PRINT "*              *"
160   PRINT "****************"
170   PRINT
180   LET N=12.3456
190   PRINT "N="; N
200   PRINT  USING 210; N
210   IMAGE "N=", DD.DDDD
220   PRINT
230   PRINT "N PACKED 3 TIMES: "N;N;N
240   PRINT  USING 250; N, N, N
250   IMAGE "N PACKED 3 TIMES: ",3(DD.DDDD)
260   PRINT
270   PRINT  USING 280; N
280   IMAGE "ROUNDING TO THE NEAREST PENNY:   $", DD.DD
290   PRINT  USING 300; N
300   IMAGE "A WIDER FIELD THAN THE NUMBER:      ", DD.DDDDDD
310   PRINT  USING 320; N
320   IMAGE "SUPPRESS LEADING ZEROES:       ", DDDDDD.DD
330   PRINT
340   PRINT  USING 350; N
350   IMAGE "INTEGER FORMAT; NO DECIMAL POINT: ", DD
360   PRINT
370   PRINT  USING 380; N
380   IMAGE "EMBEDDED BLANKS WITHIN THE NUMBER: ", DXDX.XDXDXDXD
390   PRINT  USING 400; N, N, N
400   IMAGE "N PACKED 3 TIMES TO AID READABILITY: ",3(DD.DDDD,XX)
410   PRINT
420   PRINT  USING 430; N
430   IMAGE "FLOATING SIGN: ", SDDDDDD.DDDD
440   PRINT  USING 450; N
450   IMAGE "F I X E D SIGN: ", DSDDDDD.DD
460   END
```

RUN


```
* * * * * * * * * * * * * * * *
*                              *
*  FIXED POINT  *
*                              *
*     FORMAT     *
*                              *
* * * * * * * * * * * * * * * *
```

N= 12.3456
N=12.3456

N PACKED 3 TIMES: 12.3456   12.3456   12.3456
N PACKED 3 TIMES:12.345612.345612.3456

ROUNDING TO THE NEAREST PENNY: $12.35
A WIDER FIELD THAN THE NUMBER: 12.345600
SUPPRESS LEADING ZEROES: 12.35

INTEGER FORMAT; NO DECIMAL POINT: 12

EMBEDDED BLANKS WITHIN THE NUMBER: 1 2 . 3 4 5 6
N PACKED 3 TIMES TO AID READABILITY: 12.3456   12.3456   12.3456

FLOATING SIGN: +12.3456
F I X E D SIGN: +   12.35

DONE

13.3 Additional Formatting Features

In Program 13-2, several additional features are shown. They include:

1. The abbreviated way of indicating a string of D's
2. The formatting of a negative number
3. The exponential format and
4. The referencing of IMAGE statements.

Program 13-2

```
100  PRINT "***************************"
110  PRINT "*                              *"
120  PRINT "*  FURTHER FORMATTING  *"
130  PRINT "*                              *"
140  PRINT "*           FEATURES          *"
150  PRINT "*                              *"
160  PRINT "***************************"
170  PRINT
180  LET Y=-9876.54
190  PRINT "Y=" ; Y
200  PRINT  USING 210; Y
```

```
210   IMAGE "Y=", 5D.2D
220   PRINT
230   PRINT   USING 240; Y
240   IMAGE "FLOATING SIGN: ", S6D.2D
250   PRINT   USING 260; Y
260   IMAGE "F I X E D SIGN: ", DS5D.2D
270   PRINT
280   PRINT   USING 290; Y
290   IMAGE "Y IN E FORMAT: ", S4D.2DE
300   PRINT "RE-ALIGNMENT OF DECIMAL POINT"
310   PRINT   USING 320; Y
320   IMAGE "AND ADJUSTMENT OF EXPONENT: ", S.6DE
330   PRINT   USING 340; Y
340   IMAGE "RE-ALIGNMENT IN THE OPPOSITE DIRECTION: ", S6DE
350   LET Y=12300
360   PRINT LIN(2); "Y="; Y
370   PRINT   USING 210; Y
380   PRINT
390   PRINT   USING 240; Y
400   PRINT   USING 260; Y
410   PRINT
420   PRINT   USING 290; Y
430   PRINT "RE-ALIGNMENT OF DECIMAL POINT"
440   PRINT   USING 320; Y
450   PRINT   USING 340; Y
460   END


RUN


**************************
*                        *
*  FURTHER FORMATTING  *
*                        *
*         FEATURES       *
*                        *
**************************

Y=-9876.54
Y=-9876.54

FLOATING SIGN:   -9876.54
F I X E D SIGN:  -  9876.54

Y IN E  FORMAT: -9876.54E+00
RE-ALIGNMENT OF DECIMAL POINT
AND ADJUSTMENT OF EXPONENT:  -.987654E+04
RE-ALIGNMENT IN THE OPPOSITE DIRECTION:  -987654E- 02

Y=  12300
Y=12300.00
```

```
FLOATING SIGN:  +12300.00
F I X E D SIGN:  +12300.00

Y IN E FORMAT:  +1230.00E+01
RE-ALIGNMENT OF DECIMAL POINT
AND ADJUSTMENT OF EXPONENT:  +.123000E+05
RE-ALIGNMENT IN THE OPPOSITE DIRECTION:  +123000E-01

DONE
```

In Program 13-2, Y is defined to be the negative quantity -9876.54. As in the previous program, the number is printed out in the common way using the PRINT instruction. It will be observed that there are, in this case, a sign and four digits for a total of five printed characters before the decimal point. It is not necessary to write a string of five D's; the abbreviated form 5D may be substituted. By the same token, 2D, which appears after the decimal point, is equivalent to DD. A *replication factor* may be used in front of a D, X, or before parentheses (as was in fact done in lines 250 and 400 of the "fixed point format" program covered earlier).

This feature may be used in combination with the floating and fixed sign specifications in which the letter S is used. Both of these are illustrated in Program 13-2 in lines 230 to 260.

It might interest the reader to know that no provision is made in BASIC for the printing out of embedded commas such as in the number 3,456.78. A comma in a format specification merely acts as a separator of variables in a print list.

In one of the early chapters of this book we explain the manner in which numbers may be represented in scientific notation. The letter E is a format symbol that may be used to specify scientific notation. It is usually placed at the extreme right of the format specification. Therefore, printing the number -9876.54 in S4D.2DE format or in its equivalent form SDDDD.DDE yields the number $-9876.54E+00$ (see line 280 to 290).

If a number that has no significant digits *before* the decimal point is printed, the digits appear *after* the decimal point. However, in order to compensate for this shift, the exponent field is automatically adjusted. For this reason, when -9876.54 is printed in S.6DE format in lines 310 to 320 it appears as $-.987654E+04$. Changing the format to S6DE specifies that the significant digits should appear *in integer form* within the scientific notation format. Thus the number -9876.54 prints out as $-987654E-02$ in lines 330 to 340.

Just as a DATA statement may be placed anywhere at all in a BASIC program and not necessarily immediately following its associated READ statement, so an IMAGE statement may appear anywhere within a program. And what is more, it may be referenced as often as one likes by different PRINT USING statements. This is shown in Program 13-2 where line 350 redefines the value Y to be 12300 and is successively printed out according to all of the previously used IMAGEs.

13.4 Changing a Format During Execution

Another aspect of the PRINT USING feature is that a format may actually be changed during the course of execution of the program. In order to do so the format must be placed in a string variable rather than in an IMAGE statement. Instead of writing

PRINT USING *line number; list*

we use the alternative form

PRINT USING *string name; list*

This is illustrated in Program 13-3.

Program 13-3

```
100  PRINT "***************************"
110  PRINT "*                         *"
120  PRINT "*  FORMATS THAT CHANGE  *"
130  PRINT "*                         *"
140  PRINT "*  DURING      EXECUTION  *"
150  PRINT "*                         *"
160  PRINT "***************************"
170  PRINT
180  DIM F$[50]
190  LET X=1.23456
200  LET F$="D.D"
210  FOR I=1 TO 5
220  PRINT "NOW THE FORMAT IS:  "; F$; TAB(27);
230  PRINT  USING F$; X
240  LET F$[3+I]=" D"
250  NEXT I
260  END
```

RUN

```
***************************
*                         *
*  FORMATS THAT CHANGE  *
*                         *
*  DURING      EXECUTION  *
*                         *
***************************

NOW THE FORMAT IS: D.D        1.2
NOW THE FORMAT IS: D.DD       1.23
NOW THE FORMAT IS: D.DDD      1.235
NOW THE FORMAT IS: D.DDDD     1.2346
NOW THE FORMAT IS: D.DDDDD    1.23456
```

DONE

The number X is defined to be 1.23456 and the character string F$ is initially defined to be "D.D." F$ is the object of the PRINT USING clause and is enclosed within a FOR/NEXT loop in which X is printed out during each iteration. When I = 1 the value of 1.2 is printed out, confirming that the string F$ is D.D. However, the string F$ is immediately changed to D.DD by simply defining the fourth format character symbol to be D. This D is appended to the previous three characters (D.D) and so the second printout becomes 1.23. This process continues until the loop is satisfied.

Notice that in the above program the string F$ is used in place of an IMAGE statement.

13.5 Alphabetic Format

Alphabetic format, or "A" format as it is commonly called, is not particularly useful because it usually requires knowing in advance the size of the character string to which it relates. Nevertheless, we shall illustrate its use in a program that has more aesthetic appeal than inherent value.

When used in an IMAGE statement, the formatting symbol A specifies that its corresponding character in the related PRINT USING statement be printed out. Since this probably sounds quite abstruse to the reader, an extra word of explanation is perhaps called for. Suppose we want to print out the character string C$ whose content is the word "BASIC." We may print this out completely using the format specification 5A, as shown:

```
100   PRINT USING 110; C$
110   IMAGE 5A
```

Substituting 3A for 5A will result in the printing of a truncated form of the string, BAS. (Alphabetic strings are left-adjusted.) The X formatting symbol may be combined with A to insert blanks into the string. Therefore, using an IMAGE of AXAXAXAXA the word BASIC would print out as B A S I C.

Referring now to Program 13-4, B$ contains the arbitrarily chosen 11-letter string COMPUTATION. The string F$, which is the object of the PRINT USING clause in statement 230, is initially composed of 11 A's. During the first iteration of the loop, F$ is dynamically changed by first deleting a trailing A specification symbol (by substituting it for a null string in statement 240). Then the leading A in F$ is replaced by the formatting symbol X. The loss of these two A's has the effect of truncating the last two letters of B$. This process is repeated until the loop is satisfied, during the course of which B$ does not change.

Beginning now in statement 320, a second loop is encountered. It is almost identical to the first loop with the exception that instead of inserting the X formatting specification symbol into F$ the string B$ is successively modified by replacing the leading character with a blank.

With each iteration around the loop a trailing "A" format specification is truncated; as a result, its corresponding letter in B$ is truncated.

Program 13-4

```
100   PRINT "******************"
110   PRINT "*                *"
120   PRINT "*  ILLUSTRATION  *"
130   PRINT "*                *"
140   PRINT "*  OF 'A' FORMAT *"
150   PRINT "*                *"
160   PRINT "******************"
170   PRINT
180   DIM B$[50], F$[50]
190   LET B$="COMPUTATION"
200   LET F$="AAAAAAAAAAA"
210   FOR I=1 TO 6
220   PRINT "THE FORMAT IS NOW: "; F$; TAB(32);
230   PRINT  USING F$; B$
```

```
240   LET F$[12-1]=" "
250   LET F$[I,1]="X"
260   NEXT I
270   PRINT
280   PRINT "SEE, B$ DOES NOT CHANGE:  "; B$
290   PRINT LIN(3)
300   LET B$="COMPUTATION"
310   LET F$="AAAAAAAAAA"
320   FOR I=1 TO 6
330   PRINT "THE FORMAT IS NOW:  "; F$; TAB(32);
340   PRINT   USING F$; B$
350   LET F$[12-1]=" "
360   LET B$[I,1]="   "
370   NEXT I
380   END
```

RUN

```
* * * * * * * * * * * * * * * *
*                             *
*   ILLUSTRATION   *
*                             *
*   OF 'A' FORMAT  *
*                             *
* * * * * * * * * * * * * * * *
```

```
THE FORMAT IS NOW:  AAAAAAAAAA      COMPUTATION
THE FORMAT IS NOW:  XAAAAAAAAA      COMPUTATI
THE FORMAT IS NOW:  XXAAAAAAA       COMPUTA
THE FORMAT IS NOW:  XXXAAAAA        COMPU
THE FORMAT IS NOW:  XXXXAAA         COM
THE FORMAT IS NOW:  XXXXXA          C
```

SEE, B$ DOES NOT CHANGE: COMPUTATION

```
THE FORMAT IS NOW:  AAAAAAAAAA      COMPUTATION
THE FORMAT IS NOW:  AAAAAAAAA       OMPUTATIO
THE FORMAT IS NOW:  AAAAAAAA        MPUTATI
THE FORMAT IS NOW:  AAAAAAA         PUTAT
THE FORMAT IS NOW:  AAAAAA          UTA
THE FORMAT IS NOW:  AAAAAA          T
```

DONE

For the reader who has the notion that writing programs in BASIC is all work and no play, we have designed Program 13-5 which uses the A format feature to print out nine gameboards for the dot-box game. As you will no doubt remember from your grade school days this is a game where the dots are connected by competing players. He who completes the most boxes wins.

Line 230 may seem a little complicated, even though it isn't. The IMAGE could have been written as

230   IMAGE 3 (A 2X A 2X A 2X A 2X A 2X A 7X)

Even though all spaces have been omitted in the program it is not ambiguous.

Program 13-5

```
100  PRINT "*****************"
110  PRINT "*               *"
120  PRINT "*  THE DOT-BOX  *"
130  PRINT "*               *"
140  PRINT "*      GAME      *"
150  PRINT "*               *"
160  PRINT "*****************"
170  PRINT LIN(3)
180  DIM A$[6]
190  LET A$=". . . . . ."
200  FOR I=1 TO 3
210  FOR J=1 TO 6
220  PRINT  USING 230; A$, A$, A$
230  IMAGE 3(A2XA2XA2XA2XA2XA7X)
240  PRINT
250  NEXT J
260  PRINT LIN(5)
270  NEXT I
280  END


RUN


*****************
*               *
*  THE DOT-BOX  *
*               *
*      GAME      *
*               *
*****************



.   .   .   .   .   .     .   .   .   .  .   .   .  .   .   .   .   .   .

.   .   .   .   .   .     .   .   .   .   .   .   .  .   .   .   .   .   .

.   .   .   .   .   .     .   .   .   .   .   .   .  .   .   .   .   .   .

.   .   .   .   .   .     .   .   .   .   .   .   .  .   .   .   .   .   .

.   .   .   .   .   .     .   .   .   .   .   .   .  .   .   .   .   .   .

.   .   .   .   .   .     .   .   .   .   .   .   .  .   .   .   .   .   .
```

.   .   .   .

.   .   .   .

.   .   .   .

.   .   .   .

.   .   .   .

.   .   .   .

.   .   .   .

.   .   .   .

.   .   .   .

.   .   .   .

.   .   .   .

.   .   .   .

DONE

No explanation is needed for Program 13-6, which merely prints out using the IMAGE statement the heading "Printing a heading using IMAGE format" in the now familiar caption setting.

Program 13-6

```
100   DIM A$[72]
110   DIM B$[72] , C$[72]
120   LET A$="******************************************************"
130   LET B$="*PRINTING A HEADING*"
140   LET C$="*USING IMAGE FORMAT*"
150   IMAGE25A
160   IMAGEA23XA
170   IMAGEA3X18A2XA
180   PRINT    USING  150; A$
190   PRINT    USING  160; A$
200   PRINT    USING  170; B$
210   PRINT    USING  160; A$
220   PRINT    USING  170; C$
230   PRINT    USING  160; A$
240   PRINT    USING  150; A$
```

RUN


```
*************************
*                       *
*   PRINTING A HEADING   *
*                       *
*   USING IMAGE FORMAT   *
*                       *
*************************
```

DONE

13.6 Illustration of the Slash

Finally, we come to the last of the formatting symbols to be discussed—the slash (/).

In Program 13-7, two strings B$ and C$ are defined. It is required to print the strings on separate, consecutive lines. Since B$ is 15 characters long and C$ is 22 characters in length, 15A and 22A may be included in a PRINT USING statement, with a slash separating them, *the whole specification being enclosed in quotes*. The effect of the slash is to return the carriage of the line printer to the beginning of the line and to advance it forward one line. The slash as used here has no relation whatever to division!

It is quite true that the ordinary PRINT statement used twice in succession could have printed out the lines as required. But this example indicates the simplest possible use of the slash.

To make this illustrative program a little more informative we experimented in line 230 to see the effect of having fewer format specifications than the list requires. The results are self-evident.

Program 13-7

```
100  PRINT "*****************"
110  PRINT "*               *"
120  PRINT "* ILLUSTRATION  *"
130  PRINT "*               *"
140  PRINT "* OF THE SLASH  *"
150  PRINT "*               *"
160  PRINT "*****************"
170  PRINT
180  DIM B$[50], C$[50]
190  LET B$="CANDY IS DANDY,"
200  LET C$="BUT LIKKER IS KWIKKER!"
210  PRINT USING " 15A/22A "; B$, C$
220  PRINT LIN(2)
230  PRINT USING "22A"; B$, C$
240  END
```

RUN


```
* * * * * * * * * * * * * * * * *
*                       *
*  ILLUSTRATION  *
*                       *
*  OF THE SLASH  *
*                       *
* * * * * * * * * * * * * * * * *
```


CANDY IS DANDY,
BUT LIKKER IS KWIKKER!

CANDY IS DANDY,   BUT LIKKER IS KWIKKER!

DONE

13.7   Formatting Matrices with PRINT USING

The editing features that we have discussed in connection with the PRINT USING feature may be used effectively when printing out matrices.

Suppose, for example, we generate a 4 × 4 matrix with elements 1 through 16, respectively. This is, in fact, done at the beginning of Program 13-8.

In line 260 the matrix M is printed out with the regular MAT PRINT statement. This has the effect of printing out the elements of the matrix, row by row, in accordance with the dimension statement (4 × 4), printing each successive element in each of the first four standard printing fields.

Next, the matrix is printed in a more compact form by terminating the MAT PRINT instruction with a semicolon.

The IMAGE statement in line 310 specifies that each line of output should contain four fields with three digits allocated to each element of the matrix. The presence of the slash terminates the line after four elements have been printed. To illustrate the effect of the slash, we have omitted it in line 340 with the result that the whole matrix is printed on one line. The same effect is achieved when the IMAGE is set to 3D instead of 4(3D), since the format is repeated until the matrix is exhausted.

Finally, in statements 390 and 400 the matrix is printed out two elements per row. This illustrates that by taking advantage of the PRINT USING statement, a matrix may be printed out in a form other than that specified by the dimension statement.

Program 13-8

```
100  PRINT "********************"
110  PRINT "*                  *"
120  PRINT "*  PRINT USING WITH  *"
130  PRINT "*                  *"
140  PRINT "*     MATRICES      *"
150  PRINT "*                  *"
160  PRINT "********************"
170  PRINT
180  DIM M[4,4]
190  LET K=0
200  FOR I=1 TO 4
210  FOR J=1 TO 4
220  LET K=K+1
230  LET M[I,J]=K
240  NEXT J
250  NEXT I
260  MAT  PRINT M
270  PRINT
280  MAT  PRINT M;
290  PRINT
300  MAT  PRINT  USING 310; M
310  IMAGE 4(3D)/
320  PRINT
330  MAT  PRINT  USING 340; M
340  IMAGE 4(3D)
350  PRINT
360  MAT  PRINT  USING 370; M
370  IMAGE 3D
380  PRINT
390  MAT  PRINT  USING 400; M
400  IMAGE 2(3D)/
410  END
```

```
RUN

********************
*                  *
*  PRINT USING WITH  *
*                  *
*     MATRICES      *
*                  *
********************

    1           2           3           4

    5           6           7           8

    9          10          11          12

   13          14          15          16
```

```
 1    2    3    4

 5    6    7    8

 9   1Ø   11   12

13   14   15   16


  1  2  3  4
  5  6  7  8
  9 1Ø 11 12
 13 14 15 16


 1 2 3 4 5 6 7 8 9 1Ø 11 12 13 14 15 16

 1 2 3 4 5 6 7 8 9 1Ø 11 12 13 14 15 16

  1  2
  3  4
  5  6
  7  8
  9 1Ø
 11 12
 13 14
 15 16


DONE
```

QUICK REFERENCE GUIDE TO CHAPTER THIRTEEN

Item	General Form	Examples
1. PRINT USING statement	*Line number* PRINT USING *line number; variable list*	100 PRINT USING 150; X 200 PRINT USING 920; A,B,C
	Line number PRINT USING *string variable; variable list*	100 PRINT USING X1; A 200 PRINT USING B$; X,Y,Z
	Line number PRINT USING *"image"; variable list*	100 PRINT USING "DDD.DD"; X 200 PRINT USING "AAA/$DD"; B$, B
2. IMAGE statement	*Line number* IMAGE *image specifications*	100 IMAGE 3D.4D 200 IMAGE 5X,6D, 4D, SD.SDE
3. MAT PRINT USING	*Line number* MAT PRINT USING $\begin{Bmatrix} \textit{line number} \\ \textit{string variable} \\ \textit{"image"} \end{Bmatrix}$ *matrix name*	100 MAT PRINT USING 150; X 200 MAT PRINT USING C$; Z 300 MAT PRINT USING "8(DD.D, 4X)/"; G

Questions

1. Rewrite the compound interest program described in Question 18 of Chapter Six with the following modifications:

   (a) Use an INPUT statement that permits the user to insert *arbitrary* values for the number of years, amount of original investment, and annual rates of interest. Provide instructions for the user.

   When this inputted data is printed out, use 2D, 5D.2D, and 2D.3D as format specifications for the number of years, amount of original investment, and annual rate of interest, respectively.

   (b) Prepare a suitable heading (include the amount of the original investment).

   (c) Label your output so that the actual interest rates are printed in the appropriate columns. For example,

YR	1.000 %	1.250 %	1.500 %	1.750 %
1	$10100.00	$10125.00	$10150.00	$10175.00
.	.	.	.	.
.	.	.	.	.
.	.	.	.	.

   (d) Run your program for the following input data:

   Case 1 number of years = 10
   original investment = $10,000.00
   rates of interest = $1\frac{1}{8}$ %, $1\frac{1}{4}$ %, $1\frac{3}{8}$ %, $1\frac{1}{2}$ %

   Case 2 number of years = 20
   original investment = $5,000.00
   rates of interest = 7%, $7\frac{1}{4}$ %; $7\frac{1}{2}$ %, $7\frac{3}{4}$ %.

CHAPTER FOURTEEN

FILES

In all the programs presented and illustrated so far, input has been entered as part of a data statement, or was "inputted" upon execution of an INPUT statement, or else was defined within the body of the program by means of a LET statement. Under certain circumstances, however, it may be convenient to separate the data from the program by means of *files*.

One such situation is when several different programs access the same data items. It would be both redundant and wasteful of computer storage space to have duplicate copies of the data for each of the accessing programs. A change in one data item would necessitate a change in all of the data sets.

A file is simply a sequence of data items (records) recorded on some storage device, such as a disk. A disk is somewhat similar (in appearance only) to a phonograph record, which incidentally is also a storage device in that it records whatever music or words has been impressed on it.

Information, in the form of magnetic spots, is recorded on the disk's surface. The common tape recorder is another good example of how magnetic spots may be used to record information. There is a further similarity between a disk and a tape recorder—information stored on both may be changed at will.

Unlike DATA statements, file information is stored separately from the program in the programmer's own, private, permanent library space. This permits direct and easy access of data information by any program that the user may write.

Once data is recorded in a file it may be modified or even erased under the control of a program. These operations, it is pointed out, cannot be done to ordinary DATA statements without manually retyping the DATA statement.

14.1 The OPEN Command

Before we can access a file in any way we must first allocate space for it on the disk. The disk is part of the hardware that comprises the computer system. It is separate from the memory, and in fact is regarded as a secondary storage device. As such it is capable of storing both numeric data and character strings. Access to the disk is initiated by an OPEN command. Since OPEN is a system command rather than an instruction, it is not part of a program and does not, therefore, take a statement number.

When a file is OPENed the user is allocated a certain area of the disk for his own use. The user is permitted to generate more than one file if need be, the only restriction being that the sum total of the space occupied by those files does not exceed his personal storage limit, as specified by his particular installation.

The general form of the OPEN command is:

OPEN-filename, #-of-records

A record is a physical subdivision of a file and may contain up to 128 numeric data items. When data takes the form of character strings, the maximum number of strings that may be stored on a file is determined by the length of the individual character strings. The shorter the strings the greater the number that may be stored. Specifically, eight 62-character strings will completely fill one record. Numeric and character strings may be intermixed within the same records. The approximate trade-off is one number for four characters.

14.2   Storing Data into a File

Once a file has been OPENed, and the space on the disk allocated, the programmer is at liberty to fill the file with the required data. Before a particular file can be accessed, it must be declared at the beginning of a program by means of the special statement:

FILES name-of-file

Once the file has been declared, data may be stored in the file. This is done by means of the following statement:

PRINT #n; list of variables (separated by comma)

when only one file is accessed, the number n should be 1. (The procedure for storing several files is discussed in Section 14.3.)

Program 14-1 is an illustration of the use of the FILES and PRINT #n; statements just described.

Program 14-1

OPEN-MIKE,1

```
100  PRINT "********************"
110  PRINT "*                  *"
120  PRINT "* A FILE GENERATING*"
130  PRINT "*                  *"
140  PRINT "*      PROGRAM      *"
150  PRINT "*                  *"
160  PRINT "********************"
170  PRINT
180  FILES MIKE
190  FOR I=1 TO 5
200  READ X,Y$
210  DATA 1,"A",5,"B",16,"X",11,"Y",5,"A"
220  PRINT #1;X,Y$
230  NEXT I
240  END
```

RUN

```
* * * * * * * * * * * * * * * * * * * * *
*                                        *
* A FILE GENERATING *
*                                        *
*         PROGRAM        *
*                                        *
* * * * * * * * * * * * * * * * * * * *
```

DONE

The effect of RUNning Program 14-1 is to store the 10 data items into the file arbitrarily labeled MIKE. To be completely sure that file MIKE contains what we think it does, it is always a good idea to check its contents by printing them out. This may be done by a special type of READ statement of the form:

READ #n; list of variable names

which must be included in a separate accessing program such as Program 14-2.

Program 14-2

```
100   PRINT "******************"
110   PRINT "*                        *"
120   PRINT "* A FILE ACCESSING *"
130   PRINT "*                        *"
140   PRINT "*      PROGRAM      *"
150   PRINT "*                        *"
160   PRINT "******************"
170   PRINT
180   FILES MIKE
190   FOR I=1 TO 5
200   READ #1;X,Y$
210   PRINT X,Y$
220   NEXT I
230   END
```

RUN

```
* * * * * * * * * * * * * * * * * *
*                              *
* A FILE ACCESSING *
*                              *
*       PROGRAM       *
*                              *
* * * * * * * * * * * * * * * * * *
```

1	A
5	B
16	X
11	Y
5	A

DONE

Once the program MIKE has been OPENed it may be filled by Program 14-1 and then accessed by Program 14-2. The file accessing program, like the file generating program, is headed by the special word FILES, followed by the name of the file being referenced.

14.3 The FILES Statement

Although Program 14-2 used only one file, the plural form of the noun FILES must still be used, as is done in line 180 of Programs 14-1 and 14-2. This, of course, implies that one does not have to restrict oneself to a single file. Indeed, on the HP-2000C a maximum of 16 files may be referenced in a single program. Following the word FILES, each file name is specified and separated by a comma.

The integer n in the READ #n; and the PRINT #n; statements is associated with the sequence number of the file being referenced in the FILES declaration statement. If n is 1, the *first*-named file is being referenced, if n is 2, it is the second file, etc. Do not forget that a semicolon must separate the value of n from the variable list.

14.4 Multifile Processing

As an example of multifile processing we present a series of programs designed to process some student-related data. In the file NAMES, student names are recorded, allowing for a maximum of 20 characters for each name. The file GPA contains the grade point average for each student named in the NAMES file. In the file called AWARDS is the value of the scholarship that each student has been awarded.

Program 14-3 generates the three data files. In order to make the program more general, the end of data is signalled by a type-in of the word END after the last name has been entered.

An Example of Multifile Processing

Program 14-3

```
OPEN-NAMES,1

OPEN-GPA,1

OPEN-AWARDS,1


100  PRINT "**************"
110  PRINT "*            *"
120  PRINT "* MULTI-FILE *"
130  PRINT "*            *"
140  PRINT "*PROCESSING *"
150  PRINT "*            *"
160  PRINT "**************"
```

```
170   PRINT
180   FILES NAMES,GPA,AWARDS
190   DIM N$[20]
200   PRINT "TYPE IN STUDENT'S NAME OR END."
210   INPUT N$
220   IF N$="END" THEN 310
230   PRINT #1;N$
240   PRINT "NOW TYPE IN THE GRADE POINT AVERAGE."
250   INPUT G
260   PRINT #2;G
270   PRINT "NOW TYPE IN THE AMOUNT OF AWARD."
280   INPUT A
290   PRINT #3;A
300   GO TO 200
310   END


RUN


*************
*           *
* MULTI-FILE *
*           *
* PROCESSING *
*           *
*************


TYPE IN STUDENT'S NAME OR END.
?ROSENTEL
NOW TYPE IN THE GRADE POINT AVERAGE.
?3.6
NOW TYPE IN THE AMOUNT OF AWARD.
?1000
TYPE IN STUDENT'S NAME OR END.
?HOROWITZ
NOW TYPE IN THE GRADE POINT AVERAGE.
?3.7
NOW TYPE IN THE AMOUNT OF AWARD.
?500
TYPE IN STUDENT'S NAME OR END.
?COURANT
NOW TYPE IN THE GRADE POINT AVERAGE.
?2.1
NOW TYPE IN THE AMOUNT OF AWARD.
?100
TYPE IN STUDENT'S NAME OR END.
?MULLISH
NOW TYPE IN THE GRADE POINT AVERAGE.
?1.7
NOW TYPE IN THE AMOUNT OF AWARD.
?50
```

TYPE IN STUDENT'S NAME OR END.
?TIER
NOW TYPE IN THE GRADE POINT AVERAGE.
?3.9
NOW TYPE IN THE AMOUNT OF AWARD.
?2000
TYPE IN STUDENT'S NAME OR END.
?END

DONE

14.5 Printing Out File Contents in a Tabular Form

Program 14-4 accesses the three files and prints their contents in tabular form. Advantage has been taken of a test to determine whether the end of the file has been reached. When the end of the file has been detected we would like to terminate the processing, because by that time the complete table has been printed.

Every BASIC system has its own method of determining whether an end of file has been encountered. On the HP-2000C it is by means of the IF END#n THEN statement, which in Program 14-4 behaves in the following way:

250 IF END #1 THEN 310

Statement 250 is executed only once during the processing of the program. From that time on the program is "alerted" to transfer to statement 310 when the end of file #1 is detected.

It will be noticed that only file #1 is tested for the end of file condition and not file #2 nor file #3. The reason for this is that file #1 in the program is the first file read and therefore will be the first whose end of file will be detected. If this statement were omitted or the file number substituted by file #2 or file #3, the end of file would have been encountered anyway, but provision for it would not have been made. As a result, the system would have printed out the error message:

END OF FILE/END OF RECORD IN STATEMENT 260

Program 14-4

```
100  PRINT "****************"
110  PRINT "*              *"
120  PRINT "* FILE CONTENTS*"
130  PRINT "*              *"
140  PRINT "*       IN     *"
150  PRINT "*              *"
160  PRINT "* TABULAR FORM *"
170  PRINT "*              *"
180  PRINT "****************"
190  PRINT
200  FILES NAMES,GPA,AWARDS
210  DIM N$[20]
220  PRINT "STUDENT", "G.  P.  A.", "AWARD"
230  PRINT "-------", "--------", "-----"
240  PRINT
```

```
250   IF END #1 THEN 310
260   READ #1,N$
270   READ #2;G
280   READ #3;A
290   PRINT N$,G,A
300   GO TO 250
310   END
```

```
RUN
FTABLE

****************
*              *
* FILE CONTENTS *
*              *
*      IN      *
*              *
* TABULAR FORM *
*              *
****************


STUDENT         G.  P.  A.         AWARD
- - - - - - -   - - - - - - - -    - - - - -


ROSENTEL        3.6               1000
HOROWITZ        3.7               500
COURANT         2.1               100
MULLISH         1.7               50
TIER            3.9               2000

DONE
```

Suppose now we were interested in examining one of the three files we have generated for the purpose of obtaining some elementary statistics on its data. For example, we might want to know the average grade point average. Therefore, only the GPA file need be accessed. Because of its position in the FILES statement, it is now designated as file #1. Obviously, we would have to make a count and a sum of the GPAs present. This is, in fact, done in the following program where C is the count and S is the sum. Notice that the IF END #1 statement obviates the need for a trailer.

Program 14-5

```
100   PRINT "****************"
110   PRINT "*              *"
120   PRINT "* TO  FIND  THE *"
130   PRINT "*              *"
140   PRINT "* AVERAGE GPA *"
150   PRINT "*              *"
160   PRINT "****************"
170   PRINT
180   FILES GPA
```

```
190  IF END #1 THEN 250
200  LET S=C=0
210  READ #1;C
220  LET C=C+1
230  LET S=S+C
240  GO TO 210
250  PRINT "THE AVERAGE GPA IS";S/C
260  END
```

RUN

```
* * * * * * * * * * * * * * * *
*                             *
* TO  FIND  THE *
*                             *
* AVERAGE GPA *
*                             *
* * * * * * * * * * * * * * * *
```

THE AVERAGE GPA IS 3

DONE

   Thus far we have not altered the contents of any of the files. Suppose, however, it were decided that the scholarship award of every student with a GPA of 3.5 or above were to be increased by 10%. In order to accomplish this, each GPA would have to be examined individually and the corresponding award multiplied by a factor of 1.1 if the GPA were 3.5 or better. Once this was done the AWARDS file could be updated.

   In Program 14-6, which actually updates the GPA file, there are several points that bear explanation.

1. The files named in the FILES statement are not in the same order as previously. This is perfectly acceptable provided the programmer takes care to properly identify the relevant files by the selected sequence number in the READ and PRINT statements.

2. In order to update the AWARDS file, a working copy of the extra file has to be made. The array X(50) is used for this purpose. The maximum number of elements allowed is set to 50 but the actual number of elements used is computed within the program. The index I of the loop in statement 210 is used as the counter. This is subsequently referred to as C.

3. The variable name used for reading file #1, the AWARDS file, is M rather than A (the name used when the file was originally generated). Although this may appear to be inconsistent, remember that the selection of variable names is quite arbitrary.

4. When G is less than 3.5 the award is not altered. Its value is merely saved in array X. For a G of 3.5 or above the value M is increased 10%, and this new incremented value is then stored in array X.

5. Before rewriting the AWARDS file we have to position it at its beginning point so that the rewrite will erase the original contents of the file. This is done by means of the READ #1,1 statement. The trailing ",1" has the effect of rewinding file #1 to the start of record #1 (i.e., to the beginning of the file). If the file is

not rewound before the rewriting begins, the original data would remain and it would be followed by the updated data, which is not the intention here.

Here then is the program to update the awards file.

Program 14-6

```
100   PRINT "*****************"
110   PRINT "*                *"
120   PRINT "* TO UPDATE THE*"
130   PRINT "*                *"
140   PRINT "* AWARDS    FILE*"
150   PRINT "*                *"
160   PRINT "*****************"
170   PRINT
180   FILES AWARDS,GPA
190   DIM X[50]
200   IF END #1 THEN 290
210   FOR I=1 TO 50
220   READ #1;M
230   READ #2;C
240   IF C<3.5 THEN 260
250   LET M=1.1*M
260   LET X[I]=M
270   NEXT I
280   LET I=51
290   LET C=I-1
300   READ #1,1
310   FOR J=1 TO C
320   PRINT #1;X[J]
330   NEXT J
340   END
```

RUN

```
*****************
*                *
* TO UPDATE THE*
*                *
* AWARDS    FILE*
*                *
*****************
```

DONE

In the output of Program 14-6, no printout apart from the caption follows the listing of the program. In order to confirm that the awards file has in fact been updated, it behooves us to rerun the program called "File Contents in Tabular Form." No change whatever is made to the program itself; nevertheless, the updated run clearly shows that the output is different from the original and reflects accurately the effect of the update program.

Program 14-7

```
100  PRINT "*****************"
110  PRINT "*               *"
120  PRINT "*FILE CONTENTS*"
130  PRINT "*               *"
140  PRINT "*        IN      *"
150  PRINT "*               *"
160  PRINT "*TABULAR FORM*"
170  PRINT "*               *"
180  PRINT "*****************"
190  PRINT
200  FILES NAMES,GPA,AWARDS
210  DIM N$[20]
220  PRINT "STUDENT","G. P. A.","AWARD"
230  PRINT "_____","_____","_____"
240  PRINT
250  IF END #1 THEN 310
260  READ #1;N$
270  READ #2;G
280  READ #3;A
290  PRINT N$,B,A
300  GO TO 250
310  END


RUN


*****************
*               *
*FILE CONTENTS*
*               *
*        IN      *
*               *
*TABULAR FORM*
*               *
*****************

STUDENT        G. P. A.       AWARD
_____        _____       _____


ROSENTEL       3.6            1100
HOROWITZ       3.7            550
COURANT        2.1            100
MULLISH        1.7            50
TIER           3.9            2200

DONE
```

14.6 The TYP Function

When accessing a file it is necessary to know in advance whether the particular data item being accessed is a number, a character string, or the end-of-file. The purpose of the TYP function is to test the data item in order to avoid a mismatch of variable type. The three possibilities are characterized by number, according to the following scheme:

1, if the next item is numeric
2, if the next item is a character string
3, if the next item is an end-of-file

For example, if we are dealing with file #4 we could write the following:

100 IF TYP(4) = 2 THEN 200

This is interpreted as meaning that if the data item about to be read on file #4 is a character string then execution should be transferred to statement 200.

Another example is the following:

400 IF TYP(8) = 3 THEN 800

this is translated to: if the data item being accessed on file #8 is an end-of-file, send control to statement 800.

As a further example of the use of the TYP function consider the following:

500 GO TO TYP(X) OF 600, 700, 800

This implies that X is a variable name associated with a file number. If the data TYP is equal to 1, meaning that the data item is numeric, control goes to statement 600, the first of the branches. If it is a character string, control is sent to the second branch, statement 700, while if it is an end-of-file that is being accessed, control is transferred to the third branch, statement 800.

If the file number is set equal to zero the TYP function will reference the DATA statements in the program. In this case TYP returns:

1 for numeric data
2 for character strings
3 for the out-of-data condition

This third alternative makes the TYP function an obvious choice for a trailer substitute.

Program 14-8 copies a random sequence of numeric and string data into two separate files, one of which will hold the numeric data and the other will hold character strings.

Program 14-8

```
100   PRINT "**************************"
110   PRINT "*                        *"
120   PRINT "*AN ILLUSTRATION OF THE*"
130   PRINT "*                        *"
140   PRINT "*TYP  FUNCTION  IN  FILES*"
150   PRINT "*                        *"
160   PRINT "**************************"
170   PRINT
180   FILES NUMER,ALPHA
190   DIM A$[72],C$[72]
200   DATA 14.9,"HELLO",57.36,"GOODBYE"
210   DATA "GLAD TO SEE YOU",1976,123456.
220   GO TO TYP(0) OF 230,260,290
230   READ N
```

```
240  PRINT #1;N
250  GO TO 220
260  READ A$
270  PRINT #2;A$
280  GO TO 220
290  READ #1,1
300  READ #2,1
310  PRINT "THIS IS THE NUMERIC DATA"
320  IF END #1 THEN 360
330  READ #1;M
340  PRINT M
350  GO TO 330
360  PRINT "THIS IS THE ALPHABETIC DATA"
370  IF END #2 THEN 410
380  READ #2;C$
390  PRINT C$
400  GO TO 380
410  END
```

OPEN-NUMBER,1
OPEN-ALPHA,1

RUN

```
**************************
*                        *
*AN ILLUSTRATION OF THE*
*                        *
*TYP  FUNCTION  IN  FILES*
*                        *
**************************
```

THIS IS THE NUMERIC DATA
 14.9
 57.36
 1976
 123456.
THIS IS THE ALPHABETIC DATA
HELLO
GOODBYE
GLAD TO SEE YOU

DONE

In Program 14-8, two files, NUMER and ALPHA, are declared in statement 180. The data statements contain a mixture of numeric constants and literals in random order. In line 220, where the TYP function is used, the file number is set equal to zero, causing direct reference to the DATA statements. If the data item is numeric, control is sent to the *first* of the three branches. That is to say, if a numeric constant is encountered in the DATA statement, control is sent to statement 230, at which point the data item is read into a numeric variable N, and written on the file named NUMER. After writing out the value of N, the TYP function is executed again as a result of looping back via the GO TO 220 statement. If, on the other hand, a character string item is encountered, control is passed to line 260 where the character data item is read into a string variable A$ and subsequently written on the file named ALPHA. Once again, we return to statement 220.

When an out-of-data condition is reached, control of execution is passed to lines 290 and 300, which has the effect of repositioning the files NUMER and ALPHA to the first data item in each file; in other words the files NUMER and ALPHA are "rewound." Subsequently, the files NUMBER and ALPHA are printed out on paper in the ordinary way.

14.7 Random Accessing of Records

14.7.1 Moving the Pointer

Until now we have created files and subsequently read the files in a sequential manner. In other words, we have conveniently ignored the fact that the file is made up of a discrete number of records. The system automatically accesses each record of the file one after the other. Actually, this procedure is perfectly satisfactory for most programming situations. Nevertheless, it is sometimes necessary to access records of a file in a *random* fashion, rather than sequentially. Obviously, it would be necessary to have the ability to access a particular record and to know in advance when the end of that record has been encountered. To achieve this, it is essential to move the pointer to the beginning of the specified record. This is done as follows:

100 READ #1, N

where N is either specifically defined or is computed. The effect of this statement is to reposition the pointer to the beginning of record N. If N happens to be equal to 1 we have our familiar rewind statement.

Corresponding to the random access file READ statement is a random access file PRINT statement of the form:

100 PRINT #1, N

However, this statement has the effect of erasing the contents of record number N.

Both the random access READ and PRINT statements have an alternative form permitting the reading and writing of a list of variables, while simultaneously positioning the file to the record numbered N. For example,

100 READ #1, N; A, B, C
200 PRINT #2, N; X, Y, Z

14.8 An Example of Random Accessing

To illustrate the use of the random access files Program 14-9 is offered. It is designed to convert the computer from a teaching machine to a learning machine. The computer "learns" by means of a game that resembles the familiar "Twenty Questions." The competitor sitting at the terminal is asked to think of an animal. The first time the program is run the computer "knows" of only one animal, a cat. Chances are that this is not the animal the user thought of. If this is the case, the com-

puter will solicit the name of the animal and will ask for a specific question capable
of identifying that animal. The name of the new animal and its associated question
are then saved in the file named (appropriately) ZOO. From this point on the computer will be able to identify the new animal. In effect the file ZOO will increase in
factual information each time it fails to identify an animal.

All the user has to do is to open the file ZOO and run the program. What follows is
a listing of the initialization program and the actual animal guessing game program
with some sample output.

Program 14-9

```
100  PRINT "******************************"
110  PRINT "*                            *"
120  PRINT "* INITIALIZATION      ROUTINE *"
130  PRINT "*                            *"
140  PRINT "* FOR ANIMAL GUESSING GAME *"
150  PRINT "*                            *"
160  PRINT "******************************"
170  PRINT
180  FILES ZOO
190  PRINT #1,1;3
200  PRINT #1,2;"IS IT A CAT",0,0
210  END


OPEN-ZOO,10

RUN


******************************
*                            *
* INITIALIZATION      ROUTINE *
*                            *
* FOR ANIMAL GUESSING GAME *
*                            *
******************************


DONE
```

Program 14-10

```
100  PRINT "*************************************"
110  PRINT "*                                   *"
120  PRINT "*ILLUSTRATION  OF  RANDOM  ACCESS*"
130  PRINT "*                                   *"
140  PRINT "*FILES USING ANIMAL GUESSING GAME*"
150  PRINT "*                                   *"
160  PRINT "*************************************"
170  PRINT
180  FILES ZOO
190  DIM Q$[70],A$[10],B$[70],C$[70]
200  PRINT "THIS IS AN ANIMAL GUESSING GAME."
```

```
210   PRINT "I WILL ASK THE QUESTIONS AND YOU WILL"
220   PRINT "RESPOND WITH YES OR NO"
230   PRINT
240   REM FIRST QUESTION IS IN RECORD NUMBER 2, Q=2
250   LET Q=2
260   LET B$="IS IT "
270   PRINT "NOW THINK OF THE NAME OF AN ANIMAL"
280   PRINT
290   REM READ IN CURRENT QUESTION Q$, YES BRANCH Y, AND NO BRANCH N
300   READ #1,Q;Q$,Y,N
310   REM ASK THE QUESTION
320   PRINT Q$;
330   INPUT A$
340   IF A$="YES" THEN 390
350   IF A$="NO" THEN 460
360   PRINT "CAN'T YOU ANSWER A SIMPLE QUESTION WITH A"
370   PRINT "SIMPLE YES OR NO?!"
380   GO TO 320
390   REM IF YES BRANCH IS ZERO WE HAVE GUESSED THE ANIMAL CORRECTLY
400   IF Y=0 THEN 440
410   REM OTHERWISE Y POINTS TO THE NEXT QUESTION TO BE ASKED
420   LET Q=Y
430   GO TO 300
440   PRINT "YIPPIE!!  BIG BROTHER GUESSED IT!"
450   GO TO 700
460   REM IF NO BRANCH IS ZERO WE HAVE FAILED TO GUESS CORRECTLY
470   IF N=0 THEN 510
480   REM ELSE LET NEXT QUESTION BE #N
490   LET Q=N
500   GO TO 300
510   PRINT "I GIVE UP.  WHAT ANIMAL WERE YOU THINKING OF";
520   INPUT B$[7]
530   PRINT
540   PRINT "NOW TYPE IN A QUESTION TO WHICH THE ANSWER WILL BE YES FOR"
550   PRINT B$[7]" AND NO FOR "Q$[7]
560   INPUT C$
570   REM NOW SET UP FOR AN UPDATE FOR ZOO FILE.
580   REM LOCATE FIRST AVAILABLE RECORD
590   READ #1,1;F
600   REM MOVE OLD QUESTION TO RECORD NUMBER F
610   PRINT #1,F;Q$,Y,N
620   REM PUT ANIMAL GUESS IN RECORD NUMBER F+1
630   PRINT #1,F+1;B$,0,0
640   REM PUT NEW QUESTION WHERE OLD QUESTION USED TO BE AND
650   REM LET YES AND NO BRANCH POINT TO ABOVE TWO RECORDS
660   PRINT #1,Q;C$,F+1,F
670   REM FIRST AVAILABLE RECORD IS NOW TWO RECORDS HIGHER
680   PRINT #1,1;F+2
690   PRINT "THANK YOU."
700   PRINT
710   PRINT "DO YOU WANT TO CONTINUE";
```

```
720  INPUT A$
730  IF A$="YES" THEN 230
740  IF A$="NO" THEN 760
750  PRINT "WELL, I DON'T FEEL LIKE PLAYING ANY MORE."
760  END
```

RUN

```
**************************************
*                                    *
*ILLUSTRATION  OF  RANDOM  ACCESS*
*                                    *
*FILES USING ANIMAL GUESSING GAME*
*                                    *
**************************************
```

THIS IS AN ANIMAL GUESSING GAME.
I WILL ASK THE QUESTIONS AND YOU WILL
RESPOND WITH YES OR NO

NOW THINK OF THE NAME OF AN ANIMAL

IS IT A CAT?NO
I GIVE UP. WHAT ANIMAL WERE YOU THINKING OF?AN ANT

NOW TYPE IN A QUESTION TO WHICH THE ANSWER WILL BE YES FOR
AN ANT AND NO FOR A CAT
?IS IT AN INVERTEBRATE
THANK YOU.

DO YOU WANT TO CONTINUE?YES

NOW THINK OF THE NAME OF AN ANIMAL

IS IT AN INVERTEBRATE?NO
IS IT A CAT?NO
I GIVE UP. WHAT ANIMAL WERE YOU THINKING OF?A SHARK

NOW TYPE IN A QUESTION TO WHICH THE ANSWER WILL BE YES FOR
A SHARK AND NO FOR A CAT
?DOES IT SWIM IN THE WATER
THANK YOU.

DO YOU WANT TO CONTINUE?YES

NOW THINK OF THE NAME OF AN ANIMAL

```
IS IT AN INVERTEBRATE?MAYBE
CAN'T YOU ANSWER A SIMPLE QUESTION WITH A
SIMPLE YES OR NO?!
IS IT AN INVERTEBRATE?YES
IS IT AN ANT?NO
I GIVE UP.  WHAT ANIMAL WERE YOU THINKING OF?AN AMOEBA

NOW TYPE IN A QUESTION TO WHICH THE ANSWER WILL BE YES FOR
AN AMOEBA AND NO FOR AN ANT
?IS IT MICROSCOPIC
THANK YOU.

DO YOU WANT TO CONTINUE?YES

NOW THINK OF THE NAME OF AN ANIMAL

IS IT AN INVERTEBRATE?YES
IS IT MICROSCOPIC?NO
IS IT AN ANT?YES
YIPPIE!!  BIG BROTHER GUESSED IT!

DO YOU WANT TO CONTINUE?LATER
WELL, I DON'T FEEL LIKE PLAYING ANY MORE.

DONE

RUN

**************************************
*                                    *
*ILLUSTRATION  OF  RANDOM  ACCESS*
*                                    *
*FILES USING ANIMAL GUESSING GAME*
*                                    *
**************************************

THIS IS AN ANIMAL GUESSING GAME.
I WILL ASK THE QUESTIONS AND YOU WILL
RESPOND WITH YES OR NO

NOW THINK OF THE NAME OF AN ANIMAL

IS IT AN INVERTEBRATE?NO
DOES IT SWIM IN THE WATER?NO
IS IT A CAT?NO
I GIVE UP.  WHAT ANIMAL WERE YOU THINKING OF?A BIRD

NOW TYPE IN A QUESTION TO WHICH THE ANSWER WILL BE YES FOR
A BIRD AND NO FOR A CAT
?CAN IT FLY
THANK YOU.
```

DO YOU WANT TO CONTINUE?YES

NOW THINK OF THE NAME OF AN ANIMAL

IS IT AN INVERTEBRATE?NO
DOES IT SWIM IN THE WATER?YES
IS IT A SHARK?YES
YIPPIE!! BIG BROTHER GUESSED IT!

DO YOU WANT TO CONTINUE?YES

NOW THINK OF THE NAME OF AN ANIMAL

IS IT AN INVERTEBRATE?NO
DOES IT SWIM IN THE WATER?NO
CAN IT FLY?NO
IS IT A CAT?YES
YIPPIE!! BIG BROTHER GUESSED IT!

DO YOU WANT TO CONTINUE?YES

NOW THINK OF THE NAME OF AN ANIMAL

IS IT AN INVERTEBRATE?YES
IS IT MICROSCOPIC?YES
IS IT AN AMOEBA?YES
YIPPIE!! BIG BROTHER GUESSED IT!

DO YOU WANT TO CONTINUE?NO

DONE

14.9   Using the TYP Function with Records

Earlier, we saw how the TYP function could be used to determine the type of data item being accessed, and also how it could be used to determine either an out-of-data condition or an end-of-file condition. The TYP function has an additional use in determining the type of the next item in a specified file. The file number is preceded by a negative sign and it returns a code 1 through 4 in accordance with the following scheme:

1 numeric data item
2 character string
3 end-of-file
4 end-of-record.

A typical example is:

100 GO TO TYP (−1) OF 200,300,400,500

QUICK REFERENCE GUIDE TO CHAPTER FOURTEEN

Item	General Form	Examples
1. OPEN command	OPEN-*file name, # of records*	OPEN-POMPA, 3
2. FILES statement	*Line number* FILES *filename, . . .*	100 FILES BOB 200 FILES *BUNNY
3. File PRINT statement	*Line number* PRINT# *expression; variable list*	100 PRINT #1; A,B,C 200 PRINT #N; X, Y$ 300 PRINT #(3*J); "BEATRICE", I2
4. File READ statement	*Line number* READ # *expression; variable list*	100 READ #1; A,B,C 200 READ #N; X, Y$ 300 PRINT #(3*J); A$, I2
5. End-of-file test	*Line number* IF END # *expression* THEN *line number*	100 IF END #3 THEN 150 200 IF END #N THEN 250 300 IF END #(3*J) THEN 350
6. Rewind statement	*Line number* READ # *expression*, 1	100 READ #1, 1 200 READ #N, 1 300 READ #(3*J), 1
7. TYP function	TYP(n), *where* n = 0 *refers to* DATA *statement* n > 0 *refers to file* #n	100 IF TYP (3) = 2 THEN 200 200 GOTO TYP (5) OF 300, 400, 500
8. Random access file READ statement	*Line number* READ # *expression, expression; variable list.*	100 READ #1, 1 200 READ #N, X; A,B,C 300 READ #2, Y; D,E
9. Random access file PRINT statement	*Line number* PRINT # *expression, expression; variable list*	100 PRINT #1, N 200 PRINT #1, Z; A,B

Questions

1. There are four means by which a value can be given to a variable: the LET assignment, the terminal INPUT statement, reading from DATA statements, and reading from files. Discuss the use of these various methods. When is each appropriate or advantageous?

CHAPTER FIFTEEN

TAKING THE PLUNGE

The fun of programming is doing it. With BASIC, doing is learning!

In this chapter we explain exactly how to transmit a BASIC program to the computer via the Teletype. Every user is assigned a unique user number and the associated password. This permits a certain amount of accounting to be done at the system level and prevents the system from confusing your program with someone else's. By carefully following the steps listed below, you should have no difficulty in running any program.

1. Sit down at the Teletype and turn it on by depressing the appropriate switch. The ON light goes on. If the LOCAL light goes on as well, turn it off. The light that illuminates the printing area should go on after a few seconds. The machine might type out a few characters before it is properly warmed up. If this happens, depress the escape key (labeled esc) to clear the machine. (When you press the esc key the computer will type a back slash (" \ ") and move to the next line.)

2. Type in the word HELLO (or HEL) followed by a dash (which is also the minus sign), the user number, a comma, and the password. Passwords may contain characters that do not print on the Teletype. These characters are referred to as "control" characters and are written with a letter of the alphabet and a superscript C. For example the character "control A" is written as A^C. Since the Olivetti terminals do not use lowercase letters, to type an "A" one need only press the A key; but to type a B^C ("control B"), one must press the B key while holding down the black "shift" key (which is therefore called the "control" key). Typed instructions are transmitted only after the return key is pressed; this causes the typed line to be sent for processing to the computer.

   Here are some typical examples of log-ins:

   ```
   HELLO-K503,QEᶜDᶜ
   HELLO-X007,USA
   HEL-A000,ST
   HELL-D747,SEX
   ```

   When typing the log-in instruction (the HELLO command) no spaces are permitted between characters. Don't forget to press the return key after logging in. Should you make a mistake by pressing the wrong key, it can be corrected by typing a "back-arrow" (←) for each character in error. To erase the whole line, press the escape key, esc. It will respond by typing a back slash, \, and advancing to the next line.

3. If everything is in order, the system will type out a message, one that will, we hope, be of interest to the user.

4. It is an excellent practice to select a name for the program you are about to write. It can be any name you like, as long as it is no more than 6 characters and does not begin with either a $ or an asterisk. The name is assigned by means of the NAMe command. (The e may be omitted.) So you could type, for example:

NAM-FIRST

NAM-CUBES

NAM-STEVE

(Don't forget the return key.)

The machine will respond by advancing to the next line.

5. Type in your program making sure that each line has a line number, and an END statement is present.

There are three kinds of error messages you may have the misfortune to receive before the program is completed.

(a) A succession of three question marks. This means that the system is hopelessly confused by your most recent instruction, which is, therefore, rejected.

(b) A short descriptive message such as: ILLEGAL ACCESS (user number or password incorrect). Or it may type: ONLY 6 CHARACTERS ACCEPTED if more than six character were used in naming the program.

(c) The machine types the word ERROR and pauses. This means that the syntax analyzer, the part of the system that checks for the legality of an instruction, has found a syntactical error in the last line. You may hit the return key and retype the line correctly, or you may type any character (one usually types a colon or a dash) and then hit the return button. The computer will then print out a diagnostic message detailing the error. It then advances to a new line and waits for you to retype the statement.

15.1 Running a Program

Having typed in a program it is usually a good idea to have the computer LISt your program for you so that you can be doubly sure that what was typed in was what you intended to type in. It is surprising how often this is *not* the case.

Assuming the program was named PROB1, one types in the instruction LISt. (The t may be omitted; it will work just as well.) Upon hitting the return key the machine will type the name of the current program and will print a complete listing of the program.

If a line contains an error, the line number should be retyped and the correct line entered. If all appears well and you wish to have the computer execute the program, the word RUN is typed. This initiates the process of compilation and execution.

If the program is correctly written and works, any output will be printed, and the program will successfully terminate, printing the word DONE, and advance to a new line, signifying that the computer is awaiting a command. To get off the computer the command BYE is typed in and the computer responds by printing out some information relating to the time you have spent on the system. At that point the ON/OFF button should be pressed and you can then rip off your paper output; pressing the round, blue paper-feed button if necessary before you press the ON/OFF switch.

On the other hand, if after typing in RUN, the computer detects errors in your program, such as a GO TO statement to a nonexistent line, the computer will print an appropriate diagnostic message and come to a grinding halt. A correction to a statement may be made directly by retyping the statement correctly. If a line is to be deleted entirely, all one need do is type the line number and nothing else. Hitting the return key will eliminate the original line from the program.

If, in the middle or a run, it becomes obvious that there is an error in the program, execution may be halted by one of two methods.

1. As long as the machine is not waiting for an INPUT command to be satisfied, the button marked BRK (for break), located in the lower right-hand corner near the ON-OFF switch, is pressed. Execution is aborted, the word STOP is printed, and the machine returns to command mode.
2. If the machine is, in fact, awaiting input, one should type in control C (i.e., shift key down while C key is pressed). Hitting the return key has the same effect as in (1) above.

15.2 RENumbering a Program

After a few corrections have been made to a program and some lines inserted and others deleted, the order of the line numbers can become quite uneven. In this case, it is usually a good idea to renumber the program. Retyping the whole program is not necessary; an infinitely better idea is to take advantage of the system's renumbering feature. To do this, you simply type in the word RENumber. This automatically refers to the current program. There are several options open to you. You can:

1. Hit the return key. This has the effect of renumbering the program from line 10 in steps of 10, changing all cross-references in GO TOs, GOSUBs etc., to refer to the correct line number. The only line numbers not affected are those included in REMark statements or enclosed within quotes.
2. REN–*integer* (return). This will cause the system to renumber the program starting from that integer and going in steps of 10. In fact, all of the programs shown in this book were renumbered by the instruction:

REN–100 (return)

3. REN–*integer$_1$*,*integer$_2$*. This has the effect of renumbering the statements of the program starting with *integer$_1$* and going up in steps of *integer$_2$*.

In the very contrived program that follows (Program 15-1), the original program was deliberately written with erratically ascending line numbers. The command REN–100 was then invoked and the program relisted. Notice that all the statement numbers have been adjusted so that, with the new listing beginning at line 100, all the branching is correct relative to this new base line number. The new listing is not only more appealing to the eye but, because the interval between each line number is 10, any future amendments may easily be made.

Program 15-1

```
 1  PRINT "*******************"
 2  PRINT "* AN EXAMPLE OF *"
 3  PRINT "* THE EFFICIENCY *"
 4  PRINT "*     OF  REN     *"
 5  PRINT "*******************"
 9  LET J=0
11  GO TO 46
15  PRINT TAB(J); "S";
18  GO TO 46
27  PRINT TAB(J); "E"
```

```
 29  GO TO 46
 46  LET J=J+5
 49  IF J=35 THEN 998
 54  IF J=5 THEN 15
 71  IF J=1Ø THEN 111
 79  IF J=15 THEN 2Ø1
 83  IF J=2Ø THEN 147
 87  IF J=25 THEN 177
 89  IF J=3Ø THEN 27
 94  GO TO 998
111  PRINT TAB(J); "I";
113  GO TO 46
147  PRINT TAB(J); "P";
148  GO TO 46
177  PRINT TAB(J); "L";
179  GO TO 46
2Ø1  PRINT TAB(J); "M";
2Ø4  GO TO 46
998  END
```

REN-1ØØ

LIST

```
1ØØ  PRINT "*******************"
11Ø  PRINT "* AN EXAMPLE OF *"
12Ø  PRINT "* THE EFFICIENCY *"
13Ø  PRINT "*     OF  REN     *"
14Ø  PRINT "*******************"
15Ø  LET J=Ø
16Ø  GO TO 21Ø
17Ø  PRINT TAB(J); "S";
18Ø  GO TO 21Ø
19Ø  PRINT TAB(J); "E"
2ØØ  GO TO 21Ø
21Ø  LET J=J+5
22Ø  IF J=35 THEN 38Ø
23Ø  IF J=5 THEN 17Ø
24Ø  IF J=1Ø THEN 3ØØ
25Ø  IF J=15 THEN 36Ø
26Ø  IF J=2Ø THEN 32Ø
27Ø  IF J=25 THEN 34Ø
28Ø  IF J=3Ø THEN 19Ø
29Ø  GO TO 38Ø
3ØØ  PRINT TAB(J); "I";
31Ø  GO TO 21Ø
32Ø  PRINT TAB(J); "P";
33Ø  GO TO 21Ø
34Ø  PRINT TAB(J); "L";
35Ø  GO TO 21Ø
```

```
36Ø  PRINT TAB(J); "M";
37Ø  GO TO 21Ø
38Ø  END


RUN

*******************
* AN EXAMPLE OF *
* THE EFFICIENCY *
*     OF  REN     *
*******************

        S      I      M      P      L      E

DONE
```

15.3 Starting from SCRatch

When one has completely finished with a program and wishes to start another or if one becomes so disgusted with a current program that he wishes to begin it again— from "scratch"—one may delete whatever has been done by typing in SCRatch. This automatically deletes the current program but retains the name that was assigned to it.

15.4 SAVe, GET, KILl and CATalog

For those frequent occasions when you have succeeded in writing an exceptionally brilliant program that you wish to preserve for posterity (or at least until the end of the semester) or you are in the midst of a complex program that you wish to continue at some other time, there is a command that allows you to SAVe the program by name. The instruction SAV will preserve the program under the name last specified by a NAMe command.

Once a program named, say, PROB1 has been SAVed, it may be recalled subsequently by typing in the name GET-PROB1. To print it out, the LISt command is used.

To irretrievably erase a program that has been saved one uses the command KILl. To erase our program PROB1 we would type in:

KIL–PROB1

All programs that have been SAVed are placed in secondary storage (such as on a magnetic disk file). In order to determine which files, if any, have been SAVed and some details about them, one can ask the computer to print a catalog of those files. This is done by typing the command CATalog. This causes the system to print out the names of the files, their lengths, and their type.

15.4.1   Amending a SAVed Program

Suppose now a program named PROG1 is SAVed and is to be recalled for modification. The command GET-PROG1 will retrieve the program and work on it may be begun immediately, perhaps after listing the program. However, when the modifications have been completed, and the program checked out by trial runs, you should remember that it is the original program PROG1, not the amended PROG1, which is still SAVed in the CATalog. A subsequent GET-PROG1 will retrieve the *original*

PROG1, before it was amended and checked out, perhaps forcing the user to duplicate all her hard work.

Assuming that PROG1 was retrieved from the CATalog and had been amended the following procedure is recommended:

KIL-PROG1

This deletes the original (SAVed) program but does not affect the current program which happens to be named PROG1.

SAV

This saves the current, amended version of PROG1 for subsequent use.

15.5 Punching Paper Tape

In order to provide for backup and transfer of a program, it is possible to copy a program by punching it on paper tape. Each Olivetti terminal has a mechanism for punching tape. (But examine the tape punch; it is quite possible that even if the mechanism is in good working order, it might be out of paper tape.) Assuming that the machine is both in working order and is supplied with paper tape, the procedure to copy a program onto paper tape is as follows:

1. GET-PROG1
2. Press the ON button on the paper tape punch (it is marked ∇)
3. Type in the command PUNCH and hit the return button
4. Grab the loose end of the paper tape as it emerges from the Teletype and as soon as an area of tape containing nothing but sprocket holes appears and passes the plastic cutting mechanism, push the tape away from you and upward, thereby cutting the lead tape.
5. Sit back and watch the program being simultaneously printed (as if a listing had been requested) and punched on the paper tape. It is a good idea to start rolling the emerging tape so as to prevent it from becoming entangled. Remember that paper tape is just paper and is easily torn.
6. When the program is completely punched onto paper tape, remember to rip off the paper in the same manner as before, and turn off the paper tape punch by pressing the button marked with a circle.

15.6 Reading Paper Tape

Now that we have a copy of a program on paper tape it may, on some future occasion, be fed into the paper tape reader, below the paper tape punch. The black button next to the reader is pressed and the reading mechanism sets itself into position. The front end of the tape (shaped like an arrow) is positioned under the bar with the sprocket holes on the right matching the bumps on the reader mechanism. Press down until the click is heard.

The SCRatch command is used to clear the current program area and the tape command TAPe is typed in. The ON button is now pressed and the computer will read in the program on the paper tape, listing it simultaneously. The command KEYboard is now typed in.

15.7 Program Libraries

Each user on the HP-2000 may access programs on three levels:

1. private library
2. group library
3. system library

The names of the programs stored in each of these libraries may be itemized by typing in the following commands.

Private library:	CATalog
Group library:	GROup
System library:	LIBrary

Programs in any of these libraries are accessed by the command

GET–program name

In order to differentiate between private, group, and system programs, the following convention has been adopted. Programs in the private library are referred to by name, programs in the group library are accessed by the appropriate name prefixed by an asterisk (*), and those in the system library are referenced by preceding the program name with a dollar sign ($).

15.8 Creating a Library Program

The accounting structure on the HP-2000 is such that the personal libraries of certain users are available to a group of users with related ID numbers. The group manager is designated by a double zero in the ID code. For example, a typical ID number for a group manager would K100. The group manager does nothing special to SAVe programs. They can be readily accessed by any user whose ID number, in this example, ranges from K101 to K199. To access any program in K100, the user merely prefixes the name with an asterisk. Once accessed, a user may work with the program, amend the copy as desired (these changes will in no way affect the program stored in K100), and, needless to say, the user cannot KILL it.

Examples

GET – *MIKE
GET – *HENRY
GET – *LOST
GET – *CONNIE

Users not provided with a group manager's ID number cannot create library programs, except within their own private library.

QUICK REFERENCE GUIDE TO CHAPTER FIFTEEN

Item	General Form	Examples
1. HELLO command	HELLO–*id code, password*	HEL-A123,$H^C E^C N^C R^C Y^C$
2. BYE command	BYE	BYE
3. LIST command	LISt	LIS
4. RUN command	RUN	RUN
	RUN–*beginning line*	RUN–119
5. NAME command	NAMe–*program name*	NAM-MIKE
	NAM	NAM
	(this unnames the program)	
6. RENumber command	REN	REN
		(renumbers from 10 in steps of 10)

QUICK REFERENCE GUIDE TO CHAPTER FIFTEEN (Continued)

Item	General Form	Examples
	REN-*beginning line*	REN-100 (renumbers from 100 in steps of 10)
	REN-*beginning line, interval*	REN-100, 100 (renumbers from 100 in steps of 100)
7. SAVE command	SAVe	SAV
8. GET command	GET-*program name*	GET-MULL
	GET-$*system program*	GET-$QUIZ8
	GET-*group program*	GET-*POMPA
9. KILL command	KILl-*program name*	KIL-LEWIS
10. CATALOG command	CAT	CAT
11. SCRATCH command	SCR	SCR
12. PUNCH command	PUN	PUN
13. TAPE command	TAP	TAP
14. KEYBOARD command	KEY	KEY
15. GROup command	GRO	GRO
16. LIBrary command	LIB	LIB

Question

1. Indicate which of the following are system commands and which are BASIC instructions. In each case, explain the role played.

   (a) LIST-95, 155

   (b) SCR

   (c) KILL–BLUE

   (d) GET-$TUT

   (e) DIM A(55)

   (f) NEXT K

   (g) the break key

   (h) PRINT TAB(25);

   (i) RUN

   (j) GOSUB 55

CHAPTER SIXTEEN

ESOTERICA

It is now possible to look back and conclude that we have covered a considerable proportion of the BASIC language. We hope that none of it was too esoteric; the intention has been to present a large body of essential material in as logical a sequence as possible. In this chapter, we break with this tradition and present a series of programs that are somewhat exotic, esoteric, complex, and some are, admittedly, difficult to follow. Readers may examine them closely if they wish, or they may merely consider the output for whatever entertainment value it may have. They may even want to write more efficient programs to solve the same problems. The first program, however, deserves careful attention because it exposes certain critical features that are, all too often, completely missed.

16.1   A Closer Look at a FOR/NEXT Loop

Essentially, Program 16-1 consists of two FOR/NEXT loops. Before the first one is encountered, a little artistry is attempted by taking advantage of the LINe function, where the argument is zero. This permits the overprinting of a line of left brackets by a line of right brackets. Next I1 and J1 are both initialized to zero and the first loop using the index I is entered.

The important point to realize here is that the index I starts at 0.1 and increments in steps of 0.1 to 1000. One would normally expect this loop to loop around $10 \times 1000 = 10,000$ times. Each time it goes around, 1 is added to I1 and a careful look at the output will reveal that the final value of I1 is one more than expected; it is 10,001.

The reason for this perhaps unexpected result is that all decimal numbers are converted to binary numbers within the computer. All integers have an *exact* binary equivalent. However, the precise value of a fraction cannot always be converted to binary. Since it is of finite length, the computer often has to deal with an *approximation* to that fraction, because of the round-off error. Round-off error is determined by the maximum size of the computer word. The larger the word is, the greater the accuracy of the computer. From the output it will be seen that at termination of the first loop the index I reaches 1000.03.

With respect to the second loop, it will be clear that the loop undergoes exactly 10,000 iterations and that the value of the index J is incremented by 1 in excess of 10,000 when the loop is satisfied. In general, on the HP-2000C, the value of the index of a "satisfied" loop is the last successful value plus whatever the step happened to be.

Program 16-1

```
100   PRINT "****************************"
110   PRINT "*                          *"
120   PRINT "*   A CLOSER EXAMINATION    *"
130   PRINT "*                          *"
130   PRINT "*   OF   A   FOR/NEXT   LOOP   *"
150   PRINT "*                          *"
160   PRINT "****************************"
170   PRINT
180   PRINT "[[[[[[[[[[[[[[[[[[[[[[[[[[[[[[[[[[[[[[[[[[[[[[[[[[[[[[[[[[[[[[[":
190   PRINT LIN (Ø);
200   PRINT "]]]]]]]]]]]]]]]]]]]]]]]]]]]]]]]]]]]]]]]]]]]]]]]]]]]]]]]]]]]]]"
210   LET I1=J1=Ø
220   FOR I=.1 TO 1000 STEP .1
230   LET I1=I1+1
240   NEXT I
250   FOR J=1 TO 10000 STEP 1
260   LET J1=J1+1
270   NEXT J
280   PRINT "  I1=";I1;"   J1=";J1;"   I=";I;"   J=";J
290   PRINT "(((((((((((((((((((((((((((((((((((((((((((((((((((((((((((";
300   PRINT LIN(Ø);
310   PRINT ")))))))))))))))))))))))))))))))))))))))))))))))))))))))))))"
320   END
```

```
RUN


****************************
*                          *
*   A CLOSER EXAMINATION    *
*                          *
*   OF   A   FOR/NEXT   LOOP   *
*                          *
****************************

[][][][][][][][][][][][][][][][][][][][][][][][][][][][][][][][][][][][][][][][]
  I1=  10001         J1=  10000       I=  1000.03       J=  10001
][][][][][][][][][][][][][][][][][][][][][][][][][][][][][][][][][][][][][][][][][]

DONE
```

16.2   The 6174 Problem

The so-called 6174 problem is nothing more than an interesting mathematical curiosity. It concerns the selection of any arbitrary four-digit integer in which not all the digits are the same. The number then undergoes the following treatment. First, the digits are sorted in descending order and then are reversed to ascending order and the difference of these two numbers is found.

Suppose our selected number was 1795. Ordering the digits in ascending order yields the number 9751. Reversing it yields 1579. Taking the difference, we get 8172.

Now exactly the same procedure is adopted with this new number 8172. It transpires that *whatever* four-digit number is originally selected the process above will terminate after a few iterations because the difference will always be 6174.

```
8721   7443   9963   6642   7641   7641
1278   3447   3669   2466   1467   1467
7443   3996   6264   4176   6174   6174
```

This number is also called Kaprekar's constant, after an Indian mathematician named Kaprekar who discovered it in the early 1950s.

We have programmed the computer to solve the 6174 problem. Our results appear in Program 16-2.

Program 16-2

```
100    PRINT "************************"
110    PRINT "*                       *"
120    PRINT "*   THE '6174' PROBLEM  *"
130    PRINT "*                       *"
140    PRINT "************************"
150    PRINT
160    DIM A$[10], V[4] ,A[4] ,S[10]
170    LET A$="0123456789"
180    PRINT "PLEASE TYPE IN YOUR 4-DIGIT NUMBER."
190    PRINT "(DO NOT USE A NUMBER WITH 4 IDENTICAL DIGITS)"
200    PRINT
210    PRINT "TO TERMINATE THE PROGRAM, TYPE IN ANY NEGATIVE NUMBER."
220    PRINT
230    INPUT N
240    IF N<0 THEN 2050
250    IF N<1000 OR N >= 10000 THEN 690
260    LET F=1
270    FOR I=1 TO 4
280    LET V[5-I] =N-10*INT(N/10)
290    IF V[5-I] =V[4] THEN 310
300    LET F=0
310    LET N=INT(N/10)
320    NEXT I
330    IF F=1 THEN 710
340    MAT S=ZER
350    GOSUB 2000
350    FOR I=1 TO 4
370    LET S[V[I]+1]=S[V[I]+1]+1
380    NEXT I
390    LET J=1
400    FOR I=1 TO 10
410    FOR K=1 TO S[I]
420    LET A[J]=I-1
430    LET V[5-J]=I-1
440    LET J=J+1
450    NEXT K
460    NEXT I
470    LET Q=0
```

```
480    GOSUB 1000
490    FOR I=4 TO 1 STEP -1
500    LET V[I]=V[I]-A[I]
510    IF V[I] >= 0 THEN 540
520    LET V[I]=V[I]+10
530    LET V[I-1]=V[I-1]-1
540    NEXT I
550    FOR I=1 TO 4
560    FOR J=1 TO 4
570    IF V[I]=A[J] THEN 600
580    NEXT J
590    GO TO 340
600    LET A[J]=-1
610    NEXT I
620    LET N=0
630    FOR I=1 TO 4
640    LET N=N*10+V[I]
650    NEXT I
660    PRINT N
670    PRINT "THERE WE GO: THE MAGIC NUMBER HAS BEEN REACHED ";N,LIN(5)
680    GO TO 180
690    PRINT "SORRY, BUT YOUR NUMBER ";N;" IS OUT OF BOUNDS."
700    GO TO 180
710    PRINT LIN(2), "AS YOU CAN SEE, YOUR NUMBER IS UNACCEPTABLE."
720    PRINT "IT HAS FOUR IDENTICAL DIGITS."
730    GO TO 180
1000   FOR I=1 TO 4
1010   PRINT TAB(1);A$[V[I]+1,V[I]+1];
1020   NEXT I
1030   PRINT
1040   FOR I=1 TO 4
1050   PRINT TAB(1);A$[A[I]+1,A[I]+1];
1060   NEXT I
1070   PRINT
1080   PRINT " ____"
1090   RETURN
2000   FOR I=1 TO 4
2010   PRINT TAB(1;A$[V[I]+1,V[I]+1];
2020   NEXT I
2030   PRINT LIN(2)
2040   RETURN
2050   END


RUN


***********************
*                     *
*   THE '6174' PROBLEM   *
*                     *
***********************
```

PLEASE TYPE IN YOUR 4-DIGIT NUMBER.
(DO NOT USE A NUMBER WITH 4 IDENTICAL DIGITS)

TO TERMINATE THE PROGRAM, TYPE IN ANY NEGATIVE NUMBER.

?6643
 6643

 6643
 3466

 3177

 7731
 1377

 6354

 6543
 3456

 3Ø87

 873Ø
 Ø378

 8352

 8532
 2358

 6174

 7641
 1467

 6174
THERE WE GO: THE MAGIC NUMBER HAS BEEN REACHED 6174

PLEASE TYPE IN YOUR 4-DIGIT NUMBER.
(DO NOT USE A NUMBER WITH 4 IDENTICAL DIGITS)

TO TERMINATE THE PROGRAM, TYPE IN ANY NEGATIVE NUMBER.

?6642
 6642

 6642
 2466

 4176

```
7641
1467
----
6174
```
THERE WE GO: THE MAGIC NUMBER HAS BEEN REACHED 6174

PLEASE TYPE IN YOUR 4-DIGIT NUMBER.
(DO NOT USE A NUMBER WITH 4 IDENTICAL DIGITS)

TO TERMINATE THE PROGRAM, TYPE IN ANY NEGATIVE NUMBER.

?0001
SORRY, BUT YOUR NUMBER   1   IS OUT OF BOUNDS.
PLEASE TYPE IN YOUR 4-DIGIT NUMBER.
(DO NOT USE A NUMBER WITH 4 IDENTICAL DIGITS)

TO TERMINATE THE PROGRAM, TYPE IN ANY NEGATIVE NUMBER.

?12345
SORRY, BUT YOUR NUMBER   12345   IS OUT OF BOUNDS.
PLEASE TYPE IN YOUR 4-DIGIT NUMBER.
(DO NOT USE A NUMBER WITH 4 IDENTICAL DIGITS)

TO TERMINATE THE PROGRAM, TYPE IN ANY NEGATIVE NUMBER.

?1795
 1795


```
9751
1579
----
8172
```

```
8721
1278
----
7443
```

```
7443
3447
----
3996
```

```
9963
3699
----
6264
```

```
      6642
      2466
      ----
      4176


      7641
      1467
      ----
      6174
```

THERE WE GO: THE MAGIC NUMBER HAS BEEN REACHED   6174

PLEASE TYPE IN YOUR 4-DIGIT NUMBER.
(DO NOT USE A NUMBER WITH 4 IDENTICAL DIGITS)

TO TERMINATE THE PROGRAM, TYPE IN ANY NEGATIVE NUMBER.

?3333

AS YOU CAN SEE, YOUR NUMBER IS UNACCEPTABLE.
IT HAS FOUR IDENTICAL DIGITS.
PLEASE TYPE IN YOUR 4-DIGIT NUMBER.
(DO NOT USE A NUMBER WITH 4 IDENTICAL DIGITS)

TO TERMINATE THE PROGRAM, TYPE IN ANY NEGATIVE NUMBER.

?- 1974

DONE

16.3   Reducing the Sum of Two Fractions to Their Simplest Form

In junior high school or even earlier we learned how to add two fractions. For
example,

$$\frac{1}{3} + \frac{2}{4} = \frac{4+6}{12} = \frac{10}{12} = \frac{5}{6}$$

The fractions are initially restructured to a common base—in this case to twelfths—and
the addition takes place, cancelling both numerator and denominator by a common
factor if at all possible.

The example cited above is one of several illustrated in Program 16-3.

Program 16-3

```
100  PRINT "****************************************"
110  PRINT "*                                      *"
120  PRINT "*  ILLUSTRATION OF REDUCTION OF TWO    *"
130  PRINT "*                                      *"
140  PRINT "*  FRACTIONS TO THEIR SIMPLEST FORM    *"
150  PRINT "*                                      *"
160  PRINT "****************************************"
```

```
170   PRINT
180   PRINT "PLEASE TYPE IN YOUR FIRST FRACTION, TWO INTEGERS SEPARATED"
190   PRINT "BY A COMMA."
200   PRINT "(TO TERMINATE THE PROGRAM, TYPE IN Ø, Ø)"
210   PRINT
220   INPUT N1,D1
230   IF N1=Ø AND D1=Ø THEN 490
240   PRINT
250   IF INT(N1)#N1 OR INT (D1)#D1 THEN 470
260   PRINT "YOU'RE DOING FINE. NOW TYPE IN YOUR SECOND FRACTION"
270   PRINT "EXACTLY THE SAME WAY."
280   INPUT N2,D2
290   IF INT(N2)#N2 OR INT(D2)#D2 THEN 470
300   LET N3=D2*N1+D1*N2
310   LET D3=D2*D1
320   LET X=N3
330   LET Y=D3
340   LET Q=INT(X/Y)
350   LET R=X-Q*Y
360   IF R=Ø THEN 400
370   LET X=Y
380   LET Y=R
390   GO TO 340
400   LET N3=N3/Y
410   LET D3=D3/Y
420   IF D3=1 THEN 450
430   PRINT LIN(2), "THE SUM OF THE TWO FRACTIONS =";N3;"/";D3
440   GO TO 170
450   PRINT LIN(2), "THE SUM OF THE TWO FRACTIONS =";N3
460   GO TO 170
470   PRINT LIN(2), "SORRY OLD CHAP, THEY HAVE TO BE INTEGERS YOU KNOW."
480   GO TO 170
490   END
```

RUN

```
*****************************************
*                                       *
*   ILLUSTRATION OF REDUCTION OF TWO    *
*                                       *
*   FRACTIONS  TO  THEIR  SIMPLEST FORM *
*                                       *
*****************************************
```

PLEASE TYPE IN YOUR FIRST FRACTION, TWO INTEGERS SEPARATED
BY A COMMA.
(TO TERMINATE THE PROGRAM, TYPE IN Ø,Ø)

?2,3

YOU'RE DOING FINE. NOW TYPE IN YOUR SECOND FRACTION
EXACTLY THE SAME WAY.
?4,5

THE SUM OF THE TWO FRACTIONS = 22   /   15

PLEASE TYPE IN YOUR FIRST FRACTION, TWO INTEGERS SEPARATED
BY A COMMA.
(TO TERMINATE THE PROGRAM, TYPE IN Ø,Ø)

?6.1,7.1

SORRY OLD CHAP, THEY HAVE TO BE INTEGERS YOU KNOW.

PLEASE TYPE IN YOUR FIRST FRACTION, TWO INTEGERS SEPARATED
BY A COMMA.
(TO TERMINATE THE PROGRAM, TYPE IN Ø, Ø)

?6,7

YOU'RE DOING FINE. NOW TYPE IN YOUR SECOND FRACTION
EXACTLY THE SAME WAY.
?11,12

THE SUM OF THE TWO FRACTIONS = 149   /   84

PLEASE TYPE IN YOUR FIRST FRACTION, TWO INTEGERS SEPARATED
BY A COMMA.
(TO TERMINATE THE PROGRAM, TYPE IN Ø,Ø)

?3,2

YOU'RE DOING FINE. NOW TYPE IN YOUR SECOND FRACTION
EXACTLY THE SAME WAY.
?1.3,3

SORRY OLD CHAP, THEY HAVE TO BE INTEGERS YOU KNOW.

PLEASE TYPE IN YOUR FIRST FRACTION, TWO INTEGERS SEPARATED
BY A COMMA.
(TO TERMINATE THE PROGRAM, TYPE IN Ø,Ø)

?3,2

YOU'RE DOING FINE. NOW TYPE IN YOUR SECOND FRACTION
EXACTLY THE SAME WAY.
?1,3

THE SUM OF THE TWO FRACTIONS = 11   / 6

PLEASE TYPE IN YOUR FIRST FRACTION, TWO INTEGERS SEPARATED
BY A COMMA.
(TO TERMINATE THE PROGRAM, TYPE IN 0,0)

?1,4

YOU'RE DOING FINE. NOW TYPE IN YOUR SECOND FRACTION
EXACTLY THE SAME WAY.
?1,2

THE SUM OF THE TWO FRACTIONS = 3   / 4

PLEASE TYPE IN YOUR FIRST FRACTION, TWO INTEGERS SEPARATED
BY A COMMA.
(TO TERMINATE THE PROGRAM, TYPE IN 0,0)

?1,3

YOU'RE DOING FINE. NOW TYPE IN YOUR SECOND FRACTION
EXACTLY THE SAME WAY.
?2,4

THE SUM OF THE TWO FRACTIONS = 5   / 6

PLEASE TYPE IN YOUR FIRST FRACTION, TWO INTEGERS SEPARATED
BY A COMMA.
(TO TERMINATE THE PROGRAM, TYPE IN 0,0)

?0,0

DONE

16.4 Converting from an Arbitrary Base to Base 10

In computer science one is often confronted with the need to convert numbers from
a particular base necessitated by a particular computer to the common representation
with which we are all familiar in the decimal system—base 10.

In order to understand how the conversion from one base to another is accomplished, it is necessary to be familiar with what each digit of the number actually
represents. As an illustration let us examine in detail the decimal number 4196. It
really represents, in a most succinct form, the following sum:

$$
\begin{array}{rcrcr}
6 \times 10^0 &=& 6 \times & 1 &=& 6 \\
9 \times 10^1 &=& 9 \times & 10 &=& 90 \\
1 \times 10^2 &=& 1 \times & 100 &=& 100 \\
4 \times 10^3 &=& 4 \times & 1000 &=& 4000 \\
\hline
&&&&& 4196
\end{array}
$$

Placing each of the digits into an array makes the number much easier to deal with because each digit becomes individually accessible.

In Program 16-4 the user types in the *base* from which she wishes to convert, and the particular integer *number* she wishes to convert from that base.

Both the base and the number are tested to determine whether they conform to the criteria set up for this program; namely, the base must not exceed 10, and the number to be converted must be six digits or less. Once the necessary tests have been passed, the number to be converted is then placed in an array D, digit by digit, with D(1) containing the least significant digit (the one farthest to the right). Each time a digit is "chopped off" it is tested to ensure that it is neither greater than nor equal to the base selected. If any digit proves to be greater than or equal to the base selected, an error message is printed out and it is assumed that the number to be converted was incorrectly entered.

Within a FOR/NEXT loop, each digit is multiplied by the specified base raised to the appropriate power. The sum of these products is accumulated under the variable name S, which represents the equivalent number in base 10.

To terminate the program, the user types in the string of six characters "I QUIT." Anything else, even "IQUIT" will be treated as an indication to continue, according to the logic of the program.

Program 16-4

```
100  PRINT "**********************"
110  PRINT "*                    *"
120  PRINT "*  BASE CONVERSION   *"
130  PRINT "*                    *"
140  PRINT "**********************"
150  PRINT
160  DIM A$[10],D[6]
170  PRINT "PLEASE TYPE IN THE BASE (NOT GREATER THAN 10) YOU WISH"
180  PRINT "TO CONVERT FROM."
190  INPUT B
200  PRINT
210  IF B >= 1 THEN 250
220  PRINT "AN ARITHMETIC BASE MUST BE A POSITIVE INTEGER.  TRY AGAIN."
230  PRINT
240  GO TO 170
250  IF B#INT(B) THEN 220
260  IF B <= 10 THEN 310
270  PRINT "THIS PROGRAM IS NOT EQUIPPED TO HANDLE ARITHMETIC"
280  PRINT "BASES GREATER THAN 10. PLEASE TRY A DIFFERENT BASE VALUE."
290  PRINT
300  GO TO 170
310  PRINT "PLEASE TYPE IN THE NUMBER (6 DIGITS OR LESS) WHICH"
320  PRINT "YOU WISH TO CONVERT";
330  INPUT N
340  PRINT
350  IF N >= 1.E+06 THEN 610
360  LET J=N
370  FOR K=1 TO 6
380  LET D[K]=N-INT(N/10)*10
390  IF D[K] >= B THEN 570
400  LET N=INT(N/10)
```

```
410   NEXT K
420   LET S=0
430   FOR M=1 TO 6
440   LET S=S+D[M]*B↑(M-1)
450   NEXT M
460   PRINT "THE NUMBER";J;",BASE";B;" IS EQUAL TO";S;",BASE 10."
470   PRINT LIN(3)
480   PRINT "(TO CONTINUE WITH THIS PROGRAM, TYPE IN 'OF COURSE!',"
490   PRINT " TO TERMINATE THE PROGRAM, TYPE IN 'I QUIT')"
500   PRINT
510   PRINT "DO YOU WANT TO GO ON WITH THIS";
520   INPUT A$
530   IF A$[1,6]="I QUIT" THEN 650
540   PRINT
550   PRINT "GOOD.  ";
560   GO TO 170
570   PRINT "SORRY, BUT YOUR NUMBER,";J;", IS NOT A LEGAL  "
580   PRINT "NUMBER IN BASE   ";B;".  TRY AGAIN."
590   PRINT
600   GO TO 310
610   PRINT "YOU KNOW THAT THE NUMBER CAN'T BE MORE THAN 6 DIGITS."
620   PRINT "HAVE ANOTHER TRY."
630   PRINT
640   GO TO 310
650   END

RUN


***********************
*                     *
*  BASE CONVERSION  *
*                     *
***********************


PLEASE TYPE IN THE BASE (NOT GREATER THAN 10) YOU WISH
TO CONVERT FROM.
?8

PLEASE TYPE IN THE NUMBER (6 DIGITS OR LESS) WHICH
YOU WISH TO CONVERT?65000

THE NUMBER 65000.   , BASE 8   IS EQUAL TO 27136   , BASE 10.

(TO CONTINUE WITH THIS PROGRAM, TYPE IN 'OF COURSE!',
TO TERMINATE THE PROGRAM, TYPE IN 'I QUIT')

DO YOU WANT TO GO ON WITH THIS?OF COURSE!

GOOD.  PLEASE TYPE IN THE BASE (NOT GREATER THAN 10) YOU WISH
TO CONVERT FROM.
?0
```

AN ARITHMETIC BASE MUST BE A POSITIVE INTEGER. TRY AGAIN.

PLEASE TYPE IN THE BASE (NOT GREATER THAN 1Ø) YOU WISH
TO CONVERT FROM.
?12

THIS PROGRAM IS NOT EQUIPPED TO HANDLE ARITHMETIC
BASES GREATER THAN 1Ø. PLEASE TRY A DIFFERENT BASE VALUE.

PLEASE TYPE IN THE BASE (NOT GREATER THAN 1Ø) YOU WISH
TO CONVERT FROM.
?2

PLEASE TYPE IN THE NUMBER (6 DIGITS OR LESS) WHICH
YOU WISH TO CONVERT?1ØØ1

THE NUMBER 1ØØ1   , BASE 2   IS EQUAL TO 9   , BASE 1Ø.

(TO CONTINUE WITH THIS PROGRAM, TYPE IN 'OF COURSE!',
TO TERMINATE THE PROGRAM, TYPE IN 'I QUIT')

DO YOU WANT TO GO ON WITH THIS?OF COURSE!

GOOD. PLEASE TYPE IN THE BASE (NOT GREATER THAN 1Ø) YOU WISH
TO CONVERT FROM.
?5

PLEASE TYPE IN THE NUMBER (6 DIGITS OR LESS) WHICH
YOU WISH TO CONVERT?63332

SORRY, BUT YOUR NUMBER, 63332.   , IS NOT A LEGAL
NUMBER IN BASE   5   . TRY AGAIN.

PLEASE TYPE IN THE NUMBER (6 DIGITS OR LESS) WHICH
YOU WISH TO CONVERT?21122424

YOU KNOW THAT THE NUMBER CAN'T BE MORE THAN 6 DIGITS.
HAVE ANOTHER TRY.

PLEASE TYPE IN THE NUMBER (6 DIGITS OR LESS) WHICH
YOU WISH TO CONVERT?2444

THE NUMBER 2444   , BASE 5   IS EQUAL TO 374   , BASE 1Ø.

(TO CONTINUE WITH THIS PROGRAM, TYPE IN 'OF COURSE!',
TO TERMINATE THE PROGRAM, TYPE IN 'I QUIT')

DO YOU WANT TO GO ON WITH THIS?I QUIT

DONE

16.5 Conversion from One Base to Another

Program 16-5 converts an integer from any given base to any other given base, assuming that both bases are <37.

The algorithm used is that of repeated division. Converting the integer 12 from base 10 to base 2, for example, one would repeatedly divide 12 by 2 in the following manner:

$$2 \overline{)12} \quad \frac{6}{} \quad \text{remainder } 0$$

$$2 \overline{)6} \quad \frac{3}{} \quad \text{remainder } 0$$

$$2 \overline{)3} \quad \frac{1}{} \quad \text{remainder } 1$$

$$2 \overline{)1} \quad \frac{0}{} \quad \text{remainder } 1$$

Thus we are left with the remainders (top to bottom, right to left) 1100. This is the binary equivalent of 12 in the decimal base.

In line 210 B$ is assigned the character string composed of the 10 decimal digits followed by the 26 letters of the alphabet, which themselves have ascending numeric values in bases greater than 10.

In line 270 the computer requests the user to type in (in decimal) the base from which the numbers are to be converted. In line 290 the user is requested to type in the base into which the number is to be printed. Finally, in line 310 a number in the original base is read into a string.

Each character in the string is converted into a numeric representation and is stored in the corresponding element of vector I.

In lines 430 to 630, the computer performs repeated extended long division by the second base B2, storing the remainders in vector F until zero is reached. Finally, vector F is printed out backward in character form.

Program 16-5

```
100  PRINT "**************************"
110  PRINT "*                        *"
120  PRINT "*  PROGRAM TO CONVERT    *"
130  PRINT "*                        *"
140  PRINT "*   A NUMBER FROM ONE    *"
150  PRINT "*                        *"
160  PRINT "*     BASE TO ANOTHER    *"
170  PRINT "*                        *"
180  PRINT "**************************"
190  PRINT
200  DIM A$[72], B$[37],I[72],F[72]
210  LET B$="0123456789ABCDEFGHIJKLMNOPQRSTUVWXYZ"
220  PRINT
```

```
230  PRINT "TO STOP THE PROGRAM, ENTER '*STOP' WHEN"
240  PRINT "'NUMBER?' APPEARS."
250  PRINT "TO CHANGE THE BASES USED' ENTER '*BASE' WHEN"
260  PRINT "'NUMBER?' APPEARS."
270  PRINT
280  PRINT "IN WHAT BASE WILL THE NUMBER BE ENTERED ";
290  INPUT B1
300  PRINT "TO WHAT BASE IS THE NUMBER TO BE CONVERTED ";
310  INPUT B2
320  PRINT
330  PRINT "NUMBER";
340  INPUT A$
350  IF A$="*BASE" THEN 280
360  IF A$="*STOP" THEN 710
370  FOR I=1 TO LEN(A$)
380  FOR J=1 TO B1
390  IF A$[I,I]=B$[J,J] THEN 430
400  NEXT J
410  PRINT "THE CHARACTER '";A$[I,I];"' IS NOT A LEGAL BASE ";B1;"DIGIT."
420  GO TO 320
430  LET I[I]=J-1
440  NEXT I
450  LET P2=LEN(A$)
460  LET P9=0
470  LET P1=1
480  LET F=0
490  LET N=0
500  FOR I=P1 TO P2
510  LET N=N*B1+I[I]
520  LET C=INT(N/B2)
530  LET N=N-B2*C
540  IF F=0 THEN 580
550  LET F=F+1
560  LET I[F]=C
570  GO TO 610
580  IF C=0 THEN 610
590  LET F=1
600  GO TO 560
610  NEXT I
620  LET P9=P9+1
630  LET F[P9]=N
640  LET P2=F
650  IF F>0 THEN 480
660  FOR I=P9 TO 1 STEP -1
670  PRINT B$[F[I]+1,F[I]+1];
680  NEXT I
690  PRINT
700  GO TO 320
710  END
```

```
**************************
*                        *
*  PROGRAM TO CONVERT  *
*                        *
*   A NUMBER FROM ONE    *
*                        *
*    BASE TO ANOTHER     *
*                        *
**************************
```

TO STOP THE PROGRAM, ENTER '*STOP' WHEN
'NUMBER?' APPEARS.
TO CHANGE THE BASES USED, ENTER '*BASE' WHEN
'NUMBER?' APPEARS.

IN WHAT BASE WILL THE NUMBER BE ENTERED ? 1Ø
TO WHAT BASE IS THE NUMBER TO BE CONVERTED ?2

NUMBER?12
11ØØ

NUMBER?1Ø
1Ø1Ø

NUMBER?HI
THE CHARACTER 'H' IS NOT A LEGAL BASE   1Ø   DIGIT.

NUMBER?5
1Ø1

NUMBER?1ØØØØ
1ØØ11 1ØØØ1ØØØØ

NUMBER?1
1

NUMBER?2
1Ø

NUMBER?3
11

NUMBER?7
111

NUMBER?8
1ØØØ

```
NUMBER?*BASE
IN WHAT BASE WILL THE NUMBER BE ENTERED ?16
TO WHAT BASE IS THE NUMBER TO BE CONVERTED  ?8

NUMBER?10
20

NUMBER?FF
377

NUMBER?4FF
2377

NUMBER?FFF
7777

NUMBER?9FF
4777

NUMBER?0
0

NUMBER?1
1

NUMBER?7
7

NUMBER?8
10

NUMBER?9
11

NUMBER?10
20

NUMBER?11
21

NUMBER?12
22

NUMBER?A
12

NUMBER?B
13

NUMBER?C
14
```

NUMBER?E
16

NUMBER?F
17

NUMBER?G
THE CHARACTER 'G' IS NOT A LEGAL BASE   16   DIGIT.

NUMBER?*STOP

DONE

16.6 Permutation of a String

The letters C, A, and T may be ordered in the following six ways:

CAT   CTA   ACT   ATC   TCA   TAC

The number of times three things may be taken three at a time is six. This is known as a permutation. In Program 16-6, the user enters any character string up to the maximum 72 characters imposed by the system. He is then asked to specify how many characters of those typed in are to be taken at a time.

The algorithm by which this is accomplished is somewhat difficult to explain but in essence it is as follows.

First, a vector I of the same length as the string is set up. Each element of I is initially set equal to the position in the string of the first occurrence of each character, reading from left to right. For example, if the string is

KEEPER

the vector would be 122426. The first character scanned is K and therefore I(1) is set equal to 1. Next, the E is found and it becomes I(2). The third character is also an E, and so I(3) is assigned the same value as the previous E, namely 2. The fourth character P, occurs for the first time and so I(4) is set equal to 4. Next, the E occurs for the third time and therefore I(5) is set equal to 2, since this letter first appeared as the second character. Finally, the letter R occurs for the first and only time, causing I(6) to be assigned the value 6. With this the initialization process is completed.

The reason for the complexity of the above procedure is to prevent strings of identical characters being printed. Assuming the word KEEPER is being manipulated 3 characters at a time, it would not make much sense to print out six strings of triple E's. The above procedure will print it out only once.

The index vector is now sorted into ascending order in a particularly efficient manner. The vector that was originally 122426 now becomes 122246. If N is set to 3 in the program, the three characters pointed to by the first three elements of vector I are assigned to B$. A space is appended to B$ for cosmetic reasons before pointing it out. (Since all three characters and the space are part of the same string, the system will not attempt to break it up before printing. If there is insufficient room left on a line, the string will be printed on the next new line. Thus we have forced the machine to cooperate in formatting our output into neat columns with the maximum number of combinations per line.)

Program 16-6

```
100   PRINT "*****************"
110   PRINT "*               *"
120   PRINT "* PERMUTATIONS *"
130   PRINT "*               *"
140   PRINT "* OF   A   STRING *"
150   PRINT "*               *"
160   PRINT "*****************"
170   PRINT LIN(2)
180   DIM A$[72],B$[72],I[72],J[72]
190   PRINT "PLEASE TYPE IN YOUR STRING."
200   PRINT LIN(2),"(TO TERMINATE THE PROGRAM, TYPE IN 'QUIT')"
210   INPUT A$
220   IF A$="QUIT" THEN 810
230   PRINT LIN(2),"SO YOU HAVE SELECTED: ";A$
240   LET M=LEN(A$)
250   PRINT LIN(2),"NOW ALL COMBINATIONS OF ";A$;" WILL BE PRINTED"
260   PRINT "N AT A TIME."
270   PRINT "TYPE IN N."
280   INPUT N
290   IF N<1 THEN 740
300   IF N <> INT(N) THEN 790
310   IF N>M THEN 760
320   PRINT
330   FOR I=1 TO M
340   FOR J=1 TO I-1
350   IF A$[J,J]=A$[I,I] THEN 380
360   NEXT J
370   LET J=I
380   LET I[I]=J
390   NEXT I
400   LET Q=0
410   GO TO 570
420   FOR Q=N TO 1 STEP -1
430   FOR K=Q+1 TO M
440   IF I[K]>I[Q] THEN 480
450   NEXT K
460   NEXT Q
470   GO TO 170
480   LET K1=I[K]
490   FOR K2=Q+2 TO M
500   IF I[K2] <= I[Q] THEN 540
510   IF I[K2]>K1 THEN 540
520   LET K=K2
530   LET K1=I[K]
540   NEXT K2
550   LET I[K]=I[Q]
560   LET I[Q]=K1
570   MAT J=ZER[M]
580   FOR K=Q+1 TO M
590   LET J[I[K]]=J[I[K]]+1
```

```
6ØØ   NEXT K
61Ø   LET K1=Q+1
62Ø   FOR K=1 TO M
63Ø   FOR K3=1 TO J[K]
64Ø   LET I[K1]=K
65Ø   LET K1=K1+1
66Ø   NEXT K3
67Ø   NEXT K
68Ø   FOR I=1 TO N
69Ø   LET B$[I,I]=A$[I[I],I[I]]
7ØØ   NEXT I
71Ø   LET B$[N+1]=" "
72Ø   PRINT B$;
73Ø   GO TO 42Ø
74Ø   PRINT LIN(2), "NO DICE!  N HAS TO BE GREATER THAN 1."
75Ø   GO TO 27Ø
76Ø   PRINT LIN(2), "IT IS IMPOSSIBLE TO TAKE ";M;"CHARACTERS"
77Ø   PRINT TAB(25),N;" AT A TIME."
78Ø   GO TO 27Ø
79Ø   PRINT LIN(2), "SORRY, BUT YOU HAVE TO TYPE IN AN INTEGER."
8ØØ   GO TO 27Ø
81Ø   END


RUN


* * * * * * * * * * * * * * * *
*                             *
* PERMUTATIONS *
*                             *
* OF   A   STRING *
*                             *
* * * * * * * * * * * * * * * *



PLEASE TYPE IN YOUR STRING.


(TO TERMINATE THE PROGRAM, TYPE IN 'QUIT')
?KEEPER


SO YOU HAVE SELECTED: KEEPER


NOW ALL COMBINATIONS OF KEEPER WILL BE PRINTED
N AT A TIME.
TYPE IN N.
?3
```

KEE KEP KER KPE KPR KRE KRP EKE EKP EKR EEK EEE EEP EER
EPK EPE EPR ERK ERE ERP PKE PKR PEK PEE PER PRK PRE RKE
RKP REK REE REP RPK RPE

PLEASE TYPE IN YOUR STRING.

(TO TERMINATE THE PROGRAM, TYPE IN 'QUIT')
?STEVE

SO YOU HAVE SELECTED: STEVE

NOW ALL COMBINATIONS OF STEVE WILL BE PRINTED
N AT A TIME.
TYPE IN N.
?7

IT IS IMPOSSIBLE TO TAKE 5   CHARACTERS
                          7   AT A TIME.
TYPE IN N.
?6.5

SORRY, BUT YOU HAVE TO TYPE IN AN INTEGER.
TYPE IN N.
?3

STE STV SET SEE SEV SVT SVE TSE TSV TES TEE TEV TVS TVE
EST ESE ESV ETS ETE ETV EES EET EEV EVS EVT EVE VST VSE
VTS VTE VES VET VEE

PLEASE TYPE IN YOUR STRING.

(TO TERMINATE THE PROGRAM, TYPE IN 'QUIT')
?TIHOR

SO YOU HAVE SELECTED: TIHOR

NOW ALL COMBINATIONS OF TIHOR WILL BE PRINTED
N AT A TIME.
TYPE IN N.
?-5

NO DICE! N HAS TO BE GREATER THAN 1.
TYPE IN N.
?4

```
TIHO   TIHR   TIOH   TIOR   TIRH   TIRO   THIO   THIR   THOI   THOR   THRI   THRO
TOIH   TOIR   TOHI   TOHR   TORI   TORH   TRIH   TRIO   TRHI   TRHO   TROI   TROH
ITHO   ITHR   ITOH   ITOR   ITRH   ITRO   IHTO   IHTR   IHOT   IHOR   IHRT   IHRO
IOTH   IOTR   IOHT   IOHR   IORT   IORH   IRTH   IRTO   IRHT   IRHO   IROT   IROH
HTIO   HTIR   HTOI   HTOR   HTRI   HTRO   HITO   HITR   HIOT   HIOR   HIRT   HIRO
HOTI   HOTR   HOIT   HOIR   HORT   HORI   HRTI   HRTO   HRIT   HRIO   HROT   HROI
OTIH   OTIR   OTHI   OTHR   OTRI   OTRH   OITH   OITR   OIHT   OIHR   OIRT   OIRH
OHTI   OHTR   OHIT   OHIR   OHRT   OHRI   ORTI   ORTH   ORIT   ORIH   ORHT   ORHI
RTIH   RTIO   RTHI   RTHO   RTOI   RTOH   RITH   RITO   RIHT   RIHO   RIOT   RIOH
RHTI   RHTO   RHIT   RHIO   RHOT   RHOI   ROTI   ROTH   ROIT   ROIH   ROHT   ROHI
```

PLEASE TYPE IN YOUR STRING.

(TO TERMINATE THE PROGRAM, TYPE IN 'QUIT')
?ROBERT

SO YOU HAVE SELECTED: ROBERT

NOW ALL COMBINATIONS OF ROBERT WILL BE PRINTED
N AT A TIME.
TYPE IN N.
?5

```
RROBE   RROBT   RROEB   RROET   RROTB   RROTE   RRBOE   RRBOT   RRBEO   RRBET
RRBTO   RRBTE   RREOB   RREOT   RREBO   RREBT   RRETO   RRETB   RRTOB   RRTOE
RRTBO   RRTBE   RRTEO   RRTEB   RORBE   RORBT   ROREB   RORET   RORTB   RORTE
ROBRE   ROBRT   ROBER   ROBET   ROBTR   ROBTE   ROERB   ROERT   ROEBR   ROEBT
ROETR   ROETB   ROTRB   ROTRE   ROTBR   ROTBE   ROTER   ROTEB   RBROE   RBROT
RBREO   RBRET   RBRTO   RBRTE   RBORE   RBORT   RBOER   RBOET   RBOTR   RBOTE
RBERO   RBERT   RBEOR   RBEOT   RBETR   RBETO   RBTRO   RBTRE   RBTOR   RBTOE
RBTER   RBTEO   REROB   REROT   RERBO   RERBT   RERTO   RERTB   REORB   REORT
REOBR   REOBT   REOTR   REOTB   REBRO   REBRT   REBOR   REBOT   REBTR   REBTO
RETRO   RETRB   RETOR   RETOB   RETBR   RETBO   RTROB   RTROE   RTRBO   RTRBE
RTREO   RTREB   RTORB   RTORE   RTOBR   RTOBE   RTOER   RTOEB   RTBRO   RTBRE
RTBOR   RTBOE   RTBER   RTBEO   RTERO   RTERB   RTEOR   RTEOB   RTEBR   RTEBO
ORRBE   ORRBT   ORREB   ORRET   ORRTB   ORRTE   ORBRE   ORBRT   ORBER   ORBET
ORBTR   ORBTE   ORERB   ORERT   OREBR   OREBT   ORETR   ORETB   ORTRB   ORTRE
ORTBR   ORTBE   ORTER   ORTEB   OBRRE   OBRRT   OBRER   OBRET   OBRTR   OBRTE
OBERR   OBERT   OBETR   OBTRR   OBTRE   OBTER   OERRB   OERRT   OERBR   OERBT
OERTR   OERTB   OEBRR   OEBRT   OEBTR   OETRR   OETRB   OETBR   OTRRB   OTRRE
OTRBR   OTRBE   OTRER   OTREB   OTBRR   OTBRE   OTBER   OTERR   OTERB   OTEBR
```

```
BRROE  BRROT  BRREO  BRRET  BRRTO  BRRTE  BRORE  BRORT  BROER  BROET
BROTR  BROTE  BRERO  BRERT  BREOR  BREOT  BRETR  BRETO  BRTRO  BRTRE
BRTOR  BRTOE  BRTER  BRTEO  BORRE  BORRT  BORER  BORET  BORTR  BORTE
BOERR  BOERT  BOETR  BOTRR  BOTRE  BOTER  BERRO  BERRT  BEROR  BEROT
BERTR  BERTO  BEORR  BEORT  BEOTR  BETRR  BETRO  BETOR  BTRRO  BTRRE
BTROR  BTROE  BTRER  BTREO  BTORR  BTORE  BTOER  BTERR  BTERO  BTEOR
ERROB  ERROT  ERRBO  ERRBT  ERRTO  ERRTB  ERORB  ERORT  EROBR  EROBT
EROTR  EROTB  ERBRO  ERBRT  ERBOR  ERBOT  ERBTR  ERBTO  ERTRO  ERTRB
ERTOR  ERTOB  ERTBR  ERTBO  EORRB  EORRT  EORBR  EORBT  EORTR  EORTB
EOBRR  EOBRT  EOBTR  EOTRR  EOTRB  EOTBR  EBRRO  EBRRT  EBROR  EBROT
EBRTR  EBRTO  EBORR  EBORT  EBOTR  EBTRR  EBTRO  EBTOR  ETRRO  ETRRB
ETROR  ETROB  ETRBR  ETRBO  ETORR  ETORB  ETOBR  ETBRR  ETBRO  ETBOR
TRROB  TRROE  TRRBO  TRRBE  TRREO  TRREB  TRORB  TRORE  TROBR  TROBE
TROER  TROEB  TRBRO  TRBRE  TRBOR  TRBOE  TRBER  TRBEO  TRERO  TRERB
TREOR  TREOB  TREBR  TREBO  TORRB  TORRE  TORBR  TORBE  TORER  TOREB
TOBRR  TOBRE  TOBER  TOERR  TOERB  TOEBR  TBRRO  TBRRE  TBROR  TBROE
TBRER  TBREO  TBORR  TBORE  TBOER  TBERR  TBERO  TBEOR  TERRO  TERRB
TEROR  TEROB  TERBR  TERBO  TEORR  TEORB  TEOBR  TEBRR  TEBRO  TEBOR
```

PLEASE TYPE IN YOUR STRING.

(TO TERMINATE THE PROGRAM, TYPE IN 'QUIT')
?QUIT

DONE

16.7 Conversion from Decimal to Roman Numerals and Vice Versa

What follows is a table of equivalence between the decimal system and Roman numerals.

$$
\begin{aligned}
M &= 1000 \\
D &= 500 \\
C &= 100 \\
L &= 50 \\
X &= 10 \\
V &= 5 \\
I &= 1
\end{aligned}
$$

It is difficult to conceive how the Romans managed with their system since it does not allow for zero, or fractions, or even negative numbers. Every positive integer is represented by a combination of the letters M, D, C, L, X, V, and I.

When the letters are written from left to right in descending order of decimal value, for example,

$$MMCCLXXI$$

their individual values are added together. In the example quoted it becomes:

$$1000 + 1000 + 100 + 100 + 50 + 10 + 10 + 1 = 2271$$

The Romans adopted the convention that when one of their seven letters is preceded by a letter representing a lesser value, that lesser value is deducted from its neighbor to the right. For example,

MXLVII

is equivalent to

$$1000 + (50 - 10) + 5 + 1 + 1 = 1047$$

The idea behind Program 16-7 is to permit the user to enter any positive decimal number and the computer will convert it to the standard form of the Roman notation.

In line 190 the seven primary Roman letters are replaced in the string R$. In line 230 the decimal number is entered for conversion to Roman. After it passes the three validity tests in lines 270 and 300, the output string B$ is initialized to the null string. Since there is no short method for the computer to print out numerals greater than 4000, the sequence of instructions 340 to 380 will print out an appropriate number of M's and reduce the value of the variable N correspondingly.

The FOR/NEXT loop beginning at line 390 separates the number N into a series of decimal digits that are successively stored into the variable M. At the same time, the position of the character in R$, which corresponds to the appropriate power of 10, is stored in the variable C.

The computed GOSUB in line 430 transfers to the routine that will add the appropriate characters to the end of B$. In line 460, B$ is printed and the program returns for more input.

Program 16-7

```
100  PRINT "*******************************"
110  PRINT "*                             *"
120  PRINT "* CONVERSION FROM DECIMAL     *"
130  PRINT "*                             *"
140  PRINT "* TO ROMAN NUMERAL SYSTEM     *"
150  PRINT "*                             *"
160  PRINT "*******************************"
170  PRINT
180  DIM R$[7],B$[72]
190  LET R$="MDCLXVI"
200  PRINT "PLEASE ENTER YOUR NUMBER FOR CONVERSION TO ROMAN
        NUMERALS."
210  PRINT "(TYPE IN THE NUMBER 1.E15 TO TERMINATE THE PROGRAM.)"
220  PRINT
230  INPUT N
240  IF N<1.E+15 THEN 270
250  PRINT "I AM ";
260  STOP
270  IF N <> 0 THEN 300
280  PRINT "SORRY, BUT THE ROMANS NEVER HAD A NUMERAL FOR ZERO."
290  GO TO 200
300  IF N>0 AND INT(N)=N THEN 330
310  PRINT "SORRY, ONLY POSITIVE INTEGERS ARE ALLOWED."
320  GO TO 200
330  LET B$=" "
340  IF N<4000 THEN 390
350  FOR I=1 TO INT(N/1000)
360  PRINT "M";
370  NEXT I
```

```
380   LET N=N-1000*INT(N/1000)
390   FOR I=3 TO 0 STEP -1
400   LET X=10↑I
410   LET C=7-I-I
420   LET M=INT(N/X)
430   GOSUB M+1 OF 490,1000,1000,1000,2000,3000,4000,4000,4000,5000
440   LET N=N-M*X
450   NEXT I
460   PRINT B$
470   PRINT
480   GO TO 200
490   RETURN
1000  FOR I1=1 TO M
1010  LET B$[LEN(B$)+1]=R$[C,C]
1020  NEXT I1
1030  RETURN
2000  LET B$[LEN(B$)+1]=R$[C,C]
2010  LET B$[LEN(B$)+1]=R$[C-1,C-1]
2020  RETURN
3000  LET B$[LEN(B$)+1]=R$[C-1,C-1]
3010  RETURN
4000  LET B$[LEN(B$) + 1]=R$[C-1,C-1]
4010  FOR I1=6 TO M
4020  LET B$[LEN(B$) + 1]=R$[C,C]
4030  NEXT I1
4040  RETURN
5000  LET B$[LEN(B$) + 1]=R$[C,C]
5010  LET B$[LEN(B$) + 1]=R$[C-2,C-2]
5020  RETURN
5030  END
```

```
****************************
*                          *
* CONVERSION  FROM DECIMAL *
*                          *
* TO ROMAN NUMERAL SYSTEM  *
*                          *
****************************
```

PLEASE ENTER YOUR NUMBER FOR CONVERSION TO ROMAN NUMERALS.
(TYPE IN THE NUMBER 1.E15 TO TERMINATE THE PROGRAM.)

```
?1974
MCMLXXIV
```

PLEASE ENTER YOUR NUMBER FOR CONVERSION TO ROMAN NUMERALS.
(TYPE IN THE NUMBER 1.E15 TO TERMINATE THE PROGRAM.)

```
?100.8
SORRY, ONLY POSITIVE INTEGERS ARE ALLOWED.
PLEASE ENTER YOUR NUMBER FOR CONVERSION TO ROMAN NUMERALS.
(TYPE IN THE NUMBER 1.E15 TO TERMINATE THE PROGRAM.)
```

```
?50
L
```

PLEASE ENTER YOUR NUMBER FOR CONVERSION TO ROMAN NUMERALS.
(TYPE IN THE NUMBER 1.E15 TO TERMINATE THE PROGRAM.)

```
?10
X
```

PLEASE ENTER YOUR NUMBER FOR CONVERSION TO ROMAN NUMERALS.
(TYPE IN THE NUMBER 1.E15 TO TERMINATE THE PROGRAM.)

```
?0
```
SORRY, BUT THE ROMANS NEVER HAD A NUMERAL FOR ZERO.
PLEASE ENTER YOUR NUMBER FOR CONVERSION TO ROMAN NUMERALS.
(TYPE IN THE NUMBER 1.E15 TO TERMINATE THE PROGRAM.)

```
?-1
```
SORRY, ONLY POSITIVE INTEGERS ARE ALLOWED.
PLEASE ENTER YOUR NUMBER FOR CONVERSION TO ROMAN NUMERALS.
(TYPE IN THE NUMBER 1.E15 TO TERMINATE THE PROGRAM.)

```
?1
I
```

PLEASE ENTER YOUR NUMBER FOR CONVERSION TO ROMAN NUMERALS.
(TYPE IN THE NUMBER 1.E15 TO TERMINATE THE PROGRAM.)

```
?1.E15
I AM
DONE
```

For the benefit of those who are limitlessly fascinated by the previous program, we present now another conversion program, this time going from Roman notation to the decimal system.

Program 16-8

```
100   PRINT "****************************"
110   PRINT "*                          *"
120   PRINT "* CONVERSION FROM ROMAN    *"
130   PRINT "*                          *"
140   PRINT "* TO  THE  DECIMAL  SYSTEM *"
150   PRINT "*                          *"
160   PRINT "****************************"
170   PRINT
180   DIM C$[7],V[7],A[73],A$[72]
190   MAT READ V
200   DATA 1,5,10,50,100,500,1000
210   LET C$="IVXLCDM"
220   PRINT "PLEASE TYPE IN YOUR ROMAN NUMERALS."
230   PRINT "(TO TERMINATE THE PROGRAM, TYPE IN 'STOP')",LIN(2)
```

```
240   INPUT A$
250   IF A$="STOP" THEN 490
260   LET Q=0
270   LET S=0
280   FOR X=1 TO 73
290   LET A[X]=0
300   NEXT X
310   FOR X=1 TO LEN(A$)
320   FOR C=1 TO 7
330   IF A$[X,X]=C$[C,C] THEN 360
340   NEXT C
350   GO TO 470
360   LET A[X]=C
370   NEXT X
380   FOR X=1 TO LEN(A$)
390   IF A[X+1]>A[X] THEN 420
400   LET S=S+V[A[X]]
410   GO TO 430
420   LET S=S-V[A[X]]
430   NEXT X
440   PRINT A$;"=";S
450   PRINT
460   GO TO 220
470   PRINT LIN(2),"INVALID INPUT-SORRY!  (CHARACTER IN ERROR-";A$[X,X];")"
480   GO TO 220
490   END
```

RUN

```
***************************
*                         *
* CONVERSION FROM ROMAN *
*                         *
* TO  THE  DECIMAL  SYSTEM *
*                         *
***************************
```

PLEASE TYPE IN YOUR ROMAN NUMERALS.
(TO TERMINATE THE PROGRAM, TYPE IN 'STOP')

?I
I = 1

PLEASE TYPE IN YOUR ROMAN NUMERALS.
(TO TERMINATE THE PROGRAM, TYPE IN 'STOP')

?X
X= 10

PLEASE TYPE IN YOUR ROMAN NUMERALS.
(TO TERMINATE THE PROGRAM, TYPE IN 'STOP')

?V
V= 5

PLEASE TYPE IN YOUR ROMAN NUMERALS.
(TO TERMINATE THE PROGRAM, TYPE IN 'STOP')

?C
C= 100

PLEASE TYPE IN YOUR ROMAN NUMERALS.
(TO TERMINATE THE PROGRAM, TYPE IN 'STOP')

?D
D= 500

PLEASE TYPE IN YOUR ROMAN NUMERALS.
(TO TERMINATE THE PROGRAM, TYPE IN 'STOP')

?M
M= 1000

PLEASE TYPE IN YOUR ROMAN NUMERALS.
(TO TERMINATE THE PROGRAM, TYPE IN 'STOP')

?DDS

INVALID INPUT-SORRY! (CHARACTER IN ERROR-S)
PLEASE TYPE IN YOUR ROMAN NUMERALS.
(TO TERMINATE THE PROGRAM, TYPE IN 'STOP')

?MCMLXXIV
MCMLXXIV= 1974

PLEASE TYPE IN YOUR ROMAN NUMERALS.
(TO TERMINATE THE PROGRAM, TYPE IN 'STOP')

?MDCCLXXVI
MDCCLXXVI= 1776

PLEASE TYPE IN YOUR ROMAN NUMERALS.
(TO TERMINATE THE PROGRAM, TYPE IN 'STOP')

?STOP

DONE

16.8   The ASCII Character Set

In order to permit information to be readily exchanged between different systems, an organization was formed called the American National Standards Institute (ANSI). ANSI provides recognized standards that have been adopted by many segments of American industry. A standardized character set was developed and called the American Standard Code for Information Interchange (ASCII—pronounced "askey").

In BASIC each character has a numeric representation that gives meaning to the comparison operations of character strings. They range in decimal value from 0 through 127. For the reader's benefit they are reproduced and are printed here. They have been taken from the book *BASIC* (sixth edition) Kiewit Computation Center, Dartmouth College.

ASCII CHARACTER SET

Graphic	Octal Value	Decimal Value	ASCII Abbreviation	Comments
	0	0	NUL	Null
	1	1	SOH	Start of heading
	2	2	STX	Start of text
	3	3	ETX	End of text
	4	4	EOT	End of transmission
	5	5	ENQ	Enquiry
	6	6	ACK	Acknowledge
	7	7	BEL	Bell
	10	8	BS	Backspace
	11	9	HT	Horizontal tabulation
	12	10	LF	Line feed
	13	11	VT	Vertical tabulation
	14	12	FF	Form feed
	15	13	CR	Carriage return
	16	14	SO	Shift out
	17	15	SI	Shift in
	20	16	DLE	Data link escape
	21	17	DC1	Device control 1
	22	18	DC2	Device control 2
	23	19	DC3	Device control 3
	24	20	DC4	Device control 4
	25	21	NAK	Negative acknowledge
	26	22	SYN	Synchronous idle
	27	23	ETB	End of transmission block
	30	24	CAN	Cancel
	31	25	EM	End of medium

Graphic	Octal Value	Decimal Value	ASCII Abbreviation	Comments
	32	26	SUB	Substitute
	33	27	ESC	Escape
	34	28	FS	File separator
	35	29	GS	Group separator
	36	30	RS	Record separator
	37	31	US	Unit separator
	40	32	SP	Space
!	41	33	!	Exclamation point
”	42	34	”	Quotation mark
#	43	35	#	Number sign
$	44	36	$	Dollar sign
%	45	37	%	Percent sign
&	46	38	&	Ampersand
’	47	39	’	Apostrophe
(	50	40	(	Opening parenthesis
)	51	41	)	Closing parenthesis
*	52	42	*	Asterisk
+	53	43	+	Plus
,	54	44	,	Comma
–	55	45	–	Hyphen (minus)
.	56	46	.	Period (decimal)
/	57	47	/	Slash (slant)
0	60	48	0	Zero
1	61	49	1	One
2	62	50	2	Two
3	63	51	3	Three
4	64	52	4	Four
5	65	53	5	Five
6	66	54	6	Six
7	67	55	7	Seven
8	70	56	8	Eight
9	71	57	9	Nine
:	72	58	:	Colon
;	73	59	;	Semicolon
<	74	60	<	Less than
=	75	61	=	Equals
>	76	62	>	Greater than
?	77	63	?	Question mark
@	100	64	@	Commercial at
A	101	65	A	Uppercase A
B	102	66	B	Uppercase B
C	103	67	C	Uppercase C
D	104	68	D	Uppercase D
E	105	69	E	Uppercase E
F	106	70	F	Uppercase F
G	107	71	G	Uppercase G
H	110	72	H	Uppercase H
I	111	73	I	Uppercase I
J	112	74	J	Uppercase J

Graphic	Octal Value	Decimal Value	ASCII Abbreviation	Comments
K	113	75	K	Uppercase K
L	114	76	L	Uppercase L
M	115	77	M	Uppercase M
N	116	78	N	Uppercase N
O	117	79	O	Uppercase O
P	120	80	P	Uppercase P
Q	121	81	Q	Uppercase Q
R	122	82	R	Uppercase R
S	123	83	S	Uppercase S
T	124	84	T	Uppercase T
U	125	85	U	Uppercase U
V	126	86	V	Uppercase V
W	127	87	W	Uppercase W
X	130	88	X	Uppercase X
Y	131	89	Y	Uppercase Y
Z	132	90	Z	Uppercase Z
[	133	91	[	Opening bracket
\	134	92	\	Reverse slash (slant)
]	135	93	]	Closing bracket
^	136	94	^	Circumflex, up-arrow
_ or ←	137	95	,UND,BKR	Underscore, back arrow
`	140	96	`,GRA	Grave accent
a	141	97	a,LCA	Lowercase a
b	142	98	b,LCB	Lowercase b
c	143	99	c,LCC	Lowercase c
d	144	100	d,LCD	Lowercase d
e	145	101	e,LCE	Lowercase e
f	146	102	f,LCF	Lowercase f
g	147	103	g,LCG	Lowercase g
h	150	104	h,LCH	Lowercase h
i	151	105	i,LCI	Lowercase i
j	152	106	j,LCJ	Lowercase j
k	153	107	k,LCK	Lowercase k
l	154	108	l,LCL	Lowercase l
m	155	109	m,LCM	Lowercase m
n	156	110	n,LCN	Lowercase n
o	157	111	o,LCO	Lowercase o
p	160	112	p,LCP	Lowercase p
q	161	113	q,LCQ	Lowercase q
r	162	114	r,LCR	Lowercase r
s	163	115	s,LCS	Lowercase s
t	164	116	t,LCT	Lowercase t
u	165	117	u,LCU	Lowercase u
v	166	118	v,LCV	Lowercase v
w	167	119	w,LCW	Lowercase w
x	170	120	x,LCX	Lowercase x
y	171	121	y,LCY	Lowercase y
z	172	122	z,LCZ	Lowercase z

Graphic	Octal Value	Decimal Value	ASCII Abbreviation	Comments
{	173	123	{,LBR	Opening (left) brace
|	174	124	|,VLN	Vertical line
}	175	125	},RBR	Closing (right) brace
~	176	126	~,TIL	Tilde
	177	127	DEL	Delete

A program that we have called ASCII was run on the terminal to demonstrate how the user can access the full ASCII character set, even though neither the Olivetti terminals presently being used nor a standard model 33 Teletype can generate a character with an ASCII value greater than 95. As will be seen by comparing the output of Program 16-9 with the preceding table, lowercase letters are printed as uppercase.

As is explained in the printout, certain ASCII characters control the motion of the printer carriage. However, only two of these characters can be included in a literal string and still maintain carriage control. One is the control N (N^c), the ASCII "shift out" character, which will cause a line feed to be generated only when it is output by the execution of a PRINT statement. The other is the control letter 0 (0^c), the ASCII "shift in," which will cause a return of the carriage without advancing the line, under the same conditions as above.

A particular convenience of the Olivetti terminal is that it has the ASCII abbreviation for each control character marked on the appropriate key.

Program 16-9

```
RUN
ASCII
READ-ONLY FILES:
#1

AFTER EXECUTING THE LINES:


10 FILES $CHARS
20 DIM A$[64],B$[64]
30 READ #1;A$,B$

  THE ASCII CHARACTER SET WILL HAVE BEEN LOADED INTO THE TWO
STRINGS AS FOLLOWS.
(NOTE: THE CHARACTERS WITH ASCII VALUES 0-31 & 127 DO NOT
HAVE A GRAPHIC REPRESENTATION SUCH AS '$' OR 'A'
INSTEAD THEY MAY CAUSE A SPECIAL ACTION TO TAKE PLACE.
THE CHARACTERS WITH ASCII NUMERICAL VALUES OF 10,11,12 & 14
WILL CAUSE A LINEFEED TO BE GENERATED WHEN THEY ARE PRINTED.
  THE CHARACTERS WITH ASCII REPRESENTATION 13 AND 15
WILL CAUSE THE CARRIAGE TO RETURN AS SOON AS THEY ARE
PRINTED. THE CHARACTER WITH ASCII VALUE 18 TURNS ON THE PAPER
TAPE PUNCH, AND THE CHARACTER WITH ASCII VALUE 20 TURNS
IT OFF. THE CHARACTER WITH ASCII VALUE 17 TURNS ON THE TAPE
READER, AND THE ONE WITH ASCII VALUE 19 TURNS IT OFF.)
```

	ASCII VALUE	CHARACTER PRINTS AS
	- - - - -	- - - - - - - - -
A$(1,1)	Ø	(NON-PRINTING)
A$(2,2)	1	(NON-PRINTING)
A$(3,3)	2	(NON-PRINTING)
A$(4,4)	3	(NON-PRINTING)
A$(5,5)	4	(NON-PRINTING)
A$(6,6)	5	(NON-PRINTING)
A$(7,7)	6	(NON-PRINTING)
A$(8,8)	7	(NON-PRINTING)
A$(9,9)	8	(NON-PRINTING)
A$(1Ø,1Ø)	9	(NON-PRINTING)
A$(11,11)	1Ø	(NON-PRINTING)
A$(12,12)	11	(NON-PRINTING)
A$(13,13)	12	(NON-PRINTING)
A$(14,14)	13	(NON-PRINTING)
A$(15,15)	14	(NON-PRINTING)
A$(16,16)	15	(NON-PRINTING)
A$(17,17)	16	(NON-PRINTING)
A$(18,18)	17	(NON-PRINTING)
A$(19,19)	18	(NON-PRINTING)
A$(2Ø,2Ø)	19	(NON-PRINTING)
A$(21,21)	2Ø	(NON-PRINTING)
A$(22,22)	21	(NON-PRINTING)
A$(23,23)	22	(NON-PRINTING)
A$(24,24)	23	(NON-PRINTING)
A$(25,25)	24	(NON-PRINTING)
A$(26,26)	25	(NON-PRINTING)
A$(27,27)	26	(NON-PRINTING)
A$(28,28)	27	(NON-PRINTING)
A$(29,29)	28	(NON-PRINTING)
A$(3Ø,3Ø)	29	(NON-PRINTING)
A$(31,31)	3Ø	(NON-PRINTING)
A$(32,32)	31	(NON-PRINTING)
A$(33,33)	32	(SPACE)
A$(34,34)	33	!
A$(35,35)	34	"
A$(36,36)	35	#
A$(37,37)	36	$
A$(38,38)	37	%
A$(39,39)	38	&
A$(4Ø,4Ø)	39	'
A$(41,41)	4Ø	(
A$(42,42)	41	)
A$(43,43)	42	*
A$(44,44)	43	+
A$(45,45)	44	,
A$(46,46)	45	–
A$(47,47)	46	.

	ASCII VALUE	CHARACTER PRINTS AS
	-----	----------
A$(48,48)	47	/
A$(49,49)	48	Ø
A$(5Ø,5Ø)	49	1
A$(51,51)	5Ø	2
A$(52,52)	51	3
A$(53,53)	52	4
A$(54,54)	53	5
A$(55,55)	54	6
A$(56,56)	55	7
A$(57,57)	56	8
A$(58,58)	57	9
A$(59,59)	58	:
A$(6Ø,6Ø)	59	;
A$(61,61)	6Ø	<
A$(62,62)	61	=
A$(63,63)	62	>
A$(64,64)	63	?
B$(1,1)	64	@
B$(2,2)	65	A
B$(3,3)	66	B
B$(4,4)	67	C
B$(5,5)	68	D
B$(6,6)	69	E
B$(7,7)	7Ø	F
B$(8,8)	71	G
B$(9,9)	72	H
B$(1Ø,1Ø)	73	I
B$(11,11)	74	J
B$(12,12)	75	K
B$(13,13)	76	L
B$(14,14)	77	M
B$(15,15)	78	N
B$(16,16)	79	O
B$(17,17)	8Ø	P
B$(18,18)	81	Q
B$(19,19)	82	R
B$(2Ø,2Ø)	83	S
B$(21,21)	84	T
B$(22,22)	85	U
B$(23,23)	86	V
B$(24,24)	87	W
B$(25,25)	88	X
B$(26,26)	89	Y
B$(27,27)	9Ø	Z
B$(28,28)	91	[
B$(29,29)	92	\
B$(3Ø,3Ø)	93	]

	ASCII VALUE	CHARACTER PRINTS AS
	- - - - -	- - - - - - - - -
B$(31,31)	94	↑
B$(32,32)	95	←
B$(33,33)	96	@
B$(34,34)	97	A
B$(35,35)	98	B
B$(36,36)	99	C
B$(37,37)	100	D
B$(38,38)	101	E
B$(39,39)	102	F
B$(40,40)	103	G
B$(41,41)	104	H
B$(42,42)	105	I
B$(43,43)	106	J
B$(44,44)	107	K
B$(45,45)	108	L
B$(46,46)	109	M
B$(47,47)	110	N
B$(48,48)	111	O
B$(49,49)	112	P
B$(50,50)	113	Q
B$(51,51)	114	R
B$(52,52)	115	S
B$(53,53)	116	T
B$(54,54)	117	U
B$(55,55)	118	V
B$(56,56)	119	W
B$(57,57)	120	X
B$(58,58)	121	Y
B$(59,59)	122	Z
B$(60,60)	123	[
B$(61,61)	124	\
B$(62,62)	125	]
B$(63,63)	126	↑
B$(64,64)	127	(NON-PRINTING)

DONE

CHAPTER SEVENTEEN

STRUCTURED PROGRAMMING

Experts in the art of programming are inclined nowadays to place a lot of emphasis on a method of programming known as *structured programming*. What is meant by this term is that a problem should be programmed such that each logical unit is self-contained, clearly separated from all the other logical units. Fundamentally, this implies that, at the minimum, the section of the program that reads the data is distinguished from the other sections by a suitable number of REM statements (which have the secondary function of documenting the program internally). The same applies to both the processing and print sections. If any of these sections is sufficiently complex in itself, then it too should be segmented with appropriate REM statements. Structured programming is more useful when dealing with sophisticated programs than with those usually discussed in the classroom situation.

To be truthful, the level of BASIC presented in this book hardly lends itself to structured programming. In fact, even the most advanced versions of BASIC can only partially satisfy the criteria demanded by structured programming. Ideally, one tries to avoid the use of GO TO statements in structured programming because of the difficulty human beings have in reading and following such programs. Experts seem to agree that the best programs do not include GO TO statements. However, in BASIC, which is highly statement-number-oriented, it is virtually impossible to avoid the use of GO TOs. They may be minimized, however, by resorting to FOR/NEXT loops as frequently as possible.

In the more advanced versions of the BASIC language (for example, Dartmouth's BASIC Version 6) elements of other higher level languages have been borrowed. Structured programming is more easily applied to these versions of BASIC.

INDEX